# NEW TESTAMENT

## EVERYDAY BIBLE STUDY SERIES

# JOHN

---

## SCOT MCKNIGHT

QUESTIONS WRITTEN BY
BECKY CASTLE MILLER

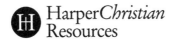

Harper*Christian*
Resources

*New Testament Everyday Bible Study Series: John*
© 2022 by Scot McKnight

Requests for information should be addressed to:
HarperChristian Resources, 3900 Sparks Dr. SE, Grand Rapids, Michigan 49546

ISBN 978-0-310-12932-5 (softcover)
ISBN 978-0-310-12933-2 (ebook)

# CONTENTS

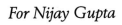
*For Nijay Gupta*

# GENERAL INTRODUCTION

Christians make a claim for the Bible not made of any other book. Or, since the Bible is a library shelf of many authors, it's a claim we make of no other shelf of books. We claim that God worked in each of the authors as they were writing so that what was scratched on papyrus expressed what God wanted communicated to the people of God. Which makes the New Testament (NT) a book unlike any other book. Which is why Christians are reading the NT almost two thousand years later with great delight. These books have the power to instruct us and to rebuke us and to correct us and to train us to walk with God every day. We read these books because God speaks to us in them.

Developing a routine of reading the Bible with an open heart, a receptive mind, and a flexible will is the why of the *New Testament Everyday Bible Studies*. But not every day will be the same. Some days we pause and take it in and other days we stop and repent and lament and open ourselves to God's restoring graces. No one word suffices for what the Bible does to us. In fact, the Bible's view of the Bible can be found by reading Psalm 119, the longest chapter in the Bible with 176 verses! It is a meditation on eight terms for what the Bible is and what the Bible does to those who listen and read it. It's laws (*torah*) instruct us, its laws (*mishpat*) order us, its statutes direct us, its precepts inform us, its decrees guide us, its command compel us, its words speak to us, and its promises comfort us, and it is no wonder that the author can sum all eight up as the "way" (119:3, 37). Each of those terms still speaks to what happens when we open our minds to the Word of God.

Every day with the Bible then is new because our timeless and timely God communes with us in our daily lives in our world and in our time. Just as God spoke to Jesus in Galilee and Paul in Ephesus and John on Patmos. These various contexts help up hear God in our context so the *New Testament Everyday Bible Studies* will often delve into contexts.

Most of us now have a Bible on our devices. We may well have several translations available to us everywhere we go every day. To hear those words we are summoned by God to open the Bible, to attune our hearts to God and to listen to what God says. My prayer is that these daily study guides will help each of us become daily Bible readers attentive to the mind of God.

# INTRODUCTION: READING THE GOSPEL OF JOHN

Please don't forget this as we read the Gospel of John together. There is something about the Gospels unlike anything else in the whole Bible. The books of the prophets of the Old Testament, often divided into major and minor prophets, record what the prophets said. We learn very little about their biographies. Our four Gospels are a bit like the vignettes of the patriarchs and Moses and kings and others in the historical books of the Old Testament. Unlike the prophets, our Gospels do not turn their pages into quotations of Jesus. Instead, the Gospels are obsessed, which is the only word for it unless there's a stronger one I don't know, with one person from verse 1:1 to the end of the Gospels. In our case, the Gospel of John. If we fail to see this shift in focus— from what the prophet said or even to some short vignettes to lengthy narratives about what Jesus did, with whom he interacted, who decided to follow him, who didn't like him, how he was arrested and crucified and raised—we fail to read this Gospel well. Every passage of the Gospel of John is about Jesus. Not us. Not you. Not me. Jesus.

Reading John's Gospel requires something counter-intuitive. What is intuitive works like this: We have a good idea of who or what God is, and we ask, "Does what we already know about God fit Jesus?" The counter-intuitive works like this: We only know who or what God is in knowing who Jesus is, so we now ask the counter-intuitive, "Does God fit what we know about Jesus?" In other words, God is Jesus. The Gospel of John invites us to a fresh reconception of God by showcasing Jesus from 1:1 to 21:25.

A Gospel has a mission: to "gospel." That is, to tell the story of Jesus in a way that compels response. In their essence, then, every paragraph in a Gospel is about Jesus. Who he is, or who the reader understands him to be, shapes how that reader responds to Jesus. In John's Gospel Jesus is first and foremost the Logos/Word, the Word spoken by the Father into the existence of a human in order that God can be revealed for who God truly is. The proper response to this Logos Jesus is faith or believing, and that faith is ongoing abiding in who he is, ongoing obedience to what he calls his followers to do, and ongoing witness to the world about who Jesus is. Those who respond to this Logos Jesus enter into nothing less than eternal life in the here and now as it opens them up to eternal life in the there and then. But there is a long list of labels or titles or terms for Jesus in this Gospel (see p. 31). In this Gospel words and ideas and people are woven together like a Celtic cross (see p. 246).

In John's Gospel we watch scenes that stun us with their simplicity and yet, upon deeper reading, an undeniable profundity. The great German New Testament scholar Martin Hengel once described this Gospel writer in such terms: "If any New Testament writer is not naïve but complex or even sophisticated, ironical and even paradoxical, and sometimes deliberately ambiguous, but at the same time one-sided and clear to the point of monomania, then he [John] is" (Hengel, *The Johannine Question*, 69).

In this Gospel we read not about the kingdom of God/heaven but about eternal life; we encounter miracles as signs, and Jesus often gives what are called "I am" sayings; instead of short punchy episodes John's Gospel sketches fewer scenes but at length and with longer discourses. He likes dualities, like light and darkness, above and below, believing and unbelieving, salvation and judgment. Miroslav Volf calls these "oppositional dualities." Jesus uses stiff and strong dualities, like good and bad—not good, mixed, and bad as we might prefer—but he does this for a reason: to present stark alternatives as he pleads for decisions about Jesus.

Which is the purpose of this Gospel: to promote believing and to enhance those who already believe. Which is why the study guide will begin at 20:30–31 (and not 1:1).

An important warning: The Gospel of John often mentions the "Jews" in derogatory terms. Not only do we know the horrific history of what happened to Jews but also Christians and Christianity are to blame for the stereotyping and othering of those whom the Christian God has chosen from Abraham on. This story may just help you. Amy-Jill Levine is one of America's finest New Testament scholars. She is a Jew, and she teaches at a mainline seminary, Vanderbilt Divinity School. I have known her for my entire career. She grew up in Boston among Roman Catholics. One day going to school, she describes for us,

> A friend on the school bus said to me, "You killed our Lord." "I did not," I responded with some indignation. Deicide would be the sort of thing I would have recalled. "Yes, you did," the girl insisted. "Our priest said so." Apparently she had been taught that "the Jews" were responsible for the death of Jesus. Since I was the only one she knew, I must be guilty.

One of the major sources for such Christian bigotry and historical ignorance is the Gospel of John. I want you to remember this story of Professor Levine's on every page of this Study Guide.

The Gospel of John's actual term, which most translate with "Jews," is *Youdaioi*, and this is most naturally translated in English as "Judeans," that is those who live in or who derive from the tribe of Judah (and Benjamin). Over time the term expanded to all those who are connected to the Judeans. Eventually "Judean/Judahite" shifted into the English term "Jew." The widest term, however, is "Israel," and "Judah" is a tribe in Israel with Judean referring to those connected to the geographical area (Judeans). In John the term is mostly used of leaders in Jerusalem so it makes sense to translate it "Judean" even more than "Jew," which refers to an ethnic group. In this Study Guide we express our sensitivity to anti-Semitism's tragic consequences by alternating in no particular order between "Jew" and "Judean."In what follows, I want to balance respect and honor for the ethnic group (Jew) as well as for the geographical connotation (Judean).

## FOR FURTHER READING

Richard Bauckham, "Dualisms," in his study *Gospel of Glory: Major Themes in Johannine Theology* (Grand Rapids: Baker Academic, 2015), 109–129.

Martin Hengel, *The Johannine Question* (trans. John Bowden; Philadelphia: Trinity Press International, 1989).

Amy-Jill Levine, *The Misunderstood Jew: The Church and the Scandal of the Jewish Jesus* (New York: HarperOne, 2006).

Miroslav Volf, "Johannine Dualism and Contemporary Pluralism," in *The Gospel of John and Christian Theology* (ed. R. Bauckham, C. Mosser; Grand Rapids: Wm. B. Eerdmans, 2008), 19–50.

**Cited in the Study Guide** (throughout the Guide you will find the author's name and title as noted in this book listing with page numbers whenever I cite something from it):

Allen Dwight Callahan, "The Gospel of John," in *True to Our Native Land: An African American New Testament Commentary* (ed. Brian K. Blount; Minneapolis: Fortress, 2007), 186–212. [Callahan, "John"]

David Ford, *The Gospel of John: A Theological Commentary* (Grand Rapids: Baker Academic, 2021). [Ford, *John*] I'm grateful to Annabel Robinson for the kind gift of Ford's book.

Steven A. Hunt, D. Francois Tolmie, Ruben Zimmermann, *Character Studies in the Fourth Gospel: Narrative Approaches to Seventy Figures in John* (Grand Rapids: Wm. B. Eerdmans, 2016). [Author of the chapter, character, *Character Studies*]

J. Ramsey Michaels, *The Gospel of John* (Grand Rapids: Wm. B. Eerdmans, 2010). [Michaels, *John*]

Kevin Quast, *Reading the Gospel of John: An Introduction* (rev. ed.; New York: Paulist, 1996). [Quast, *John*]

Rodney Reeves, *Spirituality according to John: Abiding in Christ in Johannine Writings* (Downers Grove: IVP Academic, 2021). [Reeves, *Spirituality*]

Marianne Meye Thompson, *John: A Commentary* (Louisville: Westminster John Knox, 2015). [Thompson, *John*]

# BELIEVING IN JESUS

## *John 20:30–31*

**Special Note to the Reader:** The purpose of the Gospel of John is explicitly stated at the end of the Gospel (20:30–31). Because that passage is so important to understand how this Gospel works, we begin with it. The purpose is to enhance faith in both believers and to promote faith among those who are not yet believers. If we keep this in mind as we read the Gospel, we will read the Gospel as John wants us to.

*30 Jesus performed many other signs in the presence of his disciples, which are not recorded in this book. 31 But these are written that you may believe that Jesus is the Messiah, the Son of God, and that by believing you may have life in his name.*

John waits until near the end of his Gospel to tell us why he wrote the Gospel. After Thomas offered the truest confession of all truths, that Jesus is both Lord and God, John closes the scene by saying Jesus did dozens of wonderful "signs" John does not even record. But what he wrote was enough. Enough that "you may believe that Jesus is the Messiah, the Son of God, and that by believing you may have life in his name" (20:30–31).

John wrote about Jesus *so people would believe*. Not in a simplistic sense of accepting Jesus into one's heart but in the Gospels' fullest sense. To believe is both to begin believing in Jesus and continuing to believe, that is, to become allegiant, faithful, ongoing believers. To promote faith like this John told stories about Jesus. For one example, the signs (miracles) and discourses of this Gospel were mapped onto the life of Jesus so readers could encounter the Lord, God enfleshed, the Lamb of God, the Glorified and Raised One, the Bread of Life, and many other titles for Jesus we will encounter. John wants such an encounter to generate believers.

We need to say more about how important believing is. In this Gospel believing is both a one-time act of trusting surrender and ongoing trust and deeper surrender. Perhaps the best English term for believing in John's Gospel is "abiding" or "indwelling." It is a life of constant communion with and participation in Jesus. John never uses the noun *pistis* ("faith" or "belief") but always the verb *pisteuō* ("to believe"). In fact, he uses that verb 98x in a NT that uses it only some 243x. But that word is surrounded by friends, which can be broken into the four categories below. As a college student I began underlining these various terms in my Bible. The result was a seriously marked-up, almost unreadable, Gospel.

To see how wide-ranging and deep-diving believing is for John, each of these terms comes into play, and by the time you get to 4x we realize believing is a massive mountain in John. Believing is:

1. Discernment
    a. seeing,
    b. hearing,
    c. remembering.

2. Decision
 a. coming to,
 b. rejecting/receiving.
3. Dependence
 a. drinking,
 b. eating,
 c. abiding.
4. Obedience
 a. disciple,
 b. keeping,
 c. serving,
 d. worshiping.

This Gospel was written so its readers would see Jesus for who he truly is and respond throughout life in all these ways. Take a moment with each and ponder how you have responded to Jesus like that, and what it did for you. What each of those terms does to us is usher us deeper into participating in a "life in his name" (20:31).

## QUESTIONS FOR REFLECTION
## AND APPLICATION

1. Why does John say he wrote his Gospel?

2. McKnight writes that in John, believing means "both a one-time act of trusting surrender and ongoing trust and deeper surrender." How does that challenge the prevailing evangelical idea that "believing in Jesus" means simply once praying a sinner's prayer?

3. What are the four major terms McKnight uses in his expanded definition of believing?

4. How have you lived out believing in Jesus over time?

5. How can you change the way you share the Gospel to better present this greater understanding of believing?

# JESUS IS THE LOGOS

## *John 1:1–18*

*¹ In the beginning was the Word, and the Word was with God, and the Word was God. ² He was with God in the beginning. ³ Through him all things were made; without him nothing was made that has been made. ⁴ In him was life, and that life was the light of all mankind. ⁵ The light shines in the darkness, and the darkness has not overcome it.*

*⁶ There was a man sent from God whose name was John. ⁷ He came as a witness to testify concerning that light, so that through him all might believe. ⁸ He himself was not the light; he came only as a witness to the light.*

*⁹ The true light that gives light to everyone was coming into the world. ¹⁰ He was in the world, and though the world was made through him, the world did not recognize him. ¹¹ He came to that which was his own, but his own did not receive him. ¹² Yet to all who did receive him, to those who believed in his name, he gave the right to become children of God—¹³ children born not of natural descent, nor of human decision or a husband's will, but born of God.*

*¹⁴ The Word became flesh and made his dwelling among us. We have seen his glory, the glory of the one and only Son, who came from the Father, full of grace and truth.*

*¹⁵ (John testified concerning him. He cried out, saying, "This is the one I spoke about when I said, 'He who comes after me has surpassed me because he was before me.'")* [16] *Out of his fullness we have all received grace in place of grace already given.* [17] *For the law was given through Moses; grace and truth came through Jesus Christ.* [18] *No one has ever seen God, but the one and only Son, who is himself God and is in closest relationship with the Father, has made him known.*

We should begin thinking together about this passage with one simple thought: there was a man in Galilee, a man with sandals and hair and a voice, a man who performed signs, a man who was embraced by some and ignored or rejected by many more, a man who was hailed before Pilate and gruesomely crucified in public, a man who, it was claimed, was raised from the dead and was seen by many. In this passage this man is God. That's utterly astounding. A man who was—no, who *is* God. God is not a human, and no human is God, at least until Jesus. That is the most astounding claim this Gospel makes, and on it the entirety of Christianity builds.

The sum of this prologue is about the Logos, translated as "Word." John explores briefly five relationships of the Logos: to God (1:1–2), to creation (1:3–5), to John the Baptist as witness (1:6–8), to the world (1:9–13), and to the community of faith (1:14–18). Each of these five units says something fiercely clear about Jesus. While there are bits and bobs for you and me in these verses, John concentrates on Jesus, the Messiah, the God's Logos.

## THE LOGOS AND GOD

John's "In the beginning" echoes but also deepens Genesis 1:1's "In the beginning." Behind Genesis 1 was the Logos, and the Logos was "with" God. That is, next to and alongside.

He was so close in being "alongside" that John breaks forth in his first verse with the astounding claim: "and the Logos was God." The word *was* can be signified like this: the Logos = God. You cannot say something simpler and more profound than with a simple use of "was" or "is." For this text Jesus is God (Harris). John then abbreviates verse one with verse two: "He was with God in the beginning." Again, the word "with" means "next to."

Why Logos? Greeks commonly used this term for Reason, for Meaning, for Logic, and for Words Spoken. The Old Testament, however, is John's world even more than the Greek world, and this term Logos/Word evokes:

1. creation (cf. 1:3–5),
2. the revelation of God's tent and glory and love at Sinai,
3. the Wisdom of God (Proverbs 1:20–33; 8—9),
4. God speaking and communicating and revealing his will and law (cf. Psalm 119:9, 25, 28, 65, 107, 169),
5. and the prophets declaring the word of God to the people of God (Isaiah 40:11; Psalm 33:6).

John baptizes these Jewish ideas into Greek waters when he uses "Logos," but his sensibilities are more Jewish than Greek. In this Gospel Jesus is the Logos who reveals the truth, the word of God, to humans (1:1, 3, 14; 5:37–38; 17:14, 17). He is then both God's revelation and the One who reveals God as the living, speaking Word. As Kevin Quast says it, "the Logos did not merely descend upon or enter into Jesus, the Logos of God became the human nature Jesus bore." Which leads him to a profound next line: "The life of Jesus is the history of God himself on earth" (Quast, *John*, 13).

We have become far too comfortable with what John writes in 1:1. Jesus is God in the flesh.

## The Logos and Creation

Not only is the Logos with God and is God, but John declares the Logos was the creator. I translate verse three with "*All things* came into being through him" and then "outside of him" or "apart from the Logos not one thing that exists came into being." John explains this a little more when he says, "in him was life," and he means life itself. The Logos is Life, and Life alone creates other life. He goes deeper again with "that life was the light" of every human being. The Logos is the Life is the Light. Light here means revelation and illumination. A hint of what is to come finds its way into verse five when John says that Logos-Life-Light "shines in the darkness" but that darkness has no power to suppress, silence, and darken the brightness of the true Light. The hint dropped is one of rejection of the Light, and John will develop this in the fourth paragraph (1:9–13).

> As Logos, he is the living, speaking Word of redemption.
> As Life, he is and creates redemptive eternal life.
> As Light, he illumines humans to redemption.

## The Logos and the Witness

Into that darkness was a "man sent from God," whom we call John the Baptist. God's commission for him was to be a "witness," a verbal testifier of Who Jesus is—Logos, Life, Light. Jesus reveals God and is God's revelation, but some words (*logoi*) are needed to make meaning of who Jesus is. John's mission is to use such words to explain Jesus so that "all might believe" (1:7). A witness is someone who points to Jesus and then verbally explains his identity and mission and accomplishment and grandeur. We can call this verbal activism for Jesus or evangelism or gospeling.

It is hard to imagine this today, but John was a rival of Jesus and for some even superior to Jesus. In fact, the order of John first and then Jesus made it at least appear that Jesus was for awhile the disciple of John! So, John has to make it doubly clear that John was "not the light" but just a "witness to the light" (1:8). Not only do witnesses become at times rivals of Jesus, they can at times upstage Jesus by becoming celebrities drunk with their own importance (Beaty). The witness's true mission is not self-promotion but to point others to Jesus.

## THE LOGOS AND THE WORLD

The hint dropped now becomes clarity. The "true light," Jesus, is sent by the Father into the world, and even though Jesus was witnessed to by other witnesses, that Light is rejected by the world even though it was created by him! This is cosmic cancelling, that is, the world of God rejecting the Word of God about the world. In fact, even Jesus' own contemporaries didn't accept him as the Logos, Life, and Light of God. In the posing of Light against Darkness/world, we touch upon one of John's favorite devices for communication: dualities. He uses stiff and strong dualities, like good and bad, to promote decisions about Jesus.

> The word "world" is important in John. World can point us to the world as God's created order (1:10; 17:5, 24) but at the same time to the world as structured rebellion against God (3:16, 17, 19–20; 7:7; 15:19). Jesus is God's envoy to the world to save the world by conquering the rebellion

(1:9; 3:16, 17, 19; 16:33; 12:31). Jesus comes to break down systemic worldliness.

My first taste of salvation, when I was a lad of about eight, was through John 1:12, and my Bible was the KJV so here it is: "But as many as received him, to them gave he power to become the sons of God, *even* to them that believe on his name:" (By the time I was eight, King James English was my second language.) Those who receive him or welcome him to be "next to" themselves, are "born . . . of God," not by human powers and decisions and actions. Christians speak of "born again" because of this verse and John 3:3.

## THE LOGOS AND THE COMMUNITY

Jesus is the Logos, the Life, and the Light. He is each of these because he is "with" God and "is" God. The astounding claim is that God became human, which we call the incarnation or the "enfleshment" of God in Jesus. Paul will tell us in Philippians 2 that Jesus, "being in very nature God . . . made himself nothing, by taking the very nature of a servant, being made in human likeness . . . he humbled himself by becoming obedient to death–even death on a cross!" (2:6–8). John says, "The Word became flesh and made his dwelling among us" (John 1:14). Which means God, the Logos, is now part of the community of humans he came to save. As Allen Dwight Callahan puts it poetically, "In this incarnation, the divine and the human sound together in a symphony of transcendence and immanence" (Callahan, "John," 187).

John says at 1:14 God "dwelt among us" or "pitched a tent among us," or as Eugene Peterson translated it, "moved into the neighborhood" (MSG). Behind the language is the image of the tent pitched by Israel in their wanderings from Egypt to the Land. Even more important than background are the claims of John about this enfleshed God: we saw his "glory" and it is the glory of the One-and-Only Son. This embodied Logos was "full of grace and truth" (1:14). The early Christians liked this notion of fullness. Paul will say "in Christ all the fullness of the Deity lives in bodily form" (Colossians 2:9).

The Gospel author degrades once again John the Baptist's status when compared with Jesus (1:15). It is only "out of his [not John's] fullness" that believers find grace flourishing with more grace (1:16). Which leads John to make yet another claim about Jesus by comparing him to Israel's hero of heroes: Moses brought the law, but Jesus brings "grace and truth" (1:17).

John 1:18 reminds his readers about 1:1 with a new emphasis. "No one has ever seen God." Yes, in fact, One has, and it is "the one and only Son." But that Son is "himself God." The One who was "next to" God is now in an even more intimate relation. The NIV's "is in closest relationship with the Father" is one attempt. The CEB has "is at the Father's side" and the NRSV has "who is close to the Father's heart." The Greek term is "garment fold," and Jesus exists alongside the Father "in" that fold. The same term is used for the disciple Jesus especially loved, who "was reclining next to him" (13:23). It can refer to a pocket, the fold of a woman's dress, the lap, the womb, or the bosom.

His proximity, yea intimacy, with the Father makes him the only true revealer of God. The Logos is God, the Logos is Life, the Logos is Light.

17

## QUESTIONS FOR REFLECTION
## AND APPLICATION

1. What are the five relationships of the Logos John explores in this section?

2. How does John tie together Jewish and Greek ideas in his use of "Logos"?

3. How does John explain Jesus' intimacy with and proximity to the Father?

4. When have you seen a supposed witness of Jesus become a rival of Jesus or upstage him? How does John the Baptist's humility as a witness contrast that?

5. Which of the three terms for Jesus in this section—Logos, Life, Light—is most meaningful to you? Why?

## FOR FURTHER READING

Katelyn Beaty, *Celebrities for Jesus: How Personas, Platforms, and Profits are Hurting the Church* (Grand Rapids: Brazos, 2022).

Murray J. Harris, *Jesus as God* (Grand Rapids: Baker, 1992) 51–71.

# JOHN THE BAPTIST'S WITNESS TO JESUS

## John 1:19–34

¹⁹ Now this was John's testimony when the Jewish leaders in Jerusalem sent priests and Levites to ask him who he was. ²⁰ He did not fail to confess, but confessed freely, "I am not the Messiah."

²¹ They asked him, "Then who are you? Are you Elijah?"

He said, "I am not."

"Are you the Prophet?"

He answered, "No."

²² Finally they said, "Who are you? Give us an answer to take back to those who sent us. What do you say about yourself?"

²³ John replied in the words of Isaiah the prophet, "I am the voice of one calling in the wilderness, 'Make straight the way for the Lord.'"

²⁴ Now the Pharisees who had been sent ²⁵ questioned him, "Why then do you baptize if you are not the Messiah, nor Elijah, nor the Prophet?"

²⁶ "I baptize with water," John replied, "but among you stands one you do not know. ²⁷ He is the one who comes after me, the straps of whose sandals I am not worthy to untie."

²⁸ This all happened at Bethany on the other side of the Jordan, where John was baptizing. ²⁹ The next day John saw Jesus coming

toward him and said, "Look, the Lamb of God, who takes away the sin of the world! [30] This is the one I meant when I said, 'A man who comes after me has surpassed me because he was before me.' [31] I myself did not know him, but the reason I came baptizing with water was that he might be revealed to Israel."

[32] Then John gave this testimony: "I saw the Spirit come down from heaven as a dove and remain on him. [33] And I myself did not know him, but the one who sent me to baptize with water told me, 'The man on whom you see the Spirit come down and remain is the one who will baptize with the Holy Spirit.' [34] I have seen and I testify that this is God's Chosen One."

When we realize that someone drawing a crowd, persuading with words, and impressing others enough to become followers is *at the same time* inevitably tempted to draw attention to himself or herself, become impressed with one's oratory, and proud of loyalty, we have the toxic brew that turns a witness into a narcissist (DeGroat). That toxic brew is not easy to resist, but John the Baptizer did. I will call him "J-B." His calling was to be a "witness," one of the Gospel's favorite words, and as a witness his mission was an "I-am-not the one but Jesus is" calling.

The biggest temptations to wallow in one's calling and detract from the witness mission are congratulations, adorations, and platforms. After teaching or preaching and advising one may receive some heartfelt appreciations that, over time, become expectations and then frustrations when not given. Repetition of those affirmations slide into adorations and before long the person on the platform has become a persona. Every person in a church with any responsibility and even a smidgeon of authority will go nose-to-nose with this temptation.

J-B faced it and stiff-armed it. How?

## Not Messiah, Not Elijah, Not the Prophet

First, he denied labels of glory. We forget J-B's charisma. A clutch of "priests and Levites" commissioned by some Judean leaders asked J-B about his identity. (The Who-do-you-think-you-are question.) Are you the Messiah, Elijah, or the Prophet? It may not be as noticeable to us as it was to them, but Elijah and the Prophet are the very persons who appeared at Jesus' transfiguration, only there the Prophet had a name, Moses. The label of labels was "Messiah."

His answers are terse and true: "I am not the Messiah" (1:20), "I am not" Elijah (1:21), and "No" he was not the Prophet (1:21). To become a true and faithful witness one has to get off the platform, poke the persona, and come to terms both with oneself and with *to Whom* one is a witness. John does just that. His I-am-nots are the foundations for genuine Jesus-is witness. John's I-am-nots will be matched by Jesus's own I-ams, where he witnesses to himself.

## Only a Voice

So, they ask J-B following his denials, *Who in the world are you then? You seem pretty big stuff to some of us.* His answer perfectly matches his mission as a witness: he's nothing but a voice. His answer locates himself in a biblical text, Isaiah 40:3, a verse from a powerful chapter that announces the end of divine discipline, the launching of forgiveness and return to the promised land, and the revelation of God's redemptive glory. So, J-B may be full of I-am-nots, but what he is taps into a very special role in history. He is the Voice that prepares for the arrival of God, which John utterly connects to Jesus, the Logos.

## WITNESS

The author John shifts from "priests and Levites" to "Pharisees" in verse twenty-four, which suggests the clutch came from the spectrum of concerns in Jerusalem about J-B's goings-on. They ask him why he is dipping people into water if he's none of the above. Their concerns were no doubt the purity concerns typical of Pharisees. Once again, J-B turns this both into an I-am-not and into a "But Jesus is" witness. J-B's calling is to dip people into the east side of the Jordan, where Joshua led the twelve tribes into the Land. Jesus, who "comes after me," he tells them, is far greater. In fact, his I-am-not reaches its true location: he's not even worthy, slave or servant like, to untie the Logos' sandals.

Christians have turned "Pharisee" into a word denoting hypocrite, legalist, judgmental, insecure before God, etc. These are false historically and dangerous socially, as the Holocaust shows. There is a drink in Germany called *Der Pharisäer* that looks like coffee but contains alcohol. In fact, a Pharisee of the first century was more of a progressive than a fundamentalist. The Pharisees sought to expand the Torah to make it more practicable for ordinary Jews. Amy-Jill Levine, in a webinar hosted by the Enoch Seminar at the University of Michigan, played with "You might be a redneck, if you . . ." comedy routine, and turned it into these very common realities that are historically accurate about the Pharisees:

You might be a Pharisee if . . . [brackets are mine]

1. You believe in a combination of fate and free will [most evangelicals]
2. You believe in the resurrection of the dead and a final judgment [evangelicals]
3. You reject elitism and favor voluntary groups over inherited positions [check]
4. You value your traditions, but you also realize they must be reinterpreted in light of new social circumstances [can't deny that]
5. You want to make it easier and more meaningful for people to engage in their traditions, and you are willing to discuss how to do so [at the heart of evangelicalism]
6. You care about multiculturalism and maintaining group identity despite assimilational pressures [check the polls]
7. You have been maligned over the centuries for your commitment to your traditions. [oy!] And now the drumroll. . . .
8. You've had dinner with Jesus. [At least they did!]

*Source: http://enochseminar.org/the-pharisees*

J-B is the Voice out in the wilderness, a Voice that witnesses to Jesus. If I can play with the terms: J-B uses words about the Word, *logoi* about the *Logos*! His gift is entirely Jesus-shaped and Jesus-directed. He labels Jesus with three counter labels to the popular labels pinned to J-B. They thought he might be Messiah, Elijah, or the Prophet. J-B says Jesus is (1) the "Lord" who returns to Zion (1:23), (2) the Lamb of God (1:29), an image that points to the one who dies an atoning death and perhaps Isaiah 53, and who will return to conquer the enemies of Jesus as in Revelation 5:6–10 and

17:14, and (3) God's Chosen One (1:34). J-B labels, and thus witnesses to, Jesus as each of these. There is no one title for Jesus. He is all these and more.

J-B can identify who Jesus is because he was in the river where it happened. He witnessed the Spirit of God "remain on" Jesus (1:32). He knew him to be the one God had told was to come: the Spirit-baptizer (not just a water-baptizer) who was God's Chosen One. (Some manuscripts have "Son of God" [NRSV, CEB, ESV] and not "Chosen One" of God.)

J-B's calling was not self-promotion but Jesus-promotion. He was good at it. It takes character to deny glory and loyalties and instead point to Jesus. J-B had such a character. In fact, J-B stands apart from all other witnesses to Jesus in this Gospel because he alone comprehends precisely who Jesus is. He has a special role, which he dispatched with efficiency and loyalty.

## QUESTIONS FOR REFLECTION AND APPLICATION

1. What does it mean to be a witness to Jesus?

2. How did John's character and series of I-am-not statements make him an excellent witness, one skilled at Jesus-promotion?

3. Why do you think the Synoptic Gospels (Matthew, Mark, Luke) see John as Elijah but the Gospel of John does not? Compare Mark 9:11–13 with John 1:19–23.

4. When have you faced the temptation of the platform to become a "persona"? How did you respond?

5. In what ways are you similar to the Pharisees, according to A.J. Levine's list? How does that impact your view of them?

### FOR FURTHER READING

Chuck DeGroat, *When Narcissism Comes to Church: Healing Your Community from Emotional and Spiritual Abuse* (Downers Grove: IVP, 2020).

# MORE WITNESSES TO JESUS

## John 1:35–51

[35] The next day John was there again with two of his disciples. [36] When he saw Jesus passing by, he said, "Look, the Lamb of God!"

[37] When the two disciples heard him say this, they followed Jesus. [38] Turning around, Jesus saw them following and asked, "What do you want?"

They said, "Rabbi" (which means "Teacher"), "where are you staying?"

[39] "Come," he replied, "and you will see."

So they went and saw where he was staying, and they spent that day with him. It was about four in the afternoon.

[40] Andrew, Simon Peter's brother, was one of the two who heard what John had said and who had followed Jesus. [41] The first thing Andrew did was to find his brother Simon and tell him, "We have found the Messiah" (that is, the Christ). [42] And he brought him to Jesus.

Jesus looked at him and said, "You are Simon son of John. You will be called Cephas" (which, when translated, is Peter[a]).

[43] The next day Jesus decided to leave for Galilee. Finding Philip, he said to him, "Follow me."

*⁴⁴ Philip, like Andrew and Peter, was from the town of Bethsaida. ⁴⁵ Philip found Nathanael and told him, "We have found the one Moses wrote about in the Law, and about whom the prophets also wrote—Jesus of Nazareth, the son of Joseph."*

*⁴⁶ "Nazareth! Can anything good come from there?" Nathanael asked.*

*"Come and see," said Philip.*

*⁴⁷ When Jesus saw Nathanael approaching, he said of him, "Here truly is an Israelite in whom there is no deceit."*

*⁴⁸ "How do you know me?" Nathanael asked.*

*Jesus answered, "I saw you while you were still under the fig tree before Philip called you."*

*⁴⁹ Then Nathanael declared, "Rabbi, you are the Son of God; you are the king of Israel."*

*⁵⁰ Jesus said, "You believe[b] because I told you I saw you under the fig tree. You will see greater things than that." ⁵¹ He then added, "Very truly I tell you,[c] you[d] will see 'heaven open, and the angels of God ascending and descending on'[e] the Son of Man."*

The first chapter of John opens with one label or title after another for Jesus. Think about what we have already noticed: Logos, Life, Light, Messiah, Lamb of God, God's Chosen One. Identity matters, and accurate titles speak to the heart of identity, so getting the right title for Jesus matters. But what the Gospel of John wants us to know is that there is no one title that tells the whole story of Jesus, so we need them all. In this section of John 1 we read of more titles for Jesus, each pointing to Jesus, but Jesus is more than the sum of his titles. How can anyone catch the Logos in a single title?

This passage, even if it describes some of the most influential early followers of Jesus, is not about them. The passage is about Jesus and who he is. The big question we can ask is, "Who do you think Jesus was and is?" As theologian David

Ford says this so well, "the key question in most of those meetings [in the Gospel] is who Jesus is . . . every other theological question is also affected by the answer to this one." I love this word of his: "Who Jesus is also changes what it means to be human" (Ford, *Gospel of John*, 51).

Knowing Jesus is life's greatest revolution.

## JESUS IS LAMB OF GOD

John the Baptist, or J-B, is with two of his own disciples. (These two would soon change teams to be with Jesus.) Jesus evidently was walking somewhere, J-B informs the two disciples that Jesus is the "Lamb of God." It is hard to erase either of the two major Lamb themes of the Jewish world: this Lamb is one who atones for sin through his death and resurrection, but this Lamb also is the one who will conquer the enemies of God to bring in the New Jerusalem.

To call Jesus Lamb of God is to affirm him as one who comprehensively liberates humans from sin's bondages.

## JESUS IS MESSIAH

Immediately after J-B points to the Lamb of God, the two disciples switch allegiances: "they followed Jesus" (1:37). Jesus notices they have started following him, so he asks them want they want (1:38), and the two—one is Andrew, brother of Simon (about to become "Cephas" or Peter)—call him "Rabbi," which means "my lord" or "my master" or "my guru" or "my teacher," and they only want to know where he's staying. They want to be with him and hear him out and get to know him. John says, "they spent that day with him" (1:39).

As family or friendship witnessing often does, Andrew invites his brother Simon Peter to meet Jesus. Andrew's introduction of Jesus to his brother is that he has "found the

Messiah" (1:41). Messiah is the climactic final leader of Israel, the one who would bring justice and peace and victory over sin, sickness, and systemic injustices. Jesus is that consummate Savior of Israel. No sooner did Jesus see Simon than he says, "You are Simon son of John. You will be called Cephas," which means Rock, which translates into "Peter" (1:42).

To call Jesus Messiah is to affirm him as the consummation of Israel's story, the king on the throne of David, the one who brings final justice and peace.

Lamb of God. Messiah. Now two or three more titles for Jesus.

## JESUS IS SON OF GOD, KING OF ISRAEL

Jesus decides to leave the Jerusalem area to head back home in the north, in Galilee. Whether on the way or after he arrived, Jesus discovers Philip and calls him to "follow me" (1:43). They find another working companion from the same hometown, Bethsaida, by the name of Nathanael, and Philip informs him they have found "the one Moses wrote about in the Law and about whom the prophets also wrote" (1:45). This sounds like what the Prophet J-B denied of himself. Just whom they had in mind from the prophets is not clear, but probably Messiah.

With some snark, Nathanael, from Cana in Galilee (21:2), opines that nothing "good" can "come from Nazareth" (1:46; see 6:42). The next words are literarily important to John 1: "Come and see" for yourself. These words are also the witness of these followers of Jesus about Jesus.

Jesus stuns Nathanael with his supernatural knowledge, revealing he knows he's a man without "deceit" (1:47). Stunned himself, the man asks Jesus how he knew such a thing, and Jesus reveals supernatural vision: "I saw you while you were still under the fig tree" (1:48). That's all the man needed to hear, and he turns the label or title "Messiah" into its synonyms: "Rabbi, you are the Son of God; you are the king of Israel" (1:49). Both of those terms are titles for the Davidic throne, for the king of Israel. Son of God, though it has often been said to point to Jesus' deity, in the Jewish world pointed to a king (Psalm 2).

To call Jesus either Son of God or King of Israel is to affirm him as Israel's true and rightful king, which inevitably means Pilate is not, Herod Antipas is not, and probably too the Roman emperor, Tiberius, is not! They are affirming that Jesus is the one anointed by God to bring in the kingdom of God.

## Words for Jesus in John

| | |
|---|---|
| Chosen One | Prophet |
| Christ | Rabbi |
| God | Savior |
| Holy One of God | Son of God, one and |
| King of Israel, Zion, |    only Son |
|    of the Jews | Son of Man |
| Lamb of God | Teacher |
| Lord and lord (sir) | Word |
| Messiah | |

## JESUS IS SON OF MAN

Lamb. Messiah. Son of God. King of Israel.

Now a wrinkle: Son of Man.

Jesus informs Nathanael that his faith and confession are rooted in the revelations of Jesus to him, but "greater things" were on their way for him (1:50). Jesus explains to

Nathanael, no doubt saying something that zipped right over his head, that he would "see heaven open" and he would thus see "the angels of God ascending and descending on the Son of Man" (1:51).[1] This sounds so much like Jacob's experience in Genesis 28, esp. 28:12, that John must be evoking that passage here. What did Jacob learn from that angelic conduit experience? That "Surely the LORD is in this place!" (28:16). And that's what Nathanael will learn: that where Jesus is, the Lord is. Jesus is the thinnest place on earth, the Person in whom one finds the very presence of God.

To call Jesus the Son of Man affirms that Jesus *is* the ladder between God and humans, that is, the Logos who communicates God's Life and Light to humans. As ladder, Jesus is like the wardrobe for the Pevensie children through which they could enter into Narnia and out of which they ended back in the home.

Which title only sums up what John has been doing since this chapter started: providing terms to identify who Jesus is.

Which title is your favorite?

## QUESTIONS FOR REFLECTION AND APPLICATION

1. What does it mean for Jesus to be Lamb of God?

2. What does it mean for Jesus to be Messiah?

3. What does it mean for Jesus to be Son of God and King of Israel?

4. What does it mean for Jesus to be Son of Man?

5. Which title for Jesus seems to be the most impactful for these disciples? Which one impacts you the most?

# JESUS AS THE FIRST SIGN

## *John 2:1–11*

[1] *On the third day a wedding took place at Cana in Galilee. Jesus' mother was there,* [2] *and Jesus and his disciples had also been invited to the wedding.* [3] *When the wine was gone, Jesus' mother said to him, "They have no more wine."*

[4] *"Woman,[a] why do you involve me?" Jesus replied. "My hour has not yet come."*

[5] *His mother said to the servants, "Do whatever he tells you."*

[6] *Nearby stood six stone water jars, the kind used by the Jews for ceremonial washing, each holding from twenty to thirty gallons.*

[7] *Jesus said to the servants, "Fill the jars with water"; so they filled them to the brim.*

[8] *Then he told them, "Now draw some out and take it to the master of the banquet."*

*They did so,* [9] *and the master of the banquet tasted the water that had been turned into wine. He did not realize where it had come from, though the servants who had drawn the water knew. Then he called the bridegroom aside* [10] *and said, "Everyone brings out the choice wine first and then the cheaper wine after the guests have had too much to drink; but you have saved the best till now."*

[11] *What Jesus did here in Cana of Galilee was the first of the signs through which he revealed his glory; and his disciples believed in him.*

Sometimes something happens that evokes another world or signifies far more than the simplicity of what happened. Like Kent State in my generation, 9/11 for a more recent generation. These are iconic moments in American history. A story unfolds—resistance to war, an attack of the USA—into an event that portrays and portends and prophesies all at once (and more). John captures stories and events that way with the term "sign."

## STORY

There's a wedding in Cana, a city not far from Nazareth, but at least one resident thinks Nazareth is for yokels (1:46). For him Cana was a long way from Nazareth. Mary, the mother of Jesus, seems to be in charge of the wedding, Jesus' disciples are present, and they run out of a wedding's major fluid: wine. Mary approaches Jesus to do something about it, Jesus rebuffs her attempt by saying "my hour has not yet come," and that "hour" is the glorification-by-crucifixion, resurrection, and ascension (12:23, 27; 13:1; 17:1). Mary turns to the servants and orders them to do whatever Jesus says. Seemingly, Jesus either shifts his mind or perceives Mary's surrender to him as sufficient for him to do exactly what she asked in exactly a surprising manner (McKnight, *Real Mary*). He speaks something into reality and turns the water in some large purification stone vessels into an abundance of wine. I once calculated it to be an equivalent of 907 bottles of wine.

The "master of the banquet" tastes it and realizes this wine is superior to the wedding's table wine (2:9–10). It is worth pondering if the water in the purification vessels has not been fulfilled and swallowed up in the wine Jesus creates. Wine is better than that water.

And the story ends.

Except for those lingering in order to understand what just happened.

## SIGN

The most important term in this passage is not found until verse eleven, and the word is "signs," and the water into wine miracle is the "first [or "beginning"] of his signs." In the Synoptic Gospels Jesus does miracles but John deepens miracles by labeling them "signs." Most think there are seven signs in John's Gospel, with the explicit mention of "sign" in brackets and two others often mentioned as signs as 8 and 9.

1. Water into wine: [2:11]
2. Healing the official's son: [4:54]
3. Feeding thousands: 6:14 [6:2]
4. Raising Lazarus: [12:18]
5. Lame man healed: 5:1–15 [6:2]
6. Healing blind man: 9:1–41 [9:16]
7. The resurrection of Jesus: 20:6–7; [2:18–19]
8. Perhaps also walking on the water: 6:16–22
9. Perhaps the miraculous fish catch: 21:4–11

To make it a little more complex, John tells us Jesus did many signs, which is his favorite term for a miracle (e.g., 2:23; 3:2; 4:48; 6:2, 26, 30; 7:31; 9:16; 11:47; 12:37; 20:30). To concentrate the signs on the first four is wise, to add a few more seems reasonable, but then to realize all of Jesus' miracles are potential signs may be the best of all.

We want to clear the air with this definition:

A sign is a public deed performed by Jesus that reveals who he is but requires faith in order to perceive its truthfulness.

As such, then, a sign is an act that, upon pondering and imagining, continues to reveal the true identity of Jesus, but only for those with faith. As God became the embodied Logos in Jesus (1:14), so God can reveal the depths of God-ness in wine. Signs are then iconic moments. The act of turning water into more than an abundance of wine iconically reveals the identity of Jesus and his abounding sufficiency, but only to those with eyes to see. Think of how the world's finest of novels and stories have been told: they tell us a story about someone and something, and we see in that telling something more than the someone or something. Good stories, whether they are Tolkien's fictions or those of Willa Cather, tap on a door that opens into deep realities. They, too, function as signs of something real-er than the story's plain telling.

The wine reveals Jesus to be the source of uber-abundant joy. Drinking is a bodily experience of slaking thirst, and drinking wine evokes sweetness and celebration. All of this, and more, forms in the minds of those who ponder the sign itself. They are the ones who "believe" like the disciples, so fulfilling the purpose of the Gospel (20:30–31). As the children of Israel saw God's glory (Exodus 13:21–22; 16:10–11; 24:15–17), so Jesus' disciples are the ones who see the "glory" of Jesus (John 2:11). The sign then is a tactile, palpable experience of the presence of God. It asks you and me to answer the question of questions: Who is Jesus?

## QUESTIONS FOR REFLECTION AND APPLICATION

1. Why do you think John chooses a wedding to open the public ministry of Jesus?

2. How do you think John's use of "sign" is different from the other Gospel writers' use of "miracle"?

3. How does McKnight define sign?

4. What are your favorite stories? How do they reveal something "real-er than the story's plain telling"?

5. In what ways do you need Jesus to bring uber-abundant joy into your life? How does this wedding sign encourage you that Jesus can do this for you?

## FOR FURTHER READING

Scot McKnight, *The Real Mary: Why Protestant Christians Can Embrace the Mother of Jesus* (Brewster, Mass.: Paraclete, 2016), 61–72.

# JESUS IS
# THE TEMPLE

## *John 2:12–25*

<sup>12</sup> *After this he went down to Capernaum with his mother and brothers and his disciples. There they stayed for a few days.*

<sup>13</sup> *When it was almost time for the Jewish Passover, Jesus went up to Jerusalem.* <sup>14</sup> *In the temple courts he found people selling cattle, sheep and doves, and others sitting at tables exchanging money.* <sup>15</sup> *So he made a whip out of cords, and drove all from the temple courts, both sheep and cattle; he scattered the coins of the money changers and overturned their tables.* <sup>16</sup> *To those who sold doves he said, "Get these out of here! Stop turning my Father's house into a market!"* <sup>17</sup> *His disciples remembered that it is written: "Zeal for your house will consume me."*

<sup>18</sup> *The Jews then responded to him, "What sign can you show us to prove your authority to do all this?"*

<sup>19</sup> *Jesus answered them, "Destroy this temple, and I will raise it again in three days."*

<sup>20</sup> *They replied, "It has taken forty-six years to build this temple, and you are going to raise it in three days?"* <sup>21</sup> *But the temple he had spoken of was his body.* <sup>22</sup> *After he was raised from the dead, his disciples recalled what he had said. Then they believed the scripture and the words that Jesus had spoken.*

<sup>23</sup> *Now while he was in Jerusalem at the Passover Festival, many people saw the signs he was performing and believed in his name.[b]* <sup>24</sup> *But Jesus would not entrust himself to them, for he knew all people.* <sup>25</sup> *He did not need any testimony about mankind, for he knew what was in each person.*

I know, and perhaps you do too, people who at one time were "on fire" or "aglow" for Jesus and then, suddenly or slowly, the fire faded, and the glow dulled, and I wonder now if they lost their faith or never had faith to begin with. When Billy Graham got off the ground as America's evangelist, he had more than a rival in Canada. His name was Chuck Templeton. The two of them were friends. At one point Chuck, whose glow was beginning to dull, tried to dissuade Billy from his evangelical faith. Billy dug in, and Chuck walked away from the faith, eventually to become a leading journalist in Canada.

There are at least two stories in the faith journey: one that begins and grows over time, not always consistently of course, and another that seems to begin, then over time the person falls away. Jesus knows this kind of response, and so does John's Gospel.

Jesus, late in chapter six, will say, "Yet there are some of you who do not believe" (6:64). Jesus, John tells us then, "had known from the beginning which of them did not believe and who would betray him." The saddest words about faith then appear in John 6: "From this time many of his disciples turned back and no longer followed him" (6:66 [what an ominous chapter and verse]). Peter's words lift our spirits: "Lord, to whom shall we go? You have the words of eternal life. We have come to believe and to know that you are the Holy One of God" (6:68–69). Willa Cather, in her wonderful novel *Death Comes for the Archbishop*, spoke of faith like Peter: "They believed they were on the right trail, for they had seen no other" (65). Two stories of faith. Always lurking in John and in the church.

John does not write about this theme to scare believers but to instruct all of us that faith is a journey, not a sip of water or wine before the journey begins.

## TROUBLE AT PASSOVER

Speaking of journeys. How about Jesus'? From a small wedding in the backwoods of Galilee to the temple of all temples in Jerusalem—at least according to Josephus. From the sign of water into wine to turning tables topsy-turvy in the temple. These shifts in Jesus's own journey themselves are signs of bigger events to come!

Passover was one of three major events on the Jewish calendar. At Passover Jerusalem flooded with people, more even than the abundance of wine at Cana. Inside the temple courts, under the stoa that ran along the perimeter of the temple edifice, one could purchase what was needed for sacrifices, which was a lot more convenient than walking or carrying farm animals on a long three-day walk from Galilee or farther (can you say Rome or Alexandria or Babylon?). Jesus discovers, and surely he had noticed this since he was a little boy, the temple had become a bazaar for trade. When I was a child, our church did not permit traveling speakers to sell books or products inside the walls of our church on Sundays. Perhaps it was a bit legalistic for some, but it was an expression of sacredness. What we have encountered in our world is that the whole world, to adapt a poet, is not a stage but a marketplace for consumers. Some call it "mammonolatry," the worship of money and possessions.

Jesus is about to call the temple "my Father's house" (2:16) because he "is in closest relationship with the Father" (1:18). So he goes all protest on the situation. He makes a "whip out of cords" to drive out the animals from sacred space (2:15). He flips the tables, and the coins spin away in all directions. He stiff-arms those selling doves in the temple courts. Quite the impression. The disciples saw in Jesus' behavior the "zeal" Jesus had for temple purity, which was a temple for his Father (2:17).

Passover was policed because the festival celebrated liberation from Egypt's pharaoh, and thus provoked Jewish enthusiasts to ponder and act for liberation from Rome. Small riots broke out that were dealt with brutally. Tense enough that for Passover, the Roman prefect, who lived on the coast at Caesarea, would come to Jerusalem to maintain order. So everyone was on edge. Jesus led the edge.

So they ask him "what sign" he could do or "show" that would "prove" his "authority" (2:18). Ever ready for an iconic moment, Jesus' response is classic: "Destroy this temple, and I will raise it again in three days" (2:19). There is no way they had the faith to see the *sign*-ificance of those words. They take them literally and wonder how anyone could destroy and rebuild in three days what took 46 years (2:20).

## SIGN-FAITHS AT PASSOVER

Faith, as we have said, works wonders at times. Barbara Brown Taylor once wrote of what I would call positive sign-faith, saying, "It is a full-bodied relationship in which mind and heart, spirit and flesh, are converted to a new way of experiencing and responding to the world. It is the surrender of one set of images and the acceptance of another. It is a matter of learning to see the world, each other, and ourselves as God sees us, and to live as if God's reality were the only one that mattered" (Taylor, *The Preaching Life*, 44).

His words are a sign. John explains them: "But the temple he had spoken of was his body" (2:21). It would be nice if the disciples could have perceived the *sign*-ificance of his words. They did, but not until "after he was raised" (2:22), at which time "they believed the scripture and the words that Jesus had spoken." Above we observed that Jesus called the temple "my Father's house" and that he was in close relationship with the Father, but now that relationship is so close Jesus is *himself* the temple! David Ford gives a list that shows how prominent this "Jesus is" theme. "John suggests figural interpretations of Abraham, Jacob, Moses and the exodus, Elijah, Isaiah, David in many psalms, Israel's festivals, many titles of Jesus, several symbols for Israel, and more" (Ford, *John*, 75). He's right. If we ponder the words of John, we will discover that his words have *sign*-ificance too!

The impact of signs, which is what chapter two of John is about, leads both to believing (2:11, 22) as well as to sign-faith or sign-believing that was inadequate (2:23–24). The words need to be read carefully. There is a seeming affirmation of the response of some people in verse twenty-three: "many people saw the signs he was performing and believed in his name." That seems positive, but verse twenty-four suggests sign-faith is not enough: "But Jesus would not *entrust* (same word as "believe") himself to them." True faith forms an intimate bond of trust between a disciple and the Messiah. In that bond each commits to the other in a way that they abide in each other. The apostle Paul will speak of being "in Christ" and Christ "in us." John's language here is like Paul's.

Why did Jesus refuse to commit himself to these people? Because he perceived like no other what was in humans (2:25). His signs divide the audiences (9:16; 11:45–48; 12:37). Some surrender to him because of signs (2:11; 3:2; 6:2; 20:30–31); others accept the reality of the miracle but do not see through it to the identity of Jesus; yet others repudiate him completely. To see his miracles as signs one must perceive the identity of Jesus beyond the material miracle itself. One could say then that sign-faith is a first but not final step in the journey of true faith (Thompson, *John*, 67–68). True faith abides over time in trusting Jesus who abides over time in nurturing the believer.

## QUESTIONS FOR REFLECTION AND APPLICATION

1. In John 2, what are the impacts of Jesus' signs that John points out?

2. What signs did Jesus give during this Passover celebration?

3. Why was Passover a time when Rome worried about the Jewish people rebelling?

4. Have you ever seen a Christian friend lose their fire or walk away from following Jesus? How did that impact you?

5. What role have signs played in your coming to faith or continuing in faith?

### FOR FURTHER READING

Willa Cather, *Death Comes for the Archbishop* (Everyman's Library; New York: A.A. Knopf, 1992).
Barbara Brown Taylor, *The Preaching Life* (Lanham, Md.: Cowley, 1993).

# JESUS BRINGS
# NEW BIRTH

## John 3:1–21

[1] Now there was a Pharisee, a man named Nicodemus who was a member of the Jewish ruling council. [2] He came to Jesus at night and said, "Rabbi, we know that you are a teacher who has come from God. For no one could perform the signs you are doing if God were not with him."

[3] Jesus replied, "Very truly I tell you, no one can see the kingdom of God unless they are born again."

[4] "How can someone be born when they are old?" Nicodemus asked. "Surely they cannot enter a second time into their mother's womb to be born!"

[5] Jesus answered, "Very truly I tell you, no one can enter the kingdom of God unless they are born of water and the Spirit. [6] Flesh gives birth to flesh, but the Spirit[b] gives birth to spirit. [7] You should not be surprised at my saying, 'You[c] must be born again.' [8] The wind blows wherever it pleases. You hear its sound, but you cannot tell where it comes from or where it is going. So it is with everyone born of the Spirit."

[9] "How can this be?" Nicodemus asked.

[10] "You are Israel's teacher," said Jesus, "and do you not understand these things? [11] Very truly I tell you, we speak of what we

*know, and we testify to what we have seen, but still you people do not accept our testimony. [12] I have spoken to you of earthly things and you do not believe; how then will you believe if I speak of heavenly things? [13] No one has ever gone into heaven except the one who came from heaven—the Son of Man. [14] Just as Moses lifted up the snake in the wilderness, so the Son of Man must be lifted up, [15] that everyone who believes may have eternal life in him."*

*[16] For God so loved the world that he gave his one and only Son, that whoever believes in him shall not perish but have eternal life. [17] For God did not send his Son into the world to condemn the world, but to save the world through him. [18] Whoever believes in him is not condemned, but whoever does not believe stands condemned already because they have not believed in the name of God's one and only Son. [19] This is the verdict: Light has come into the world, but people loved darkness instead of light because their deeds were evil. [20] Everyone who does evil hates the light, and will not come into the light for fear that their deeds will be exposed. [21] But whoever lives by the truth comes into the light, so that it may be seen plainly that what they have done has been done in the sight of God.*

The Pharisees have suffered from both bad press as well as from overt stereotyping that has at times turned into anti-Semitism and violence against Jews. Christians are the perpetrators. Here's how they do their nasty work. Step one: Pharisees, they say, were legalistic, picayune, scrupulous fundamentalists who thought they could earn their way to heaven by their good works. This denies the Christian gospel of grace and faith. Step two in the fatal pattern is to say all Jews are Pharisees. Step three is overt anti-Semitism. The Final Step is Jews are "Jesus killers" and deserving of whatever happens to them. Most Christians take some of these steps. Not all take each step, but the first step is the trouble-making step. The Gospel of John is one of their sources.

The evidence from the 1st Century counters nearly every inch of every step taken here. The Pharisees liberalized law observance by adding rules that made the law do-able. They were not then hide-bound, inflexible conservatives. A recent Jewish scholar on a webinar said the Pharisees were 1st Century progressives! Here's a surprise for many Christians: Pharisees were confident in their place in God's covenant and not concerned about going to heaven when they died. In fact, the Christian understanding of heaven was not their understanding of the afterlife at all. They thought the future was a kingdom on earth, centered of course in Jerusalem where everyone would observe the Torah. They *knew* they were destined for the kingdom because they were God's elect and observant as covenant people. Pharisees were law-observant Jews who formed home Bible studies (or the 1st Century equivalent) and worked hard to help all people follow the law. Recent studies, in fact, would say the Pharisees were "more liberal" than Jesus and that Jesus was more Bible-based (Sievers and Levine).

And they were not all alike. Some were like Nicodemus who was clearly impressed by Jesus, who wanted to get to know him and have some conversations. Nicodemus then represents a Pharisee-seeker.

## NICODEMUS COMES TO JESUS

Nicodemus was one of Jerusalem's prominent Pharisees, and he was a "member of the Jewish ruling council," which is paraphrase for "ruler of the Judeans" (3:1).[1] He comes at night, which for John *sign*-ifies spiritual darkness posed over against Jesus as the Light of the world (3:19, 21). He's a seeker pondering that Jesus must be "from God" because of the "signs" he was performing (3:2). Nicodemus is on the journey of faith, and that he continued to grow in faith shows up in 7:50 and 19:39. Did he ever get there? As Alan Culpepper has said, "The reader has good reason to be hopeful about Nicodemus" (Culpepper, "Nicodemus," 259). Perhaps many Pharisees were like Nicodemus when it came to responding to Jesus.

Jesus jumps a hurdle or two, responding with "no one can see the kingdom of God unless they are born again" (3:3). The expression "born again" could be translated "born anew" or "born from above," indicating not only a rebirth but also a fusion with the God who has come to us in his Son, the Logos (1:14; Thompson, *John*, 79). Nicodemus has not yet arrived at full faith: he hears those words of Jesus and can't make sense of a second birth, whether as born again or born from above.

So Jesus explains what he means.

## JESUS EXPLAINS

Instead of simplifying what he had just said, as one might expect, Jesus dives into the depths of Who he is and the Life he offers. Readers need to be on full alert because Jesus swims fast and changes directions a few times. You might just mark in your Bible the various images Jesus uses in John 3:5–15.

First, Jesus **defines "born again"** with "unless they are born *of water and the Spirit*" (3:5), or perhaps "born of water, that is, Spirit." The meaning of "of water and the Spirit" could be first water, then Spirit. In which case, *water* points to baptism by water, and *Spirit* would point to the indwelling of the Spirit of the new covenant. Or this may be a singular act of God's regenerating work of a person. As a singular act we might translate it as "water, that is, Spirit," that is, purification by the Spirit (Ezekiel 36:25–28). The first option seems more likely to me.

Second, Jesus **explains two cosmic powers at work in the world**: "flesh" and "Spirit/spirit," each with its own capacity to reproduce. But flesh cannot reproduce into Spirit, only Spirit can do that. Spirit-rebirth here is a surprising, uncalculated, unearned act of God (3:8). The Greek word for "spirit" and "Spirit" and "wind" is *pneuma*, and John plays with the term here. God's Spirit (*pneuma*) works in the human spirit (*pneuma*) in mysterious yet wholly surprising ways like the wind (*pneuma*). David Ford must be quoted here. He says verse eight:

> *evokes imaginatively a God who is free (the wind/Spirit* **blows where it chooses***), who overflows our categories, who challenges ours knowledge of origins and purposes* **(where it comes from or where it goes)***, who has an energy we cannot harness, who can spring endless surprises, who is unseen yet effective, and who can blow us in new directions* (his italics and bold; Ford, *John*, 89).

Third, Jesus **challenges Nicodemus**, who remains confused (3:9) even if he is "Israel's teacher" (3:10). In fact, Jesus points a long finger at the man: "you people do not accept our testimony" (3:10–11). Then Jesus asks him how someone stuck in "earthly things" can comprehend or believe in "heavenly things" (3:12). Jesus probes Nicodemus more. The only one who can speak of such heavenly things is the one who has come down, the "Son of Man" (3:13; cf. 1:51), and the one who will be "lifted up," that is crucified (3:14; 8:28; 12:32–33). Those who "believe" in that Son of Man "may have eternal life in him" (3:15; again, 20:30–31 and 1:4).

We cannot be overly surprised Nicodemus has trouble keeping up with Jesus. Most of us have to read the paragraph (3:10–15) a couple times to catch it all.

## GOD'S MISSION
## EXPLAINED BY JOHN

Jesus is not done, and he changes directions again with some new themes and metaphors about God's mission in this world. Or should we say *John* expands on what Jesus said to Nicodemus? It is hard to know who is now speaking: would you put John 3:16–21 in red letters or black letters? (I suggest black letters.)

First, God's mission expresses God's *love for the world*. Jesus was sent into the world because God *loves* the world (3:16). As Murray Harris defines it, this divine love is "clearly a strong, selfless, gift-giving love that is totally focused on the welfare of others" and he adds that "God's love knows no bounds in its intensity (it is limitless) or in its scope (it includes all humans) (Harris, *John 3:16*, 11, 13). God's love-mission means God gave "his one and only Son" to redeem the world, and that redemption is both "beyond imagination" and "beyond calculation" in giving his Son (Harris, *John 3:16*, 18). The power of that love-mission is that anyone and everyone who "believes in him" is gifted "eternal life." John characteristically repeats himself: God's mission is not a mission of condemnation but a mission of salvation (3:17), but salvation is only for those who turn to Jesus in faith (3:18).

Second, God's mission enters into *cosmic battle*. John backs up to chapter one now with the imagery of Light and Darkness. In John 1 his own people rejected Jesus, but that repudiation is now cosmic: "Light has come into the *world*, but *the humans* [my translation; NIV has "people"] loved darkness" (3:19). Not only is it cosmic, that rejection occurs in the midst of a cosmic battle: "everyone who does evil hates the light" (or "The Light"; 3:20) because it exposes their unbelief and sin. The alternative is redemption for those who live "by the truth" (3:21) and open themselves to divine exposure.

Now back up to the beginning. This is a conversation with a Pharisee who is a leader in Jerusalem. His concerns were spiritual, and everything about this late-night discussion shows Jesus's profound respect for the Pharisee as well as the Pharisee's genuine seeking. Nicodemus is more typical of a Pharisee than most Christians think. Nicodemus will show up on Jesus' side later in the Gospel and again when 3,000 people get baptized at Pentecost (Acts 2), most likely many of them Pharisees. Jesus blew apart stereotypes, and we'd do well to learn from him.

## QUESTIONS FOR REFLECTION AND APPLICATION

1. What have you been taught about the Pharisees before? How does that compare with the ideas in this lesson?

2. Why does Nicodemus come to see Jesus?

3. How does John explain God's mission in the world? How does this teaching impact Nicodemus?

4. Have you ever memorized John 3:16? How does this context help you make more sense of that verse?

5. How do you think Nicodemus felt when he left that meeting?

## FOR FURTHER READING

R. Alan Culpepper, "Nicodemus: The Travail of New Birth," in *Character Studies in the Fourth Gospel: Narrative Approaches to Seventy Figures in John*, ed. S.A. Hunt, D.F. Tolmie, R. Zimmermann (Grand Rapids: Wm. B. Eerdmans, 2016), 249–259.

Murray J. Harris, *John 3:16: What's It All About?* (Eugene, Oregon: Cascade, 2015).

Joseph Sievers, Amy-Jill Levine, editors, *The Pharisees* (Grand Rapids: Wm. B. Eerdmans, 2021).

# JOHN'S WITNESS
# ABOUT JESUS

## John 3:22–36

22 After this, Jesus and his disciples went out into the Judean countryside, where he spent some time with them, and baptized. 23 Now John also was baptizing at Aenon near Salim, because there was plenty of water, and people were coming and being baptized. 24 (This was before John was put in prison.) 25 An argument developed between some of John's disciples and a certain Jew over the matter of ceremonial washing 26 They came to John and said to him, "Rabbi, that man who was with you on the other side of the Jordan—the one you testified about—look, he is baptizing, and everyone is going to him."

27 To this John replied, "A person can receive only what is given them from heaven. 28 You yourselves can testify that I said, 'I am not the Messiah but am sent ahead of him.' 29 The bride belongs to the bridegroom. The friend who attends the bridegroom waits and listens for him, and is full of joy when he hears the bridegroom's voice. That joy is mine, and it is now complete. 30 He must become greater; I must become less."

31 The one who comes from above is above all; the one who is from the earth belongs to the earth, and speaks as one from the

earth. *The one who comes from heaven is above all.* *32 He testifies to what he has seen and heard, but no one accepts his testimony.* *33 Whoever has accepted it has certified that God is truthful.* *34 For the one whom God has sent speaks the words of God, for God gives the Spirit without limit.* *35 The Father loves the Son and has placed everything in his hands.* *36 Whoever believes in the Son has eternal life, but whoever rejects the Son will not see life, for God's wrath remains on them.*

I memorized "Repetition is the mother of all learning" in a college Greek class, which in Greek was (if my memory serves me right): *meletē to pan*. Which could be translated, "Practice (or repetition) is everything!" What John writes in this passage rehearses and repeats what John has already said so far, yet this passage is not identical to others. Instead, it repeats the same tune in a new key. There's improvisation of familiar tunes, tones, and rhythms.

In John 1 we encountered John the Baptist, whom we there dubbed "J-B." He was a witness who said, "I am not, but Jesus is what you are hoping for." He's back at it in this passage with a memorable saying: "He must become greater; I must become less," which the KJV had in a more memorizable form as, "He must increase, but I must decrease" (3:30). That one verse is J-B's entire witness. (I hope they put that on his gravestone or bone box.) His witness was one of deflection and confession, and it all began with a dispute about baptism. (Who knew?!)

The heart of Christian witness is that Jesus is the point of it all.

## DISPUTE ABOUT J-B

In the wilderness of Judea, to the east of Jerusalem and approaching River Jordan, Jesus spent time being with his disciples. Jesus was baptizing as well. J-B was doing the same in Samaria not far from Jesus. A Judean man got into an argument with J-B's disciples about "ceremonial washing" (3:25). All this as a perfect set up for J-B and for us to perceive what it means to be a witness.

## J-B's Witness to Jesus

This Judean man wants to know what J-B thinks of people flocking to Jesus. J-B, with enthusiasm, speaks up. His first theme denies he's the source of redemptive attraction: "I am not the Messiah" (3:28).

His second theme explains who he is: I "am sent ahead of him" (3:28), which takes us back to 1:23, where he explained he was the Voice sent to prepare for the coming of the Lord himself. J-B brokered the relationship of Jesus to the disciples, and he continues to broker a similar relationship with others and Jesus (Ford, *John*, 103). He then says he "belongs to the bridegroom" (Jesus) as a "friend" or the Best Man (3:29). As such J-B simply "attends" and "waits" and "listens" for the bridegroom's arrival so his "joy" can be "full" upon arrival. In fact, J-B's witness is so full of Jesus' presence he can say "That joy is mine, and it is now complete" (3:29). J-B sounds like Simeon, the old man in the temple, who, once having seen Jesus, announces he can now die (Luke 2:29). John's ultimate witness, already cited above, is "He must become greater; I must become less" (John 3:30). Or, "it's necessary for that One to grow but for me to lessen" (my translation). J-B surrenders both to God's plan ("it's necessary"; see 3:27 too) and to the superiority of Jesus to himself. Why do some witnesses think it's all about themselves?

His third theme affirms who Jesus is. Jesus is the Messiah (3:28), the bridegroom (3:29), and the greater one (3:30). These three then open origami-like to an assortment of glowing expressions about Jesus:

1. Jesus "comes from above" or "heaven" and is "above all" (3:31).
2. Jesus "testifies to what he has seen and heard" in God's closest presence (3:32).
3. Jesus is rejected by humans in spite of who he is (3:32).
4. Jesus' testimony, when accepted by humans, certifies that "God is truthful" (3:33).
5. Jesus "speaks the words of God" (3:34).
6. Jesus has God's "Spirit without limit" (3:34; cf. 1:32–33 and the word "remain").
7. Jesus as God's Son is loved by the Father (3:35).
8. Jesus has been given all things in his hands by the Father (3:35).
9. Jesus is the source of eternal life for believers (3:36).
10. Jesus is the source of God's judgment and wrath for those who reject him (3:36).

J-B was a gifted prophet, a powerful preacher, an immerser for purification, but he was nothing but a preparer for Someone Else. He deflects his giftedness in order to draw attention and audience to Jesus alone. Jesus is the One in whom the Spirit and the Word dwell (6:63), so J-B was a "It's not me but Jesus" kind of witness.

Appropriately, the man and his ministry disappear from John's Gospel at this point. He "diminishes to nothing" (Callahan, "John," 191).

## QUESTIONS FOR REFLECTION
## AND APPLICATION

1. What is the importance of John the Baptist in the story of Jesus?

2. What is the heart of Christian witness?

3. In what ways does J-B show us how to be a witness to Jesus?

4. Of J-B's expressions about Jesus listed here, which is the most meaningful for you?

5. What is the significance of J-B not showing up in John's Gospel after this point in the story?

# A SAMARITAN
# WOMAN'S WITNESS
# ABOUT JESUS

## John 4:1–42

¹ Now Jesus learned that the Pharisees had heard that he was gaining and baptizing more disciples than John—² although in fact it was not Jesus who baptized, but his disciples. ³ So he left Judea and went back once more to Galilee.

⁴ Now he had to go through Samaria. ⁵ So he came to a town in Samaria called Sychar, near the plot of ground Jacob had given to his son Joseph. ⁶ Jacob's well was there, and Jesus, tired as he was from the journey, sat down by the well. It was about noon.

⁷ When a Samaritan woman came to draw water, Jesus said to her, "Will you give me a drink?" ⁸ (His disciples had gone into the town to buy food.)

⁹ The Samaritan woman said to him, "You are a Jew and I am a Samaritan woman. How can you ask me for a drink?" (For Jews do not associate with Samaritans. )

¹⁰ Jesus answered her, "If you knew the gift of God and who it is that asks you for a drink, you would have asked him and he would have given you living water."

¹¹ "Sir," the woman said, "you have nothing to draw with and the well is deep. Where can you get this living water? ¹² Are you greater than our father Jacob, who gave us the well and drank from it himself, as did also his sons and his livestock?"

¹³ Jesus answered, "Everyone who drinks this water will be thirsty again, ¹⁴ but whoever drinks the water I give them will never thirst. Indeed, the water I give them will become in them a spring of water welling up to eternal life."

¹⁵ The woman said to him, "Sir, give me this water so that I won't get thirsty and have to keep coming here to draw water."

¹⁶ He told her, "Go, call your husband and come back."

¹⁷ "I have no husband," she replied.

Jesus said to her, "You are right when you say you have no husband.

¹⁸ The fact is, you have had five husbands, and the man you now have is not your husband. What you have just said is quite true."

¹⁹ "Sir," the woman said, "I can see that you are a prophet. ²⁰ Our ancestors worshiped on this mountain, but you Jews claim that the place where we must worship is in Jerusalem."

²¹ "Woman," Jesus replied, "believe me, a time is coming when you will worship the Father neither on this mountain nor in Jerusalem. ²² You Samaritans worship what you do not know; we worship what we do know, for salvation is from the Jews. ²³ Yet a time is coming and has now come when the true worshipers will worship the Father in the Spirit and in truth, for they are the kind of worshipers the Father seeks. ²⁴ God is spirit, and his worshipers must worship in the Spirit and in truth."

²⁵ The woman said, "I know that Messiah" (called Christ) "is coming. When he comes, he will explain everything to us."

²⁶ Then Jesus declared, "I, the one speaking to you—I am he."

²⁷ Just then his disciples returned and were surprised to find him talking with a woman. But no one asked, "What do you want?" or "Why are you talking with her?"

<sup>28</sup> *Then, leaving her water jar, the woman went back to the town and said to the people,* <sup>29</sup> *"Come, see a man who told me everything I ever did. Could this be the Messiah?"* <sup>30</sup> *They came out of the town and made their way toward him.*

<sup>31</sup> *Meanwhile his disciples urged him, "Rabbi, eat something."*

<sup>32</sup> *But he said to them, "I have food to eat that you know nothing about."*

<sup>33</sup> *Then his disciples said to each other, "Could someone have brought him food?"*

<sup>34</sup> *"My food," said Jesus, "is to do the will of him who sent me and to finish his work.* <sup>35</sup> *Don't you have a saying, 'It's still four months until harvest'? I tell you, open your eyes and look at the fields! They are ripe for harvest.* <sup>36</sup> *Even now the one who reaps draws a wage and harvests a crop for eternal life, so that the sower and the reaper may be glad together.* <sup>37</sup> *Thus the saying 'One sows and another reaps' is true.* <sup>38</sup> *I sent you to reap what you have not worked for. Others have done the hard work, and you have reaped the benefits of their labor."*

<sup>39</sup> *Many of the Samaritans from that town believed in him because of the woman's testimony, "He told me everything I ever did."* <sup>40</sup> *So when the Samaritans came to him, they urged him to stay with them, and he stayed two days.* <sup>41</sup> *And because of his words many more became believers.*

<sup>42</sup> *They said to the woman, "We no longer believe just because of what you said; now we have heard for ourselves, and we know that this man really is the Savior of the world."*

Because Jesus' reputation was climbing social scales, mostly due to the baptisms of so many by Jesus' own followers (4:1–2), he grabbed the attention of the Pharisees of Jerusalem. Which meant pressure on his ministry from the authorities, so he decided to return to Galilee, which meant, for one such trip, traveling through Samaria (4:3). In Samaria about noon one day, he was near a well and had a stunning conversation with a woman. In this chapter we have two stories woven together: one about the disciples (4:1–3, 27, 31–38) and one about the woman (4:4–26, 27–29, 30–42). As Rodney Reeves has written, she becomes the witness while the ones sent to witness are dumbfounded (Reeves, *Spirituality*, 82–93).

People gain reputations over time and not all of them are accurate and most of them are exaggerations. For some Martin Luther was a hothead; John Calvin a dry, mean-spirited legalist; John Wesley an inattentive husband; Jonathan Edwards a fierce, loveless preacher of a fierce, wrathful God; D.L. Moody a huckster of the gospel; and Billy Graham a wannabe politician. One woman after another in the history of the church has been diminished by exaggerations and distortions, including Phoebe Palmer and Mary Bethune and Anne Graham Lotz and Beth Moore and Kristin Kobes Du Mez and Beth Allison Barr and Aimee Byrd. Men have written nearly all the stories and men have given prominence to other men and not to women. But some of these women have been trashed.

John 4 tells a story about a woman whom Christians have distorted.

## CLEARING RUBBLE TO SEE THE WITNESS TO JESUS

So we have to clean out some nasty rubble that has accumulated around the Samaritan woman (Cohick, *Women in the World of the Earliest Christians*, 122–128; Reeder). Her statement trades in a stereotype when she says to Jesus, "You are a Jew [or Judean] and I am a Samaritan woman. How can you ask me for a drink?" (4:9). Yes, Jews of Jerusalem and Samaritans were often at odds with one another, but there is nothing that unusual for Jesus to cross boundaries, which is why the disciples didn't even bother to ask (cf. 4:27). Rubble.

What is unusual is how intense the conversation is between Jesus and this woman, as if there's nothing one bit unusual about it. What makes it unusual is many live in a stereotype that Jesus and teachers don't talk with women. Rubble.

There is no evidence that dissolute women went to water wells alone because other women couldn't associate with them. Rubble.

The rubble has especially collected around one simple statement, and we read it in verse eighteen: "You have had [or you had] five husbands. (The NIV adds "The fact is.") For most this means she was sexually promiscuous and unfaithful. Add to this another simple statement that gathers rubble: "and the man you now have is not your husband" (4:18). Rubble, rubble.

The text does not say any of this.

Samaria is a large region north of Jerusalem, between Judea and Galilee, and Mt. Gerizim, the sacred site of the Samaritans (who continue to exist there to this day), is about thirty miles from Jerusalem. Samaritans are considered by some biblical writers to be transplanted idolaters when the northern kingdom was conquered (2 Kings 17; but see also 2 Chronicles 30:6, 10–11). They have always rooted their faith in the Five Books of Moses. The Samaritans today see themselves as the true descendants, not just of Joshua's worship center, but of the tribes of Joseph, Ephraim, and Manasseh.

The rubble is that many . . . no, scratch that, *almost all* have seen the woman as sexually promiscuous and read the entire passage through the lens of an immoral woman. To quote a summary reading of this sort, Lynn Cohick writes, "the Samaritan woman has been harshly treated by centuries of commentators who have labeled her a promiscuous vixen bent on seducing unsuspecting men, and who therefore becomes the village pariah" (Cohick, *Women in the World of Earliest Christians*, 128). Caryn Reeder runs us through the history of Christian readings of this woman and most have interpreted her as an erotic, as sexually promiscuous, and as an adulterer. She mentions Tertullian, Origen, and John Chrysostom, influential theologians of the early church. From other periods in church history, she finds the same degrading reading in John Calvin, Clara Lucas Balfour, D.L. Moody, and in the contemporary church she mentions Liz Curtis Higgs, Barbara J. Essex, and John Piper. Not many are like Mary DeMuth who see her more in terms of victim.

Back to the rubble of assuming she was an erotic and sexually promiscuous woman. Not once is that suggested in this passage. Not once. Christian readers have destroyed this woman's character on the basis of a presumption without evidence. Why would a woman have five husbands and now a man who is not her husband? Anyone who knows Judaism can think of more than the sexually promiscuous or immoral-woman view. Her husbands could have died. Not at all impossible. She could have been passed around through the laws of levirate marriage in which if a man died, his brother took under his care his brother's wife. Not at all impossible. She could have been divorced a time or two, perhaps especially if she was a barren woman. Not at all impossible. She could be said to "have" a man, and the word could mean nothing more than "man" and not "husband," because she was a concubine of a Roman leader who could not marry a woman of lower class. Committed cohabitation was a known institution in that world, too. Or, more likely, she was under the care of her brother, her former husband's brother, or an uncle. Such explanations are not only possible but should be our first instincts.

---

### Five women given special attention in John:

Mary, mother of Jesus: 2:1–11; 19:25–27
Samaritan woman: 4:1–42
Martha: 11:20–44
Mary, sister of Martha: 12:1–8
Mary Magdalene: 20:1–18

---

Perhaps more telling against the traditional reading of the woman as immoral are the following: (1) Jesus carries on an extensive back-and-forth with her, (2) she becomes a witness of Jesus (3) without Jesus ever saying she needed to repent from something, (4) her story and Nathanael's are very much alike (1:43–51), (5) no one in the village seems to distrust her as a promiscuous woman. In fact, (6) she wields powerful influence in the community. What seems most likely is that she's a leader in the community.

## THE CONVERSATION ABOUT JESUS

Jesus engages the Samaritan woman in a conversation, but it's not a fireside chat about Roman emperors. Jesus' back-and-forth was shaped for her to see who he was so she could become a witness about Jesus. The conversation moves through four phases, with the woman responding to Jesus' metaphors with literal misperceptions (as Nicodemus did in chapter three) that climb their way into an overt confession of who Jesus is (way beyond what Nicodemus did). We might ask ourselves why we adore Nicodemus and denigrate this woman.

**Phase one** (4:7–12). Jesus had asked the woman for a drink of water. She pushed back a bit, wondering why he, a Jew, would ask such from a Samaritan. His answer shifts a few lanes over with considerable speed. If she but knew the "gift of God" and "who it is" that wanted a drink, he could have given her "living water." (These terms are clarified at 7:37–39 and go back to Jeremiah 2:13; 17:13, if not also other prophets.) The speed shifts here, and even for well-read Bible people the shifts are not immediately clear. But the three expressions just quoted are all pointing her to think about Who Jesus Is. Like Nicodemus, she thinks literally: Jesus has no bucket, the well is deep, and so she asks where he can draw this "living water." She's on her way to comprehending Jesus because she overtly wonders aloud if Jesus is greater than Jacob, whose well it was originally. Jacob dug a well; Jesus is the spring that provides running water (Thompson, *John*, 99–100).

**Phase two** (4:13–15). Jesus doesn't back up to clarify what "living water" meant. He moves on to another revelatory saying that challenges her even more. The well water slakes thirst for a moment but those who drink his living water "will never thirst" because it wells up to "eternal life." The Samaritan woman, clearly not yet perceiving the revelation of who Jesus is, realizes forever-water is the best offer yet: "Give me this water" but her reason is "so that I won't get thirsty and have to keep coming here." She's stalled in her perceptions of Jesus.

**Phase three** (4:16–20). Jesus hops lanes when he responds to her request for forever-water with "Go, call your husband and come back." Another Nathanael moment. He knows about her without her having said one word about husbands. Her response is that she has no husband, and Jesus' is that she's had five of them and the one she's with now is not a husband—so she's right, she has no husband. She's beginning to realize even more Who Jesus Is when she says he's a "prophet." But she shifts lanes to the issue between Samaritans and Jews over which mountain is God's.

**Phase four** (4:21–26). Jesus transforms the terms of her question from either Mt Gerizim or Mt Zion to "neither on this mountain nor in Jerusalem," even though he sees the Samaritans as unorthodox and the Jews as orthodox. In fact, "salvation is from the Jews [Judeans]." True worship transcends geographical location because (1) "God is spirit [or Spirit]" and (2) the right worshipers "must worship in Spirit and truth." The Samaritan woman realizes Jesus is talking eschatology, that is, the time when all truth will be embraced because the Messiah will settle all old scores. He will "explain everything to us."

Four phases now come to one single conclusion, and it's from the mouth of Jesus: "I, the one speaking to you–I am he." This is the first "I am" statement of Jesus in the Gospel. (See p. 103.) Jesus is that Messiah. The entire conversation, despite lane shifting and speed changes, was led by Jesus so she could see that he, the man asking for water and talking with her, was himself the "living water" and more than a prophet. The question shaping the entire Gospel is "Who is Jesus?" and one of the answers is "Messiah." Revelations like this lead to confession and witness.

## JESUS TEACHES THE DISCIPLES

The account is not yet complete.

Before we get to anything like a confession or witness, John interrupts the narrative with the return of the disciples, who had gone into the city to acquire food (4:8). They are surprised Jesus was talking with the woman but unwilling to break the ice by asking about that. So they turn to food: "eat something," they say to their "Rabbi" (4:31).

One more time Jesus shifts lanes with a loud voice when he utters, "I have food to eat that you know nothing about" (4:32). Like Nicodemus, like the woman, they go all literal on him when they wonder aloud if someone else brought him food. (We, the readers, know just how shallow their response is, but had we been there, we'd have said the same.)

Jesus explains. "My food . . . is to do the will of him who sent me and to finish his work" (4:34). That metaphor explained so directly must have led to perception by the disciples. But he changes lanes again, this time to the metaphor of fields, harvests, sowers, and reapers. They are about gospeling, witnessing to Jesus, one person sowing and another person reaping, they are the reapers, and they get to harvest people for eternal life (4:35–38). Instead of eating their food he is casting images for them to see their mission is to be witnesses.

Like the Samaritan woman's mission.

While they sit there thinking about food and why Jesus was talking to the woman and what he meant by the word "food."

## THE WITNESS ABOUT
## JESUS AND BY JESUS

The interruption of the narrative is over. The Samaritan woman, seemingly so joyous over Jesus's claim to be Messiah (4:26), forgets her water vessel (4:28), returns to the city and solicits the folks to come out to the well and meet the Messiah (4:29). So they did. Her witness to Jesus led to "many" turning to believing in Jesus (4:39), and it was all because of her experience with Jesus as the one who knew her life (4:39). Revelation, confession, and witness lead to a city wanting Jesus to reside with them, which he does for two days, which led to even more believers (4:40–41).

Their reasons, however, were not just because of her witness but because they had seen Jesus up close and personal. Which is what reading this Gospel does to people: they encounter the Logos, the Life, the Lord, the Lamb of God–the Messiah. For them he was the "Savior of the world" (4:42; a favorite term in Isaiah, note 43:3; 45:15, 21–22; 49:26).

Now we need to back up yet again. Some people acquire unjust, demeaning, degrading reputations because Christians sit in judgment on them. In the case of the Samaritan woman, we need to repent, and we need to restore her to her true character: a Samaritan seeker who met Jesus and became a powerful witness to Jesus as their Messiah. When we clear out the rubble by repentance and restoration, we find yet another admirable woman in the Gospels.

## Questions for Reflection and Application

1. What have you been taught about this woman before? How does this chapter confront those previous ideas? What are some possible explanations for her having had five husbands?

2. How does the woman at the well take on the task of the disciples while they are "dumbfounded"?

3. What happens to your reading of the passage if the woman is seen as a community leader instead of a promiscuous woman?

4. Review: What are the names/titles/labels that have been applied to Jesus from chapter one through chapter four?

5. Further study: Notice how versatile "water" is in John: 1:33; 2:7–9; 3:5, 23; 5:7; 7:38; 13:5; 19:34.

## FOR FURTHER READING

Lynn Cohick, *Women in the World of the Earliest Christians, Illuminating Ancient Ways of Life* (Grand Rapids: Baker Academic, 2009).
Caryn A. Reeder, *The Samaritan Woman's Story: Reconsidering John 4 After #ChurchToo* (Downers Grove, Ill.: IVP Academic, 2022).

# A FATHER WITNESSES
# ABOUT JESUS

## John 4:43–54

⁴³ *After the two days he left for Galilee.* ⁴⁴ *(Now Jesus himself had pointed out that a prophet has no honor in his own country.)* ⁴⁵ *When he arrived in Galilee, the Galileans welcomed him. They had seen all that he had done in Jerusalem at the Passover Festival, for they also had been there.*

⁴⁶ *Once more he visited Cana in Galilee, where he had turned the water into wine. And there was a certain royal official whose son lay sick at Capernaum.* ⁴⁷ *When this man heard that Jesus had arrived in Galilee from Judea, he went to him and begged him to come and heal his son, who was close to death.*

⁴⁸ *"Unless you people see signs and wonders," Jesus told him, "you will never believe."*

⁴⁹ *The royal official said, "Sir, come down before my child dies."*

⁵⁰ *"Go," Jesus replied, "your son will live."*

*The man took Jesus at his word and departed.*

⁵¹ *While he was still on the way, his servants met him with the news that his boy was living.* ⁵² *When he inquired as to the time when his son got better, they said to him, "Yesterday, at one in the afternoon, the fever left him."* ⁵³ *Then the father realized that this*

*was the exact time at which Jesus had said to him, "Your son will live." So he and his whole household believed.*

*54 This was the second sign Jesus performed after coming from Judea to Galilee.*

Taking someone at their word can become a serious challenge if it is (1) someone with a huge reputation and (2) you know the person well enough to doubt that reputation. Jesus is a Galilean from small town Nazareth. Nathanael has already opened the window onto what Cana's villagers thought of any religious leader from Nazareth. John shoves Jesus into the midst of that degrading attitude in our passage by reminding us that Jesus was aware that a prophet would be honorless among his own. But Jesus returns with at least one surprising consequence. He informs us that Jesus, after a mind-blowing set of miracles in big-city Jerusalem at a national festival (Passover), had returned back home, where he experienced *a surprising welcome.* In fact, enough of the locals had been at Passover that John can, no doubt with some hyperbole, say they "had seen *all that he had done in Jerusalem*" (4:43–45).

## A SON

With such an opening, Jesus makes a new move—what John calls the "second sign," also done in Cana (4:54). Cana is north of the normal route to Capernaum from Nazareth, but a gentile "royal official," or just "a royal," searched out where Jesus was and found Jesus in Cana.[1] His concern was his son, "who was close to death," so he pleads with Jesus to come down to Capernaum to heal him (4:46–47).

Jesus seems never to respond quite the way we expect. Jesus' response to the royal is like his response to his mother. In fact, Jesus' response is that these people don't receive him well unless they see "signs and wonders" (4:48). We now have to think that initial Galilean response of "welcome" after his return from Jerusalem in verse forty-five was actually a shallow, not-yet-believing response. This challenges a response from the man, and respond he does with "come down before my child dies" (4:49). Jesus puts a serious challenge before the man: "Go, your son will live" (4:50). The Logos speaks in Galilee, the Light flashes in the darkness.

True faith in John takes Jesus at his word and acts upon that word. The heart of this passage is in the middle line. The NIV's translation mutes the significance of the words. It is not "the man took Jesus at his word" but "the man believed the word [*logos*] that Jesus said to him" (4:50). How do we know he believed? He turned around and descended back to Capernaum, showing that believing means obeying. He hoped to get Jesus to come to Capernaum; he returns without Jesus (Reeves, *Spirituality*, 64). It was a two-day walk, and during those two days this desperate father, a bit like parents who take a child with serious illness from doctor to doctor or scroll through Google searches to find a medical solution, wondered if his son was alive and if Jesus' word was worth trusting. He could not know until he got back down to Capernaum.

On his way back his servants meet up with him to inform him that his son was living, which means he had been healed (4:51). Noticeably, and this is one of the secrets to reading the Gospel of John, the man's attention is not on his healed son but on the Healer. He inquires *when* that happened and realized it was the moment the Life-giving Logos uttered the word (*logos*) (4:52–53). Like the Samaritan woman, the official returns to his home, tells them about Jesus, and "he and his whole household believed" (4:53). Anyone who experiences redemption from Jesus can become a witness to Jesus simply by telling one's story.

## A Sign

John calls this the "second sign," and to repeat,

> A sign is a public deed performed by Jesus that reveals
> who he is but requires faith in order to perceive its
> truthfulness.

A sign, when a believer ponders and imagines by turning it over and over, reveals the deeper identity of Jesus. Signs are then iconic revelations of Jesus. In John's prologue (1:1–18) we read that "in" the Logos/Jesus "was life" that is also "Light" that pierces the darkness, and here that darkness is unbelief in Cana and Galilee. Healing with only the word of the Logos reveals the power of the Life at work in Jesus. To perceive this sign and experience that Life one must believe Jesus and act upon the *logos* of the Logos. That man talked about Jesus the rest of his life because he saw the sign, maybe the only one who did!

## Questions for Reflection and Application

1. This is the second sign at Cana. Compare the accounts of the two signs in Cana (John 2:1–11; 4:43–54). What similarities do you notice?

2. What does this sign reveal about Jesus' identity?

3. How did this man's experience with Jesus turn him into a witness?

4. Compare this story with 1 Kings 17:17–24. Is Jesus like Elijah? (You can also compare John 1:21, 25 and 6:7–14 with 2 Kings 4).

5. Why does "believing mean obeying"? Have you ever taken a step of faith when you have shown your belief with your obedience?

# A HEALED MAN
# AND JESUS

## *John 5:1–18*

*¹ Some time later, Jesus went up to Jerusalem for one of the Jewish festivals. ² Now there is in Jerusalem near the Sheep Gate a pool, which in Aramaic is called Bethesda and which is surrounded by five covered colonnades. ³ Here a great number of disabled people used to lie—the blind, the lame, the paralyzed. ⁵ One who was there had been an invalid for thirty-eight years. ⁶ When Jesus saw him lying there and learned that he had been in this condition for a long time, he asked him, "Do you want to get well?" ⁷ "Sir," the invalid replied, "I have no one to help me into the pool when the water is stirred. While I am trying to get in, someone else goes down ahead of me."*

*⁸ Then Jesus said to him, "Get up! Pick up your mat and walk." ⁹ At once the man was cured; he picked up his mat and walked.*

*The day on which this took place was a Sabbath, ¹⁰ and so the Jewish leaders said to the man who had been healed, "It is the Sabbath; the law forbids you to carry your mat."*

*¹¹ But he replied, "The man who made me well said to me, 'Pick up your mat and walk.'" ¹² So they asked him, "Who is this fellow who told you to pick it up and walk?" ¹³ The man who was healed had no idea who it was, for Jesus had slipped away into the crowd that was there. ¹⁴ Later Jesus found him at the temple and said to him, "See, you are well again. Stop sinning or something worse may happen to you." ¹⁵ The man went away and told the Jewish leaders that it was Jesus who had made him well.*

*¹⁶ So, because Jesus was doing these things on the Sabbath, the Jewish leaders began to persecute him. ¹⁷ In his defense Jesus said to them, "My Father is always at his work to this very day, and I too am working." ¹⁸ For this reason they tried all the more to kill him; not only was he breaking the Sabbath, but he was even calling God his own Father, making himself equal with God.*

It is common to think we can achieve a level of gospel accomplishment and then move steadily onward, upward, and forward. Not so fast. Much, if not most, success is accompanied by stress, obstacles, opposition, and disappointments. In this passage Jesus does the impossible and the Judean leaders work at getting rid of him. At the heart of this passage then is the core theme of Light opposed by the Darkness (1:9–13), and at times the Darkness will weaponize conventional practices or the Bible against those working for the Light. At times even those who are healed by Jesus walk away, which is the lurking disappointment in this passage.

## A Man in Need

Not far off the north end of the temple area in Jerusalem is the Church of St. Anne, built near the visually stimulating ruins of the Pool of Bethesda. Bethesda means "house of mercy." John tells us that at this site many in need of healing ("the blind, the lame, the paralyzed") gathered, awaiting the stirring of the waters, which was understood to be a merciful, healing visitation by God (5:7).[1] One man had been coming to the Pool for 38 years but had never been able to plunge into the waters in time for a healing (5:5–7).

## THE HEALER SPEAKS THE WORD

The question of Jesus contains words the man wanted to hear when he asks the weakened man, "Do you want to get well?" (5:6). The man explains his struggle and Jesus intervenes with "Get up!" and "Pick up your mat and walk" (5:8). The Logos who created, the Logos with Life, speaks the word and "at once the man was cured" and was able to walk! The healing reveals who Jesus is, and is another sign (see at 2:1–11 above). Signs reveal Jesus to the one with faith. "Who is this Jesus?" is the right question. Some people comprehend who Jesus is but turn on him.

## THE HEALED MAN BECOMES AN INFORMANT

Conventions can be weaponized to discredit a person's reputation. John tells us this happened on a Sabbath, the day of rest (5:9). The man carried his mat, and according to the conventions of the day carrying a mat was work, and work was not suitable to a Sabbath (cf. Jeremiah 17:19–27). Indeed, deliberate disobedience carried the penalty of death by stoning (Numbers 15:32–36), and even accidental violations required the sin offering prescribed in Leviticus 4:27–31. Here's a man walking for the first time in 38 years, but some get stuck on the man carrying his mat on Sabbath! Yes, of course, they had convention on their side. Jesus disagreed. Life transcends such conventions (Mark 3:1–6).

The healed man blamed the healer. The healed man knew that the one who "made me well" told me to carry the mat (John 5:11). The leaders wanted him to identify the healer, but Jesus was an incognito healer so the healed man could not identify him. "Later," the NIV reads, they encounter one another again and Jesus summons the man to "stop sinning," insinuating perhaps that the man's weakness was the result of his sins (5:14). (The connection between the man's weakness and sin stands in contrast to Jesus's words in John 9:3.) Sad to read, the man, concerned perhaps about his own life and reputation, turns informant and identified Jesus to the Judean powers (5:15). Ramsey Michaels thus wonders in print with these words: "The man said nothing in reply, no word of thanks, no expression of belief, no commitment to stop sinning" (Michaels, *John*, 299).

He simply walked away.

## THE HEALER REVEALS

Jesus both healed on the Sabbath and commanded a man to carry his mat on the Sabbath. Jesus obviously knew Sabbath conventions. He worked this miracle to provoke discussion and revelation. He reveals two things: (1) he can work on the Sabbath because God works on the Sabbath, and (2) the God of the Sabbath is the Father and Jesus is the Son. The opposition also knows Jesus crossed the line into dangerous territory: "he was even calling God his own Father, making himself equal with God" (5:18).

Signs, like windows and doors, open a room to the Light. The revelation of this sign is that Jesus, the source of Life, can work redemption on the Sabbath because, like the Father, he works the work of God. How close is that kind of relationship? Real close. As our next passage will reveal, this healing opens the windows on a Jesus who is ready to reveal.

## QUESTIONS FOR REFLECTION AND APPLICATION

1. What is the conflict between Jesus and the Judean leaders in this instance?

2. How does John use this story to further support his themes of Light and Logos?

3. What did this sign teach about Jesus?

4. If Jesus asked you, "Do you want to get well?" what would come to mind for you? In what ways do you need God's healing word today?

5. Do you have a personal Sabbath practice? To what extent do you feel a tension between resting and doing kingdom works during your Sabbath?

# FATHER, SON, AND FOUR WITNESSES TO JESUS

## *John 5:19–47*

[19] *Jesus gave them this answer: "Very truly I tell you, the Son can do nothing by himself; he can do only what he sees his Father doing, because whatever the Father does the Son also does.* [20] *For the Father loves the Son and shows him all he does. Yes, and he will show him even greater works than these, so that you will be amazed.* [21] *For just as the Father raises the dead and gives them life, even so the Son gives life to whom he is pleased to give it.* [22] *Moreover, the Father judges no one, but has entrusted all judgment to the Son,* [23] *that all may honor the Son just as they honor the Father. Whoever does not honor the Son does not honor the Father, who sent him.*

[24] *"Very truly I tell you, whoever hears my word and believes him who sent me has eternal life and will not be judged but has crossed over from death to life.* [25] *Very truly I tell you, a time is coming and has now come when the dead will hear the voice of the Son of God and those who hear will live.* [26] *For as the Father has life in himself, so he has granted the Son also to have life in*

himself. <sup>27</sup> And he has given him authority to judge because he is the Son of Man.

<sup>28</sup> "Do not be amazed at this, for a time is coming when all who are in their graves will hear his voice <sup>29</sup> and come out—those who have done what is good will rise to live, and those who have done what is evil will rise to be condemned. <sup>30</sup> By myself I can do nothing; I judge only as I hear, and my judgment is just, for I seek not to please myself but him who sent me.

<sup>31</sup> "If I testify about myself, my testimony is not true. <sup>32</sup> There is another who testifies in my favor, and I know that his testimony about me is true.

<sup>33</sup> "You have sent to John and he has testified to the truth. <sup>34</sup> Not that I accept human testimony; but I mention it that you may be saved. <sup>35</sup> John was a lamp that burned and gave light, and you chose for a time to enjoy his light.

<sup>36</sup> "I have testimony weightier than that of John. For the works that the Father has given me to finish—the very works that I am doing—testify that the Father has sent me. <sup>37</sup> And the Father who sent me has himself testified concerning me. You have never heard his voice nor seen his form, <sup>38</sup> nor does his word dwell in you, for you do not believe the one he sent. <sup>39</sup> You study the Scriptures diligently because you think that in them you have eternal life. These are the very Scriptures that testify about me, <sup>40</sup> yet you refuse to come to me to have life.

<sup>41</sup> "I do not accept glory from human beings, <sup>42</sup> but I know you. I know that you do not have the love of God in your hearts. <sup>43</sup> I have come in my Father's name, and you do not accept me; but if someone else comes in his own name, you will accept him. <sup>44</sup> How can you believe since you accept glory from one another but do not seek the glory that comes from the only God?

<sup>45</sup> "But do not think I will accuse you before the Father. Your accuser is Moses, on whom your hopes are set. <sup>46</sup> If you believed Moses, you would believe me, for he wrote about me. <sup>47</sup> But since you do not believe what he wrote, how are you going to believe what I say?"

The accusation that Jesus made himself "equal" to God closed our previous passage (5:18). Our passage affirms in many ways that the Father and the Son are intimately unified. Jesus is being summoned before the Jewish leaders in Jerusalem, almost like he is put on trial. Jesus in this passage becomes both a witness to himself by explaining himself, a lawyer who produces witnesses for himself, and then—to flip the script—he becomes the judge! All for his claim to be equal to the Father. Readers of John know the Gospel presents Jesus as God (from 1:1 on) but we will once again need to back up before this Gospel to hear these words as the first century hearers experienced them. What they experienced was a man claiming way too much.

Jesus needs to explain himself so in John 5:19–47 we are treated to a lengthy discourse of Jesus. John's habit is to weave in and out of his favorite terms and ideas. He provides in this discourse nothing less than a network of Father and Son, that is, an explanation of their intimate relationship. The simple language masks the complexity and profundity of theology, and it takes several careful readings of these verses even to begin to comprehend them. It is one of the most profound revelations of who Jesus is in the entire New Testament. David Ford, a theologian at Cambridge University, puts it like this: "Who can fathom that 'self' of the Father? The attempt to do so never ends, leading through Israel's Scriptures, the Synoptic Gospels, this Gospel, and then through centuries of prayer and worship, theology, philosophy, poetry and other arts, and experience. That need not be an overwhelming and intimidatingly difficult prospect or project, but rather an endlessly attractive one, trusting that little by little . . . understanding can grow, and that no one ever finishes fathoming and being amazed and delighted by who God is" (Ford, *John*, 131).

Jesus ushers into this fathoming.

## THE SON'S RELATIONSHIP
## WITH THE FATHER

All the Son does is from the Father, so the Son's equal status with the Father is measured by the Son's dependence on the Father. We see this in four ways. First, the Father *sent* the Son ("believe him who sent me"); second and third, the Father has *given* the Son both "to have life in himself" and has given to him the "authority to judge" (5:26–27). Fourth, the Son openly admits "By myself I can do nothing" (5:30). At 5:19 Jesus says it this way: the "Son can do nothing by himself; he can do only what he sees the Father doing because whatever the Father does the Son also does." Notice how the Father's "doing" flows into the Son's doing. What the Son does the Father does, which means the Son reveals the Father. Around and around this Gospel takes us. It's how he rolls.

The language that follows in John's Gospel will open a window for light but the light is so bright it can blind us or at least shock us enough to close our eyes. This is my attempt to say get ready for how Jesus networks himself and the Father.

Because God is always at work (5:17), Jesus, the Son, can work on the Sabbath, which pulls Jesus into a uniquely special relationship with the Father. But this relationship is more than human surrender to the divine. This relationship commissions of the Son to participate in the Father's work. The early theologians at times called this *perichoresis*, or mutual indwelling of Father and Son. Our passage is one of the earliest reflections on what came to be called the Trinity, and what later was called "inseparable operations." It is again a mistake to say we know who God is and then ask if Jesus fits our definition of God. Instead, the Logos is Jesus and the Logos is God, and that means Jesus is God. But here Jesus reveals how he, the Son, is related to the Father, and the best term for it is *perichoresis*, a Father indwelling the Son and the Son the Father. Around and around.

## THE ACTS OF THE FATHER AND THE SON

Remember John 1:2 where we learned the Logos/Son was "with the Father." That "with the Father" will now be filled out with some particulars. What the Father does, the Son does. They act in unity. The heart of this participation in the Father's work is because "the Father loves the Son and shows him all he does" (5:20). That is, the Father's love requires sharing that love with the Son. The Father shares his very self with the Son. That love communicates the Father's doings or acts to the Son. Including Jesus' doing "even greater works" than healing, and those greater works will lead to astonishment (5:20). Those greater works are the crucifixion-resurrection-ascension.

This is all a lot to take in for a first century listener. This is why we need to pause again to remember how utterly stunning, if not way over the line, these words of Jesus were (and are).

This communication is so full that the Father's power to *raise the dead* is given to the Son (5:21) just as *judgment* is entirely entrusted to the Son (5:22 see also at 5:25–27). Resurrection only can occur because the Father and the Son have life in themselves and the judgment occurs because the Son is the "Son of Man" (Daniel 7). Those who "have done what is good" will experience resurrection into eternal life while evildoers will experience a resurrection into judgment (5:29). But the communication of divine tasks—resurrection and judgment—is not the end of it. The Son also participates in the *honor* that is due the Father (5:23), which is yet one more dimension of what "equal with God" (5:18) means.

This remarkable section in 5:19–30 explains the relationship of the Father and the Son. Jesus explains this because he's been challenged not only for (1) healing on the Sabbath but far more for (2) claiming he can do so because of his relationship with the Father. Which creates the problem of a self-witness. How can one believe someone who says *I am one with God because I say I am.* So instead of being a self-witness (5:31), Jesus turns to four witnesses to who he is. Perhaps you note the irony: in saying he is not witnessing about himself, it is *Jesus himself* who tells them about four who do witness about himself! A little bit more round and round, but stay with it. We don't get dizzy so much as we get educated by repetition.

## THE SON'S WITNESSES

**First witness**: John the Baptist "testifies" (or witnesses) about me (the NIV's "in my favor" says more than "about me," and Jesus knows that what J-B says about Jesus is "true" (5:32). Jesus' opponents queried J-B about Jesus and, again, Jesus says J-B's witness was true (5:33)–not that Jesus needed a human witness to prove the truth about himself (5:34). Jesus' intention in explaining the truthfulness of J-B's witness is they can be "saved" (5:34), which here means being rescued from the final judgment for evil acts (5:29). Jesus then turns J-B's true witness into an image, and I paraphrase: *J-B was on fire and you warmed up to the truth in the fire* (5:35).

**Second witness**: Jesus ramps up the witnesses by saying "I have testimony weightier than that of John": "the very works that I am" *bringing to completion or perfection.* Jesus' works, which sends us straight back to the beginning of chapter five to the healing at the Bethesda pool, are signs that reveal who Jesus is to the eye of faith. That act and those like that act tell others "that the Father has sent me" (5:36). Why? Because Jesus the Son does what the Father does.

First witness, J-B; second, the works of Jesus in consort with the Father. Now the **third witness**: the Father (5:37). At the baptism and the transfiguration (Mark 1:11; 9:7), though not mentioned in John, the Father witnessed publicly to who Jesus was: God's beloved, royal Son. The third witness then rises to the highest possible level: God the Father has identified Jesus. "God alone is an adequate witness to God," so says David Ford (Ford, *John*, 134). Ford's words penetrate deeper than what is seen on a first reading.

The **fourth witness** turns to the authority for the Judean leaders: Moses (5:45–47). By the time Jesus gets to his fourth witness, Moses has become a man whose law witnesses both *against these opponents* while also telling the truth about Jesus' identity. Jesus says Moses "wrote about me" (5:46).

Four witnesses, however, do not convince the Jewish leaders. Why?

## JESUS THE JUDGE

Between the third and fourth witness Jesus looks the leaders in the eyes, uttering piercing words that both explain why they don't embrace the four witnesses and, at the time, judges them. These are very strong words, the kind of words you and I need to be very, very judicious in using or repeating. These are not directed at Jews in general or at Pharisees but at the Judean leaders who oppose Jesus. Again, read carefully and solemnly these tragic words:

1. they "have never heard [God's] voice nor seen his form" (5:37),
2. God's Logos/logos does not "dwell in" them (5:38),
3. they do not "believe" (5:38, 46–47),
4. they "refuse to come to" Jesus (5:40),

5. they "do not have the love of God" in their hearts (5:42),

6. they accept other human witnesses but not the Son's (5:43),

7. and they do not "accept" or "seek the glory that comes from the only God" (5:44).

Very serious words indeed, and they are a microscope analytic of what unbelief means in John's Gospel. Hence, it won't be Jesus but Moses who will file charges against them (5:45). Jesus, called into the dock by these leaders, turns the entire scene inside out and becomes the judge who puts them in the dock.

In his own work as judge Jesus reveals that apart from believing there is no understanding of the fullness of who God is, who Jesus is, and what the works of the Son reveal as signs. The classic expression in the history of the church is "faith seeking understanding." Faith can't be reduced to a logical conclusion. Rather, it is a love-based, faith-shaped knowing. Only lovers and believers can know Jesus for who he is.

The bedrock reality of this passage is that responding to God is responding to Jesus, and to respond to the Son is a response to the Father. The Father and Son's relationship forms a unity so intimate that they are, as Jesus will say in a few chapters, "one" (10:30).

## QUESTIONS FOR REFLECTION AND APPLICATION

1. In what ways does Jesus serve in three roles in this section, as witness, lawyer, and judge?

2. What are the four ways we see the Son's dependence on the Father?

3. How would you explain *perichoresis* in your own words after reading this section?

4. Who are the four witnesses Jesus presents for himself? Which would be most compelling to you?

5. How does love factor in to leading a person from unbelief to belief? How has your love for Jesus helped you believe in him?

# JESUS PERFORMS
# TWO SIGNS

## *John 6:1–21*

[1] *Some time after this, Jesus crossed to the far shore of the Sea of Galilee (that is, the Sea of Tiberias),* [2] *and a great crowd of people followed him because they saw the signs he had performed by healing the sick.* [3] *Then Jesus went up on a mountainside and sat down with his disciples.* [4] *The Jewish Passover Festival was near.*

### Multiplying Bread and Fish

[5] *When Jesus looked up and saw a great crowd coming toward him, he said to Philip, "Where shall we buy bread for these people to eat?"* [6] *He asked this only to test him, for he already had in mind what he was going to do.*

[7] *Philip answered him, "It would take more than half a year's wages to buy enough bread for each one to have a bite!"*

[8] *Another of his disciples, Andrew, Simon Peter's brother, spoke up,* [9] *"Here is a boy with five small barley loaves and two small fish, but how far will they go among so many?"*

[10] *Jesus said, "Have the people sit down." There was plenty of grass in that place, and they sat down (about five thousand men were there).* [11] *Jesus then took the loaves, gave thanks, and*

JESUS PERFORMS TWO SIGNS

*distributed to those who were seated as much as they wanted. He did the same with the fish.*

*¹² When they had all had enough to eat, he said to his disciples, "Gather the pieces that are left over. Let nothing be wasted." ¹³ So they gathered them and filled twelve baskets with the pieces of the five barley loaves left over by those who had eaten.*

*¹⁴ After the people saw the sign Jesus performed, they began to say, "Surely this is the Prophet who is to come into the world." ¹⁵ Jesus, knowing that they intended to come and make him king by force, withdrew again to a mountain by himself.*

### Walking on the Water

*¹⁶ When evening came, his disciples went down to the lake, ¹⁷ where they got into a boat and set off across the lake for Capernaum. By now it was dark, and Jesus had not yet joined them. ¹⁸ A strong wind was blowing and the waters grew rough. ¹⁹ When they had rowed about three or four miles, they saw Jesus approaching the boat, walking on the water; and they were frightened. ²⁰ But he said to them, "It is I; don't be afraid." ²¹ Then they were willing to take him into the boat, and immediately the boat reached the shore where they were heading.*

John 6 is an amazing chapter, reveling in while revealing who Jesus is. It opens with his miraculous feeding of 5,000 men, which means at least 10–15,000 people! The men had wives and children, after all. Then Jesus walks on the water. The first is called a sign at 6:14, and at 6:26 Jesus referred to "signs," so most think there are two signs here. (I sure do.) Signs, again, are public deeds of Jesus that reveal who he is but to perceive them as signs a person must enter into the deed by faith, trusting in what that deed reveals. Which is not always obvious, truth be told. And thus, after the two signs John has a lengthy discourse that, like chapter five, explains who Jesus is (6:22–59). Tragically, some observe the signs but walk away (6:60–71).

John provides a brief context to get the two sign-scenes started: (1) Jesus goes to the eastern side of the Sea of Galilee to get away from the crowds; (2) many follow him anyway "because they saw the signs"; (3) Jesus was on a mountainside and "sat down," which was a customary posture for teaching; and (4) the "Jewish Passover was near" (6:1–4). Passover indicates it was a year since the previous Passover event (2:13, 23; Exodus 12). Remember the original Passover led to the manna miracles in the wilderness (Exodus 16), which anticipates Jesus's provision of bread.

## THE BREAD SIGN

Jesus tests the faith perceptions of his followers but those closest to Jesus fail (6:5–9). Jesus, unperturbed by their lack of perception, orders them to get the crowds to sit down, and then Jesus utters words that are now familiar to us because they are part of the Lord's supper: "Jesus then took the loaves, gave thanks [*eucharistein*], and distributed to those who were seated" (6:11). As with the wine at Cana, there was plenty left over (6:12–13; cf. Exodus 16:4–18). Twelve baskets were filled with the leftovers (one basket for each of the apostles/disciples).

The "people" experiencing this abundance openly express that Jesus had to be "the Prophet who is to come into the world," that is, the future Moses (Deuteronomy 18:15; cf. 1:21). For John this is a thin perception because John's comment is that Jesus perceived that the people wanted to make him "king" and to do so "by force," which means a *coup d'etat* (John 6:15; see 1:49). Their sign perception fails sight test.

What does this sign reveal about Jesus? Jesus will explain the Bread sign in our next passage (6:25–59), but for now we note that he is revealing himself as the abundant divine provider of both material sustenance, like the provision of manna, and eternal redemption that satisfies the deepest human hunger. He is more than that prophet and more than and different than any king they may want. His kingdom, we will read later, is not of this world (18:36), which is why he "withdrew again to a mountain by himself" (6:15). They want a king, he wants a different kind of king and kingdom.

## THE WALKING ON WATER SIGN

That very evening the disciples decide to return back to the western side of the Sea of Galilee, that is to their mission headquarters, to Capernaum (which is more the northern end of the Sea). A "strong wind" breaks out and the "waters grew rough" (6:18). On a recent tour with Northern students in Galilee we crossed the Sea in the midst of a rain storm. While listening to a wonderful reflection by Julie Murdock on this story, I was more than once distracted by imagining how dangerous it would have been without a motor and in a much smaller boat. The storm's fierceness spelled danger for the disciples.

Enter Jesus. At 3–4 miles away they spot Jesus "approaching the boat, walking on the water" (6:19), and instead of the disciples saying, "Of course, the One who can stir water into wine, who can speak healing into a man's bones, and who can multiply bread and fish, could also walk on the water." But, no, they were scared. Jesus reveals himself with, not "It is I" (NIV) but simply "I am" (*ego eimi*; 6:20 as at 4:26; cf. Exodus 3:14), which indicates the presence of God. Jesus does more than identify himself as a water-walker. (See p. 103 for the I Am statements in John.) Then comes a calming "Do not be scared" (my translation). The words of the Logos himself pierce their fears, they invite him into the boat and then, what seems to be another miracle, "immediately the boat reached the shore" (6:21). Or were they so pumped the time flew by?

Signs reveal Jesus to the eye of faith. What that eye perceives here is at least that Jesus, like God, is Lord of nature and the winds and the waves (Psalms 77:16–19; 107:29–30). As Lord of the sea, like the exodus, he rescues humans in the midst of the dangers of water and ushers them into the tranquilities of safety. Those who thought Jesus was the Prophet or a king (John 6:15) perhaps now see that Jesus is more than that, he is the I Am, the incarnation of God (6:20).

## QUESTIONS FOR REFLECTION AND APPLICATION

1. Why do you think Jesus' disciples and followers continually failed to rightly perceive him?

2. What does the bread sign reveal about Jesus?

3. Compare God's provision of manna in Exodus 16 to Jesus' provision of bread and fish. What is similar? What is not?

4. What does the water sign reveal about Jesus?

5. Look again at the definition here of a sign: "public deeds of Jesus that reveal who he is but to perceive them as signs a person must enter into the deed by faith, trusting in what that deed reveals." What role does faith play in interpreting signs? What signs of God's work in your life have increased your faith?

# JESUS IS THE BREAD OF LIFE

## *John 6:22–59*

[22] *The next day the crowd that had stayed on the opposite shore of the lake realized that only one boat had been there, and that Jesus had not entered it with his disciples, but that they had gone away alone.* [23] *Then some boats from Tiberias landed near the place where the people had eaten the bread after the Lord had given thanks.* [24] *Once the crowd realized that neither Jesus nor his disciples were there, they got into the boats and went to Capernaum in search of Jesus.*

[25] *When they found him on the other side of the lake, they asked him, "Rabbi, when did you get here?"*

[26] *Jesus answered, "Very truly I tell you, you are looking for me, not because you saw the signs I performed but because you ate the loaves and had your fill.* [27] *Do not work for food that spoils, but for food that endures to eternal life, which the Son of Man will give you. For on him God the Father has placed his seal of approval."*

[28] *Then they asked him, "What must we do to do the works God requires?"*

[29] *Jesus answered, "The work of God is this: to believe in the one he has sent."*

[30] So they asked him, "What sign then will you give that we may see it and believe you? What will you do? [31] Our ancestors ate the manna in the wilderness; as it is written: 'He gave them bread from heaven to eat.'"

[32] Jesus said to them, "Very truly I tell you, it is not Moses who has given you the bread from heaven, but it is my Father who gives you the true bread from heaven. [33] For the bread of God is the bread that comes down from heaven and gives life to the world."

[34] "Sir," they said, "always give us this bread."

[35] Then Jesus declared, "I am the bread of life. Whoever comes to me will never go hungry, and whoever believes in me will never be thirsty. [36] But as I told you, you have seen me and still you do not believe. [37] All those the Father gives me will come to me, and whoever comes to me I will never drive away. [38] For I have come down from heaven not to do my will but to do the will of him who sent me. [39] And this is the will of him who sent me, that I shall lose none of all those he has given me, but raise them up at the last day. [40] For my Father's will is that everyone who looks to the Son and believes in him shall have eternal life, and I will raise them up at the last day."

[41] At this the Jews there began to grumble about him because he said, "I am the bread that came down from heaven." [42] They said, "Is this not Jesus, the son of Joseph, whose father and mother we know? How can he now say, 'I came down from heaven'?"

[43] "Stop grumbling among yourselves," Jesus answered. [44] "No one can come to me unless the Father who sent me draws them, and I will raise them up at the last day. [45] It is written in the Prophets: 'They will all be taught by God.' Everyone who has heard the Father and learned from him comes to me. [46] No one has seen the Father except the one who is from God; only he has seen the Father. [47] Very truly I tell you, the one who believes has eternal life. [48] I am the bread of life. [49] Your ancestors ate the manna in the wilderness, yet they died. [50] But here is the bread that comes down

*from heaven, which anyone may eat and not die.* [51] *I am the living bread that came down from heaven. Whoever eats this bread will live forever. This bread is my flesh, which I will give for the life of the world."*

[52] *Then the Jews began to argue sharply among themselves, "How can this man give us his flesh to eat?"*

[53] *Jesus said to them, "Very truly I tell you, unless you eat the flesh of the Son of Man and drink his blood, you have no life in you.* [54] *Whoever eats my flesh and drinks my blood has eternal life, and I will raise them up at the last day.* [55] *For my flesh is real food and my blood is real drink.* [56] *Whoever eats my flesh and drinks my blood remains in me, and I in them.* [57] *Just as the living Father sent me and I live because of the Father, so the one who feeds on me will live because of me.* [58] *This is the bread that came down from heaven. Your ancestors ate manna and died, but whoever feeds on this bread will live forever."* [59] *He said this while teaching in the synagogue in Capernaum.*

The second part of John 6, our passage, opens a number of windows, each window revealing Jesus as Life's Bread. Some of the crowd on the eastern shore realized Jesus was gone so they took off for Capernaum by boat (6:24, 59). The entire conversation in our passage occurs in the large-ish synagogue in Capernaum, though we don't know this until verse fifty-nine.

Finding Jesus, they ask him a question. Asking questions of Jesus put one's questions and intelligence at risk. Jesus responds to their simple question—"Rabbi, when did you get here?"—by not answering it, by unmasking the motive of their query, and by opening up a revelation of who he was that was far more than they asked for. The answer to their question was "Last night, late." By the time Jesus was done with his instructions, they had surely forgotten even what they had asked! Have you ever asked someone a question that the person, in answering, takes the conversation to a new level and by the time the person is done you can't even remember what you had asked? I can tell you that teachers do this often with beginning students. Without saying "Not a good question," good teachers shift the answer to the topic that actually answers the question they were groping for. Jesus does just that here.

## QUESTIONS AND REVELATION

Jesus reveals in 6:25–40 the meaning of the Bread Sign he has just performed, but this revelation occurs in a question-and-answer conversation with those who accompanied Jesus. They ask questions, Jesus answers. His answers respond to questions they don't even know they have and as such become revelations. At times the questioners appear to be forming faith and at other times not. Once again, we encounter that Who we see (Jesus) is more than What we see (miracles), but the Who can only be seen by believing. Jesus will not play the apologetic game of proving who he is, nor by giving scientific or logical arguments that lead to convincing proof. Jesus calls people to look at him, to listen to him, to watch him, and to trust Who he is. The only way to comprehend Jesus in love is to surrender to him, and so discover who he is. *Trusting him for who he is leads to greater understanding.* To use philosophical terms, it is an *epistemology of faith.* C.S. Lewis once said it this way: "I believe in Christianity as I believe that the Sun has risen, not only because I see it but *because by it, I see everything else*" (C.S. Lewis, *The Weight of Glory,* 140; emphasis added).

They ask three, yea four, questions (underlined in the translation above), each one provoked by something Jesus has done or said.

1. "When did you get here?" (6:25).
2. "What must we do to do the works God requires?" (6:28).
3. "What sign then will you give that we may see it and believe you? What will you do" (6:30).

To each question Jesus' answer pushes them deeper and deeper into Who he is. Jesus corrects their first question (6:25). They want to know *when* he arrived, but Jesus contends they want to find him "not because you saw the signs" but because their bellies were full (6:26). He pushes them to *work* "for food that endures to eternal life," which he alone can provide for them (6:27).

To their second question Jesus' response turns their term "work" inside out by revealing that "The work of God is this: to believe in the one he has sent" (6:29). Their third and fourth question yearns for a sign to convince them who he is. They appeal to Moses' provision of manna (6:31), quoting from scripture "He [Moses] gave them bread from heaven to eat," suggesting they don't think his (stunning!) feeding arrives at the level of Moses' miraculous provisions of manna. Jesus corrects that perception by revealing that it was not Moses but the Father who provides "true bread from heaven" and that bread "gives life to the world" (6:33)–and he is the new Manna!

Are they ready to perceive, to embrace, to believe?

Their three questions lead us to think they are perhaps ready to perceive Jesus. Their words sound right: "Lord" is a right label for Jesus, and "Always give us this bread" is also right. But Jesus is not satisfied. Pushing them deeper into the mysteries of who he is, Jesus responds with a stunning revelation: "I am the Bread of Life" (6:35). He explains that believing in him leads to a hunger-less and thirst-less life, a life not sustained by ordinary bread but by the True Bread. He alone satisfies the seeker, the spiritually hungry. Think, too, of this: he is not saying he "gives" that bread but that he *is* the Bread.

---

## The Seven "I Am" Sayings of Jesus

1. Bread of life (6:35, 51)
2. Light of the world (8:12; 9:5)
3. Gate/Door (10:7, 9)
4. Good Shepherd (10:11, 14)
5. Resurrection and life (11:25)
6. Way, truth, life (14:6)
7. True vine (15:1, 5)
8. Plus: absolute I Am Sayings (4:26; 6:20; 8:24, 28, 58; 13:19; 18:6).

---

Having revealed himself as Life's True Bread, Jesus returns to his opening contradiction of their question (6:25–26) by probing where their faith actually is or isn't (6:36–40). He reveals that true believers are those drawn to Jesus by the Father and that those who believe in Jesus are secure in the Father's grace and will be raised to eternal life, which sets up the next paragraph (6:41–51).

## CRITICISM AND REVELATION

What looked like a blooming perception of Who Jesus is flips into a classic response by the children of Israel in the wilderness (Exodus 15:24; 16:2, 7, 8, 9, 12; 17:3): they "grumble" in unbelief about Jesus thinking he is "the bread that came down from heaven"–they know who he is and who he's from. He's "the son of Joseph" (6:41–42). They see a man from Galilee; believers see the Bread from Heaven.

He contradicts them again and orders them to knock off the grumbling. His response wends in and out of what he said in 6:35–40, which I summarize here in these basic ideas from 6:43–51:

1. The Father draws people to the Son.
2. The Son raises people at the resurrection.
3. In the future, Isaiah predicted, Israel would be taught by God, and that time is now and the Father is teaching Israel through the Son.
4. Those responding truly to the Father come to the Son.
5. Only the Son has seen the Father.
6. The Son is the Bread of Life, the One giving eternal life to believers.
7. The Israel that ate manna died; the Son's Bread leads to eternal life.
8. The Bread of which the Son speaks "is my flesh" (6:51).

This paragraph is a mesh network of connections, with one central idea: Jesus is sent by the Father to be the Father's revelation in this world, the Son who is the Bread of Life. Right behind that revelation of Who he is we hear his summons to believe in him to enter into eternal life. One term in this mesh of eight statements trips them up: "flesh." On to that term Jesus goes.

## CHALLENGE AND REVELATION

"How can this man give us his flesh to eat?" (6:52). From the moment of the water stirred into wine at Cana on, God reveals Jesus through ordinary elements of life—wine, water, healing bodies, bread, and walking on water. The eye of faith sees through the ordinary into the super-ordinary and sees the ordinary as a sign, an icon that takes the eye beyond the colors and textures and shapes into the very heart of who God is and what God is doing. They see the word "flesh" and think cannibal. Jesus has to explain himself.

Faith cannot be reduced to one term—not even faith or believing. Jesus uses metaphors *to help his audiences imagine and think of faith from different angles*. It's a matter of getting someone to think about one thing (believing) by referring to it as something else (drinking). Metaphors do that. Think of "make yourself at home" or that word "cut my heart open" or John 6's discourse is a "mesh network." You are not at home; that word did not cut physically into your heart; and John 6 is not an actual electronic mesh network. Those metaphors, however, help us think of your presence in our home, the pain that word caused, and the relationships of terms and ideas in John 6. Richard Bauckham says the words here are "deliberate riddling" (Bauckham, *Gospel of Glory*, 101). I like that.

It has often been said that John 6 is *about the Lord's Supper*, or perhaps only an echo of the Eucharist. The words in 6:11 ("Jesus then took the loaves, gave thanks, and distributed") do sound like Matthew 26:26–28. Perhaps they are about the Lord's Supper, but there is a wiser approach: why not say the Lord's Supper *is about Jesus as Life's True Bread*? Believing in Jesus means opening the mouth to receive him, ingesting him, and allowing his life to permeate our bodies. Faith is union with Christ described with metaphors.

In this paragraph (6:52–59) the metaphors are **eating** and **drinking**. As a human knows the experience of taste, of the crunch of food, of the smooth sensations of wine, and of the satisfaction in the stomach of food doing its work in our bodies, so faith can be tasted, munched, digested, and it also soothes us. Jesus challenges them to think of eating him, of drinking him, and through those terms to give the metaphors room to work in their minds. His body (bread) and his blood (wine) are "eternal life" (6:54) because they are the "true" food and drink (6:55), and "true" is a much better translation than "real" (NIV). As food enters into the body and nourishes it, so those who eat his flesh and drink his blood abide "in" Jesus and, don't ignore this, Jesus "in" them (6:56). Richard Bauckham calls this the "in-one-anotherness" in the Gospel (Bauckham, *Gospel of Glory*, 9–13). The metaphor keeps on going: Jesus says eating and drinking him fuses the believer to himself and Jesus to the believer (Bauckham, *Gospel of Glory*, 1–19).

Those who believe in Jesus, those who read the Gospel to see and hear Jesus are those who know that drinking and eating the Bread of Life himself is what satisfies most.

## QUESTIONS FOR REFLECTION AND APPLICATION

1. Why do you think Jesus wants people to work to understand him by faith rather than giving them convincing arguments and clear proof of who he is? What development do you see in the unbelief of those with whom Jesus is talking in this passage?

2. How is Jesus' promise here that "whoever feeds on this bread will live forever" similar to and different from his promise to the Samaritan woman about his living water?

3. What are some of the ordinary elements of life through which God reveals Jesus? What are your favorite spiritual metaphors?

4. What can we learn from the Lord's Supper about this passage? What can we learn from this passage about the Lord's Supper?

5. Think about participating in communion/the Eucharist/ the Lord's supper at your church. What new insights does this section give you that you want to recall the next time you join that remembrance with your community?

## FOR FURTHER READING

Richard Bauckham, *Gospel of Glory: Major Themes in Johannine Theology* (Grand Rapids: Baker Academic, 2015).

C.S. Lewis, *The Weight of Glory, and Other Addresses* (San Francisco: HarperSanFrancisco, 1980).

# JESUS IS BELIEVED AND NOT BELIEVED

## John 6:60–71

⁶⁰ On hearing it, many of his disciples said, "This is a hard teaching. Who can accept it?"

⁶¹ Aware that his disciples were grumbling about this, Jesus said to them, "Does this offend you? ⁶² Then what if you see the Son of Man ascend to where he was before! ⁶³ The Spirit gives life; the flesh counts for nothing. The words I have spoken to you—they are full of the Spirit and life. ⁶⁴ Yet there are some of you who do not believe." For Jesus had known from the beginning which of them did not believe and who would betray him. ⁶⁵ He went on to say, "This is why I told you that no one can come to me unless the Father has enabled them."

⁶⁶ From this time many of his disciples turned back and no longer followed him.

⁶⁷ "You do not want to leave too, do you?" Jesus asked the Twelve.

⁶⁸ Simon Peter answered him, "Lord, to whom shall we go? You have the words of eternal life. ⁶⁹ We have come to believe and to know that you are the Holy One of God."

⁷⁰ *Then Jesus replied, "Have I not chosen you, the Twelve? Yet one of you is a devil!"* ⁷¹ *(He meant Judas, the son of Simon Iscariot, who, though one of the Twelve, was later to betray him.)*

John's Gospel calls for a singular response by a human to Jesus: to believe. But this term has been at times diminished into a quick formula that takes care of eternity. "Accept Jesus and be on with it." A kind of "I do" as the only thing needed in marriage. As said in the opening passage to this Study, believing is both a one-time act of trusting surrender and ongoing trust and deepening surrender. Faith is a life of constant communion with and participation in Jesus.

Believing, being more than a one-and-done event, means some respond right away to Jesus but do not then follow up with a living allegiance to Jesus. Some then renew their commitment and enter into a genuine sense of faith while others will walk away. The same happened during the life of Jesus, and it bewildered the closest disciples of Jesus when some walked away.

## SOME DISCIPLES WALK AWAY FROM JESUS

There is a shocking shift from "the Judeans" (NIV: "Jews") of the last passage (6:41–59), who were the ones chasing Jesus from one place to another (6:22–40), to "many of his disciples" in 6:60 and "his disciples were grumbling" in 6:61. The development of unbelief we observed in our previous passage seems to have penetrated the immediate circle around Jesus. Many of those in that circle found his teachings "hard" enough that they wondered if they could "accept it," which means continuing on the path of faithful following of Jesus.

He pushes back to their grumbling with "Does this

offend you?" (6:61), which could be "Does this scandalize or cause you to trip up?" He again explains that he has been sent by God and has revealed the truth, which means that he is the Bread of Life, and he can sustain them. Some are not so sure, so he counters that with "What if you see the Son of Man," that is me, "ascend to where he was before"?! Could they embrace that truth? Which asserts again his majestic Who-am-I truth. True faith, he goes to explain, is from the Spirit and not from the flesh [the word shifts in meaning from 6:53–56; see 3:6], and his words "are full of the Spirit and life" (6:63). These are bold claims indeed, but he is pressing home to these would-be leavers that their decision is one about who he is. He knew, as John says, that some would not continue, and that Judas was among them (6:70–71). Genuine faith is a work of the Father (6:65).

Sad words: "many of his disciples turned back and no longer followed him" (6:66; notice too 8:31). The term "disciple" here means those who had a genuine interest in Jesus but were not among the Twelve as true believers. Yes, it is true: some wonder if a believer can lose faith and forfeit faith, and in that sense forfeit salvation. Yes, there is much debate about this. What there is no debate about is that true faith is not a one-time "I do" but a lifetime of loving commitment, surrender, and service to Jesus.

## SOME DISCIPLES REMAIN
## WITH JESUS

Some wanted Jesus to know they were committed, including Peter. As we know, he was no perfect disciple, but Peter speaks up and tosses onto the screen what true believing looks like. Three points.

First, genuine faith is about a personal relationship to

Jesus: "To *whom* shall we go?" (6:68), is the question asked. Genuine faith transcends *what we think and what we believe to be true* because it is trusting a Person, Jesus. True faith is belief in Jesus, commitment to Jesus, and union with Jesus.

Second, genuine faith orients life toward "eternal life" (6:68). The ache of the human heart is for what transcends our life and our world, not by escaping it but by seeing through it into the inner mysteries of what God is up to in this world. Genuine faith sees in Jesus the mystery of all creation. Only Jesus, Peter acknowledges, has "the words of eternal life" (6:68). "It's gonna take a lot to drag me away from you," as Toto sang in "Africa."*

Third, genuine faith perceives, or grows in knowledge of who Jesus really is. Each of the four Gospels, especially the Gospel of John, constantly pushes its readers to answer this question: "Who is this Jesus?" Peter's confession in John is that Jesus is "the Holy One of God" (6:69). In the Synoptic Gospels Peter confesses Jesus as the long-awaited Messiah but in John Messiah is reshaped to "Holy One of God," which gives Messiah an even more glorious label.

But Peter's words are that "we have come to believe" or more simply, "we have believed" in the sense that you are the One on whom our hearts are fixed. Who else compels our love? Perhaps we are left wondering, but perhaps that's the intent of Jesus. He is sifting the true from the false, the believer from the unbeliever, and he moves forward in this Gospel (and he did in the pages of history) with fewer followers, but those left were in it for the long haul. The challenge is to get in behind him to follow him.

From our next passage to the end of this Gospel that challenge becomes increasingly difficult.

---

* David F. Paich, Jeffrey T. Porcaro Lyrics © Universal Music Publishing Group, Spirit Music Group

## QUESTIONS FOR REFLECTION
## AND APPLICATION

1. What do you observe as big-picture differences between the disciples who walk away and the disciples who stay?

2. What is the key question that John's Gospel keeps asking readers to answer?

3. How does Peter illustrate what true believing can look like?

4. In what ways is your faith experience similar to Peter's? In what ways is it different?

5. What has kept you from walking away from Jesus in your discipleship journey?

# JESUS AND BROTHERS WHO DO NOT BELIEVE IN HIM

## *John 7:1–13*

¹ *After this, Jesus went around in Galilee. He did not want to go about in Judea because the Jewish leaders there were looking for a way to kill him.* ² *But when the Jewish Festival of Tabernacles was near,* ³ *Jesus' brothers said to him, "Leave Galilee and go to Judea, so that your disciples there may see the works you do.* ⁴ *No one who wants to become a public figure acts in secret. Since you are doing these things, show yourself to the world."* ⁵ *For even his own brothers did not believe in him.*

⁶ *Therefore Jesus told them, "My time is not yet here; for you any time will do.* ⁷ *The world cannot hate you, but it hates me because I testify that its works are evil.* ⁸ *You go to the festival. I am not going up to this festival, because my time has not yet fully come."* ⁹ *After he had said this, he stayed in Galilee.*

¹⁰*However, after his brothers had left for the festival, he went also, not publicly, but in secret.* ¹¹ *Now at the festival the Jewish leaders were watching for Jesus and asking, "Where is he?"*

¹²*Among the crowds there was widespread whispering about him. Some said, "He is a good man."*

*Others replied, "No, he deceives the people."*
[13] *But no one would say anything publicly about him for fear of the leaders.*

A wonderful pastor friend with two children who don't follow Jesus, a respected Christian with an adult child who walked from the faith years ago and has shown no interest of returning, and a former student's life on Facebook that revealed a commitment to follow Jesus "no matter what" with now a "no longer matters" kind of life—these stories unsettle. Not that I am shocked about children without faith nor am I sitting in judgment on the parents or pastors.

But think about this question: How could the most sterling example of all, Jesus, *not have persuaded* his own brothers to embrace who he was and his kingdom mission? He had four brothers—named James, Joseph, Judas, and Simon—and "sisters" but they are unnamed (Mark 6:3). John tells us "even his own brothers did not believe in him" (7:5). Our text provokes us to consider that very question, provides some helpful perspectives as answers, and this short passage also gives us pause about judging others.

## LEADERS HAVE POWER

Notice that John both begins and ends this section by noting the power of the Judean leaders to halt commitment to Jesus. In verse one we read they were "looking for a way to kill him." And in verse thirteen "no one" in Jerusalem when the subject of Jesus arose "would say anything publicly about him *for fear of the leaders*" (italics added). We finished chapter six of John observing that even many of Jesus' own disciples "turned back and no longer followed him" (6:66). No doubt the opposition to Jesus by the Judean leaders was a major

115

reason for such decisions, and it factored into why his own brothers wouldn't commit to their brother.

Put in one word: fear. In four words: fear for one's life. At least that's part of why his brothers did not believe.

## FUTURE FOLLOWERS CAN HAVE PASSIONATE PASTS

Think of the apostle Paul. Paul himself persecuted the followers of Jesus so perhaps we should think more carefully about the brothers of Jesus who taunt their brother. They want him to go to Jerusalem, even knowing the danger at the gates for him (7:3). Their publicity taunt is that someone with the extravagant claims Jesus has for himself—and John has been making those claims clear from 1:1—should shout it fearlessly, frankly, and freely from Mount Zion. He should go up to Jerusalem for "Tabernacles" because it was the most popular festival. A perfect time for a public proclamation. In their cajoling, they suggest public performances in Jerusalem will encourage his disciples (7:3).

Three dates on the Jewish calendar called masses of pilgrims to Jerusalem to celebrate. The three festivals were two Spring or early summer events, Passover and Pentecost, and a fall celebration called Tabernacles, at which festival they made small booths or huts to remember how the children of Israel lived in the wilderness after the exodus (Leviticus 23:33–43). Three features of Tabernacles illuminate John 7: at that festival the law was read, they poured water on the altar, and they lit golden candlesticks.

We only grant these boys relief because we know what became of them. James became the leader of the church in Jerusalem (see Acts 15). Were it not for that we'd all see their taunting as repulsive. Yet, they too become believers. Perhaps you were that type too and know both the kindness of God's grace and the power of his love.

## JESUS WAS FREE TO DISCERN WHAT TO DO AND WHEN TO DO IT

We encounter in John 7 Jesus changing his mind. He tells his brothers what he told his mother: "My time is not yet here" (7:6, 8; cf. 2:4; see sidebar). This indicates Jesus knows it is not the Father's time for his final public actions, namely, his crucifixion, resurrection, and ascension. Since the brothers are harmless figures, they can go to Jerusalem anytime they want. Jesus turns to his customary strong rhetoric by connecting his brothers to the "world" that "hates" Jesus. We are reminded of John 1:11, too.

### "HOUR" AND "TIME" IN JOHN

**John 2:4** "Woman, why do you involve me?" Jesus replied. "My hour has not yet come."

**John 7:6** Therefore Jesus told them, "My time is not yet here; for you any time will do.

**John 7:8** You go to the festival. I am not going up to this festival, because my time has not yet fully come."

**John 7:30** At this they tried to seize him, but no one laid a hand on him, because his hour had not yet come.

**John 8:20** He spoke these words while teaching in the temple courts near the place where the offerings

> were put. Yet no one seized him, because his hour had not yet come.
>
> **John 12:23** Jesus replied, "The hour has come for the Son of Man to be glorified.
>
> **John 12:27** "Now my soul is troubled, and what shall I say? 'Father, save me from this hour'? No, it was for this very reason I came to this hour.
>
> **John 13:1** It was just before the Passover Festival. Jesus knew that the hour had come for him to leave this world and go to the Father. Having loved his own who were in the world, he loved them to the end.
>
> **John 17:1** After Jesus said this, he looked toward heaven and prayed: "Father, the hour has come. Glorify your Son, that your Son may glorify you.

After the brothers leave, Jesus discerns he should go to Jerusalem "not publicly, but in secret" (7:10). A time to stay, a time to go; a time to reveal in public, a time to lurk in the shadows. We will learn that upon discerning it was God's will to go to Jerusalem he also discerned it was time to go public at the same festival (7:14).

## PEOPLE ARE SPLIT ON JESUS

In Jerusalem discussions about Jesus led to people on two sides. One side has the leaders who are scouting for him in order to kill him (7:1, 11). On the other side are those who think he is a "good" man (7:12). On the other side, too, are those who think he's a charlatan, a false prophet, a teacher who leads people to wander from the way (7:12).

## Patience with the Brothers

In that situation, what do you think you would have done had you been one of Jesus' siblings? He's a dangerous man to be connected to, especially in Jerusalem around its leaders. He seems a bit indecisive on how to go public with who he is and when to do it. From Capernaum to Jerusalem there are leaders who are warning people about Jesus.

The brothers were mistaken, but perhaps we should empathize a bit with their situation. Maybe Jesus' little story of the two brothers, found in Matthew 21:28–32, was told about his own brothers! One says he won't follow but eventually does; another says he will but later turned back. Jesus approves of the first. For some, repentance and faith come early; for others it takes time. The question then is not "Why did the brothers not believe?" but "Why did the brothers come to believe?" Their reason is the only one given in John.

*Because of who Jesus is.*

## Questions for Reflection and Application

1. What are some reasons Jesus' brothers might not have believed in him?


2. Why do you think Jesus was such a divisive figure, leading some people to hate him and others to love him?

3. What do you think changed for James that moved him from not believing to believing?

4. Have you ever experienced leaders—religious or secular—who made you afraid to believe certain things about Jesus?

5. What was your life like before you became a follower of Jesus? Why did you disbelieve? Did you taunt or insult his followers? What changed your mind?

# JESUS ANSWERS QUESTIONS

## *John 7:14–44*

<sup>14</sup> *Not until halfway through the festival did Jesus go up to the temple courts and begin to teach.*

### First Question
<sup>15</sup> *The Jews there were amazed and asked, "How did this man get such learning without having been taught?"*

<sup>16</sup> *Jesus answered, "My teaching is not my own. It comes from the one who sent me. <sup>17</sup> Anyone who chooses to do the will of God will find out whether my teaching comes from God or whether I speak on my own. <sup>18</sup> Whoever speaks on their own does so to gain personal glory, but he who seeks the glory of the one who sent him is a man of truth; there is nothing false about him. <sup>19</sup> Has not Moses given you the law? Yet not one of you keeps the law. Why are you trying to kill me?"*

### Second Question
<sup>20</sup> *"You are demon-possessed," the crowd answered. "Who is trying to kill you?"*

<sup>21</sup> *Jesus said to them, "I did one miracle, and you are all amazed. <sup>22</sup> Yet, because Moses gave you circumcision (though actually it did*

*not come from Moses, but from the patriarchs), you circumcise a boy on the Sabbath.* ²³ *Now if a boy can be circumcised on the Sabbath so that the law of Moses may not be broken, why are you angry with me for healing a man's whole body on the Sabbath?* ²⁴ *Stop judging by mere appearances, but instead judge correctly."*

### Third Question

²⁵ *At that point some of the people of Jerusalem began to ask, "Isn't this the man they are trying to kill?* ²⁶ *Here he is, speaking publicly, and they are not saying a word to him. Have the authorities really concluded that he is the Messiah?* ²⁷ *But we know where this man is from; when the Messiah comes, no one will know where he is from."*

²⁸ *Then Jesus, still teaching in the temple courts, cried out, "Yes, you know me, and you know where I am from. I am not here on my own authority, but he who sent me is true. You do not know him,* ²⁹ *but I know him because I am from him and he sent me."*

³⁰ *At this they tried to seize him, but no one laid a hand on him, because his hour had not yet come.*

### Fourth Question

³¹ *Still, many in the crowd believed in him. They said, "When the Messiah comes, will he perform more signs than this man?"*

³² *The Pharisees heard the crowd whispering such things about him. Then the chief priests and the Pharisees sent temple guards to arrest him.*

³³ *Jesus said, "I am with you for only a short time, and then I am going to the one who sent me.* ³⁴ *You will look for me, but you will not find me; and where I am, you cannot come."*

### Fifth Question

³⁵ *The Jews said to one another, "Where does this man intend to go that we cannot find him? Will he go where our people live scattered among the Greeks, and teach the Greeks?* ³⁶ *What did he mean*

when he said, 'You will look for me, but you will not find me,' and 'Where I am, you cannot come'?"

[37] On the last and greatest day of the festival, Jesus stood and said in a loud voice, "Let anyone who is thirsty come to me and drink. [38] Whoever believes in me, as Scripture has said, rivers of living water will flow from within them." [39] By this he meant the Spirit, whom those who believed in him were later to receive. Up to that time the Spirit had not been given, since Jesus had not yet been glorified.

### Sixth Question and Decisions

[40] On hearing his words, some of the people said, "Surely this man is the Prophet."

[41] Others said, "He is the Messiah."

Still others asked, "How can the Messiah come from Galilee?

[42] Does not Scripture say that the Messiah will come from David's descendants and from Bethlehem, the town where David lived?"

[43] Thus the people were divided because of Jesus. [44] Some wanted to seize him, but no one laid a hand on him.

What one person thinks is the greatest thing on earth another may think is ho-hum, ordinary, routine. Other situations crank it up to full throttle. When that Person is Jesus, the responses are not "great" vs. "ho-hum" but "Messiah" vs. "demonic." He is so self-oriented, leading to what can only be called "Ego-centricity" when one ponders the signs and I Am claims, that his teachings force total surrender or total opposition. He's an either-or prophet. Is he Messiah or does he embody opposition to God? Questions abound about Jesus, and he seems intent on subverting their questions by going two levels deeper.

For some Jesus had very little going for him: he was from backwater Galilee and had no formal education into conventions. He was therefore easy to discredit. Discrediting the Messiah has consequences, especially when his actions and words provoke imaginations, expectations, hopes, and stunning on-point and to-the-point wisdom. People were flummoxed about how to respond to Who he was, and going public with an answer pitched a battle with those with different answers. As his audiences were formulating questions and answers, Jesus was pushing the conversation into deeper topics. With eyes of faith, we can see that Jesus answers life's deep questions with answers revealing that the questions being asked form the problem.

## QUESTIONS

Like John 6's long discourse, this discourse in John 7 is also punctuated and moved forward with questions. I underlined each question, or set of questions, in the translation above. Each question emerges from something said or done and then leads to Jesus' answers that provoke yet more questions. The questions will be explained first.

1. The Jews there were amazed and asked, "How did this man get such learning without having been taught?" (7:15)
2. "You are demon-possessed," the crowd answered. "Who is trying to kill you?" (7:20)
3. At that point some of the people of Jerusalem began to ask, "Isn't this the man they are trying to kill? Here he is, speaking publicly, and they are not saying a word to him. Have the authorities really concluded that he is the Messiah? But we know where this man is from; when the Messiah comes, no one will know where he is from." (7:25–27)

4. Still, many in the crowd believed in him. They said, "When the Messiah comes, will he perform more signs than this man?" (7:31)

5. The Jews said to one another, "Where does this man intend to go that we cannot find him? Will he go where our people live scattered among the Greeks, and teach the Greeks? What did he mean when he said, 'You will look for me, but you will not find me,' and 'Where I am, you cannot come'?" (7:35–36)

6. Still others asked, "How can the Messiah come from Galilee? Does not Scripture say that the Messiah will come from David's descendants and from Bethlehem, the town where David lived?" (7:41–42)

Questions about Jesus simultaneously and ironically become confessions of who he is. There is an admission of how well he knows the law of Moses without formal training, which reveals that he is Logos (#1); how he discerns the motives of others to kill him (#2); that he might be the Messiah (#3, #4); that he knows some mystery about where he is going in the future (#5); and, that he is the Messiah but not from Bethlehem, but really is (#6).

Each of these questions boils down to a complex question: Who is Jesus, and if he is who we think he might be, what does that mean for us? Jesus' answers clarify who he is and what that means for them: they are challenged to believe in him.

## ANSWERS (IN ITALICS)

Jesus boldly answers #1 with a claim bolder than the words: "My teaching is not my own" because it "comes from the one who sent me" (7:16). The claim stuns. How does one disagree with God? He offers them a challenge: *if you are truly those who want to do God's will, then you will know that what I teach is God's will*. In fact, he contends that those who claim personal authority or individual brilliance hop off the path. Truth is found in the One sent by the Father (7:17–18). That first question (7:15) is prompted, we only discover at the end of Jesus' answer in 7:19, by the emphasis in Jerusalem at Tabernacles on the law of Moses. Jesus pushes Moses forward to accuse them of (1) not observing his laws by (2) trying to kill him (7:19).

That second point provokes a strong accusation against Jesus: "you have a demon" (my translation; 7:20). They demand to know who is trying to kill him. He doesn't answer that question but instead shifts to their misguided judgment and puts them on their heels. They justify circumcising a boy on the Sabbath but—here he appeals from a lesser to a greater good—find no justification for Jesus healing a man on the Sabbath (5:1–15). *Jesus reveals he does greater works than they can permit.*

The jumps from questions and answers to more questions are not always clear in John. It is what it is. From wondering if Jesus is not the one the leaders want to kill, to their fear of doing anything to him in spite of public teaching, to his perhaps being Messiah, to the oddity that no one knows where the Messiah will come from . . . all of these indicate they are asking Jesus in various ways if he is the Messiah (7:25–27). To which Jesus says, *You think you know where I'm from (Galilee) but you don't know that I'm from the Father and have been sent by the Father* (7:28–29).

The leaders want to kill him (cf. 7:1, 19, 20, 25, and now 7:30) but God prevents such an action because it is not time. Yet others "believed in him" because, *even if he is not Messiah*, the Messiah would never do more "signs than him" (7:31). The camera shifts from believers to Pharisees who, along with the chief priests, "sent temple guards to arrest him" (7:32). Jesus' response to the decision to arrest him contains revelatory if mysterious words. He knows he will not be with them long because he will return to the Father who sent him. They have to know this is what we call heaven. But he pierces their bubble by saying they will not find him because they "cannot come" to where he is going. Why? Because they do not believe in him. It had to be mystifying to be listening to this conversation.

The sign-words of Jesus are understood literally and materially instead of metaphorically and *Spirit*-ually. They wonder if he might be heading out to the diaspora (7:35–36). None of Jesus' words in 7:33–34 strike home for them. Jesus now offers a powerful challenge, once again turning to ordinary matter as metaphors for the proper response of faith, and the ordinary matter is the pouring of water on the altar as a prayer for rains for the crops. He challenges them with "Let anyone who is thirsty come to me and drink" (7:37). That is, "whoever *believes in me*" will discover living water flowing "within them" (7:38; like 4:14). John knows they could not comprehend his metaphor or the time so he explains it: The Living Water is the Holy Spirit to come, after Jesus' crucifixion and ascension, who will become an endless stream (7:39).

Sent by the Father, turning festivals into signs and revelations of who he is, puncturing fragile egos with answers that transcend the questions, and at the same time barely lifting the envelope to see the redemption to come.

## DECISIONS

Jesus, remember where this passage began, was not embraced by his brothers or Jerusalem's leaders. By the end of the festival Jesus draws out opinions about who he might be:

(1) the Prophet,

(2) the Messiah,

(3) not the Messiah because he comes from Galilee (so they assume) and

(4) others wanted to "seize him" to kill him (7:40–44).

I translate the summary of John: "Therefore, a split happened among the people because of him" (7:43). The opening Prologue said this, but it takes chapters of watching the split occur to see that Light is not always welcomed by Darkness. What Jesus reveals in this chapter is summarized in verse twenty-four: "Stop judging by mere appearances, but instead judge correctly." Or, "Don't judge by what you see on the face. Judge what is right." The opponents looked at the "face" of Jesus and saw a Galilean, an ordinary man, one they knew, and they judged he could not be the Messiah. They saw flesh, but the eye of faith saw Jesus heal a man on the Sabbath and recognized who he was, the Logos become flesh, the glory of God, the Life, the Light, the Lamb, the Messiah, the Son of God.

## QUESTIONS FOR REFLECTION AND APPLICATION

1. What do the people's questions for Jesus reveal about their knowledge (and lack of knowledge) of him?

2. What does Jesus try to teach them about himself with his redirecting answers?

3. Why did people dismiss that Jesus could be the Messiah?

4. If you could ask Jesus any question about himself, what would it be?

5. Who do you believe Jesus is? What difference does that make in your life?

# JESUS DIVIDES

## John 7:45–52

[45] *Finally the temple guards went back to the chief priests and the Pharisees, who asked them, "Why didn't you bring him in?"*

[46] *"No one ever spoke the way this man does," the guards replied.*

[47] *"You mean he has deceived you also?" the Pharisees retorted.* [48] *"Have any of the rulers or of the Pharisees believed in him?* [49] *No! But this mob that knows nothing of the law—there is a curse on them."*

[50] *Nicodemus, who had gone to Jesus earlier and who was one of their own number, asked,* [51] *"Does our law condemn a man without first hearing him to find out what he has been doing?"*

[52] *They replied, "Are you from Galilee, too? Look into it, and you will find that a prophet does not come out of Galilee."*

John is like a drone who can fly from one scene to another, and here he buzzes over to the offices of the "chief priests and the Pharisees" on the southwestern side of Jerusalem. Their conversations with the "temple guards" reveal both the irony of the guards and the determination of the authorities.

This passage works with the theme of justice. We have two problems with this word because in public statements "bringing someone to justice" equates the term with punishment, while in many public statements the term refers to a nation's constitutional documents. To be sure, exacting justice at times entails judgment according to public laws with serious consequences. But justice is one of the Bible's great words and refers to moral behaviors that conform, not to a modern nation's legal codes, but to God's revealed will. That will has three major expressions in the Bible: the law of Moses, the teachings of Jesus, and life in the Spirit. To do justice, then, is to do what God wants. I add one small clarification: justice is to do what God wants *at the right time.*

We encounter in this text three named do-ers: the temple guards, the authorities, and an outlier who gets it right, Nicodemus. Two do the right thing at the right time.

## SOME CONSIDER JESUS

The guards can't dismiss Jesus' powerful speaking, and if one reads that last discourse one can easily agree with them: "no one ever spoke the way this man does" (cf. 7:47 with 7:14–44). The irony is that the guards' "no one" penetrates behind the veil of who Jesus truly is. The guards do the right thing at the right time by speaking up with a simple "no one ever spoke the way this man does."

At the bottom of this passage, we meet Nicodemus again (cf. 3:1–21), who is one of the authorities but, unlike the authorities and like the temple guards, thinks Jesus should be given a fair hearing (7:50–51). He, too, did justly by saying the right thing to the right people at the right time. His fellow authorities dismiss him, too.

In most situations that involve a moral challenge, voices will emerge from the back of the room or a side seat or from a marginalized person. Those voices often perceive what is right. Such persons often speak with a soft voice because of their lack of status and because of the power at work in the room, and soft voices can be shouted down by the loudmouths. They were in this text. In most cases those soft voices are only perceived to have said the right thing at the right time too late to have made a difference.

## SOME DON'T

The authorities perceive Jesus (1) as a false prophet and deceiver (7:47). (2) They appeal to authority: "Have any of the rulers or of the Pharisees believed in him?" They then (3) go all elitist and dismissive of the crowd, which the NIV over-translates with "mob." The elites think of the crowd as the *hoi polloi*, uneducated country bumpkins, who know "nothing of the law" and so are "cursed" (7:49). And (4) they degrade Jesus to Nicodemus with a slur by saying he's nothing but a "Galilean," who can have no status with the Jerusalem elites (cf. 7:15). Yet their remark is "snide and inaccurate" (Callahan, "John," 196). After all, Jonah and Nahum were prophets from Galilee (cf. 2 Kings 14:25; Nahum 1:1). Perhaps Jesus is too.

To put this in modern categories, the "chief priests and the Pharisees" *gaslit* the temple guards and Nicodemus. To gaslight is to exercise power in the use of words designed to confuse a person's perceptions in such a manner that the person questions the reality of their own memories and perceptions. They tried to manipulate the guards and Nicodemus into thinking they were crazies. I doubt it worked, but it did, as it does today often, silence the softer voices.

## QUESTIONS FOR REFLECTION AND APPLICATION

1. What does "justice" mean in the Bible?

2. How do the guards do justice?

3. How does Nicodemus do justice?

4. How do the religious authorities fail to do justice?

5. Have you ever spoken up with a "soft voice" and been right but not been heard? When have you seen others attempt to do justice by speaking and get shouted down or ignored?

**Special Note to the Reader:** John 7:53–8:11 is not original to the Gospel of John though most think the passage "sounds just like Jesus." The NIV 2011, accordingly, prints it in small italics with a note indicating why they do not include it as original to John's Gospel. If included, the story illustrates judgment on the woman's accusers, the just judgment of Jesus in offering grace and forgiveness to the woman.

# JESUS DISPUTES

## *John 8:12–59*

**Special Note to the Reader:** There is so much back and forth in this passage I have identified the speakers. John's narrative explanations are in italics.

### Jesus

*12 When Jesus spoke again to the people, he said,* "I am the light of the world. Whoever follows me will never walk in darkness, but will have the light of life."

### Unbelieving Pharisees

*13 The Pharisees challenged him,* "Here you are, appearing as your own witness; your testimony is not valid."

### Jesus

*14 Jesus answered,* "Even if I testify on my own behalf, my testimony is valid, for I know where I came from and where I am going. But you have no idea where I come from or where I am going. 15 You judge by human standards; I pass judgment on no one. 16 But if I do judge, my decisions are true, because I am not alone. I stand with the Father, who sent me. 17 In your own Law it is written that the testimony of two witnesses is true. 18 I am one who testifies for myself; my other witness is the Father, who sent me."

## They [Unbelieving Pharisees]

*19 Then they asked him,* "Where is your father?"

## Jesus

*"You do not know me or my Father," Jesus replied. "If you knew me, you would know my Father also."*

*20 He spoke these words while teaching in the temple courts near the place where the offerings were put.*
*Yet no one seized him, because his hour had not yet come.*

## Jesus

*21 Once more Jesus said to them,* "I am going away, and you will look for me, and you will die in your sin. Where I go, you cannot come."

## Unbelieving Jews/Judeans

*22 This made the Jews ask,* "Will he kill himself? Is that why he says, 'Where I go, you cannot come'?"

## Jesus

*23 But he continued,* "You are from below; I am from above. You are of this world; I am not of this world. 24 I told you that you would die in your sins; if you do not believe that I am he, you will indeed die in your sins."

## They [Unbelieving Jews/Judeans]

*25* "Who are you?" they asked.

## Jesus

"Just what I have been telling you from the beginning," *Jesus replied.* 26 "I have much to say in judgment of you. But he who sent me is trustworthy, and what I have heard from him I tell the world."

²⁷ *They did not understand that he was telling them about his Father.*

### Jesus

²⁸ *So Jesus said,* "When you have lifted up the Son of Man, then you will know that I am he and that I do nothing on my own but speak just what the Father has taught me. ²⁹ The one who sent me is with me; he has not left me alone, for I always do what pleases him."

³⁰ *Even as he spoke, many believed in him.*

### Jesus

³¹ *To the Jews who had believed him, Jesus said,* "If you hold to my teaching, you are really my disciples. ³² Then you will know the truth, and the truth will set you free."

### They [Unbelieving Jews/Judeans]

³³ *They answered him,* "We are Abraham's descendants and have never been slaves of anyone. How can you say that we shall be set free?"

### Jesus

³⁴ *Jesus replied,* "Very truly I tell you, everyone who sins is a slave to sin. ³⁵ Now a slave has no permanent place in the family, but a son belongs to it forever. ³⁶ So if the Son sets you free, you will be free indeed. ³⁷ I know that you are Abraham's descendants. Yet you are looking for a way to kill me, because you have no room for my word. ³⁸ I am telling you what I have seen in the Father's presence, and you are doing what you have heard from your father."

### They [Unbelieving Jews/Judeans]

³⁹ "Abraham is our father," *they answered.*

### Jesus

"If you were Abraham's children," *said Jesus,* "then you would do what Abraham did. [40] As it is, you are looking for a way to kill me, a man who has told you the truth that I heard from God. Abraham did not do such things. [41] You are doing the works of your own father."

### They [Unbelieving Jews/Judeans]

"We are not illegitimate children," *they protested.* "The only Father we have is God himself."

### Jesus

[42] *Jesus said to them,* "If God were your Father, you would love me, for I have come here from God. I have not come on my own; God sent me. [43] Why is my language not clear to you? Because you are unable to hear what I say. [44] You belong to your father, the devil, and you want to carry out your father's desires. He was a murderer from the beginning, not holding to the truth, for there is no truth in him. When he lies, he speaks his native language, for he is a liar and the father of lies. [45] Yet because I tell the truth, you do not believe me! [46] Can any of you prove me guilty of sin? If I am telling the truth, why don't you believe me? [47] Whoever belongs to God hears what God says. The reason you do not hear is that you do not belong to God."

### Unbelieving Jews/Judeans

[48] *The Jews answered him,* "Aren't we right in saying that you are a Samaritan and demon-possessed?"

### Jesus

[49] "I am not possessed by a demon," *said Jesus,* "but I honor my Father and you dishonor me. [50] I am not seeking glory for myself; but there is one who seeks it, and he is the judge. [51] Very truly I tell you, whoever obeys my word will never see death."

### They [Unbelieving Jews/Judeans]

*52 At this they exclaimed*, "Now we know that you are demon-possessed! Abraham died and so did the prophets, yet you say that whoever obeys your word will never taste death. 53 Are you greater than our father Abraham? He died, and so did the prophets. Who do you think you are?"

### Jesus

*54 Jesus replied*, "If I glorify myself, my glory means nothing. My Father, whom you claim as your God, is the one who glorifies me. 55 Though you do not know him, I know him. If I said I did not, I would be a liar like you, but I do know him and obey his word. 56 Your father Abraham rejoiced at the thought of seeing my day; he saw it and was glad."

### They [Unbelieving Jews/Judeans]

57 "You are not yet fifty years old," *they said to him*, "and you have seen Abraham!"

### Jesus

58 "Very truly I tell you," *Jesus answered*, "before Abraham was born, I am!"

> *59 At this, they picked up stones to stone him,*
> *but Jesus hid himself, slipping away from the temple*
> *grounds.*

This relentless back-and-forth dispute with Jesus is unmatched in the Gospels. The design of the entire passage is to present Jesus for who he is and to challenge different audiences to render the right decision about who he is. The dispute in this chapter is so spiritually intense, however, that the language spills over into what, in the history of the church, became virulent anti-Semitism. The term "Jews" became "opponents of Jesus," which became "Christ-killers," which led to atrocities spewed and spilled out against all Jews. It is no exaggeration to claim the European Holocaust under Hitler owes some of its despicable hatred to this passage. The language in this chapter should make us uncomfortable even if that discomfort can be softened by realizing this is one Jew, Jesus, disputing with his fellow Jews over what makes a person a faithful Jew. Our passage is not Jesus vs. Judaism. Instead, it is Jesus the Jew vs. Jewish, or Judean, leaders in Jerusalem. We would do well to read this Gospel with Jewish friends.

The entire dispute can be seen as Jesus speaking truth to power. In this dispute discourse Jesus will use a number of either-or bold contrasts: above and below, light and darkness, truth and lie, this world and the Father's side, slaves and free, and the strongest one in the Father and the father (devil). This language shapes listeners' and readers' hearing to face the alternative of following Jesus or walking away from Jesus. It also leads to strong stereotypes that, when wielded in our world, become dangerous and diabolical.

Jesus responds to four groups: Pharisees, Unbelieving Jews/Judeans, Believing Jews/Judeans, and then to Unbelieving Jews/Judeans again. The Gospel of John, and this is especially important for our day and too often a surprise to many Christian readers, does not depict all Jews as unbelieving opponents of Jesus (though many read it that way). Each of the responses includes a claim by Jesus about who he is. Some are tempted to turn this chapter into anger and finger-pointing, wrinkled-nose, watery eyes, red-faced, mucus-spewing rhetoric. That's a serious mistake. Yes, this is a dispute, but we might try reading it with a measured calmness, viewing Jesus with a tranquil face and his disputants as perplexed by him enough to ask their deepest questions about him. David Ford urges us to shift this chapter into the living room as "the language of family quarreling" (Ford, *John*, 185). In which case, Jesus and his disputants remain family.

## RESPONDING TO
## UNBELIEVING PHARISEES

John 8:12 continues the discourse of John 7 with Jesus making a bold claim. He opens with "I am the light of the world," and those following him "will never walk in darkness" because "they will have the light of life" (8:12). This is the second major I Am statement (see p. 103 in 6:22–59), and it is perhaps anchored in the memory of the lighting of candles in the temple on the first day of Tabernacles. He will say this same I Am in 9:5. Light both illumines and dispels darkness. As the Light of the World, Jesus illumines the world of God's Logos, Life, Lamb, and Messiah as he dispels the world's sin, sicknesses, and systemic evils. He does so like Isaiah's servant (Isaiah 42:6; 49:6).

The Pharisees deconstruct Jesus on his own words because he has said a person cannot witness to their own truthfulness (8:13;[1] 5:31). A later rabbinical text, called *Mishnah*, expresses this directly: "But a person is not believed to testify in his own behalf" (*m. Kethubot* 2:9). Jesus rebuts their deconstruction because (1) he knows his origins and destiny (8:14), (2) he does not judge by the flesh (NIV has "human standards") and does not judge others (8:15) and, because (3) the "Father" sent him into the world (8:16), there are actually two witnesses—Father and Son (8:17–18)!

The Pharisees, again one group among Jerusalem's authorities, want to know where his father is, and here they could be raising an issue about the rumor of his supposed illegitimate birth (8:19). Jesus' response is direct and clear: he has been sent by the Father, he represents the Father, they don't know that Father, and if they knew who he was they would actually know the Father! Father and Son are, as

John 6 and John 10 show, unified in revelation and witness and oneness.

John, inserting himself into the drama of this chapter, wants his readers to know that Jesus uttered all these claims in the open and "no one seized him" because "his hour had not yet come" (8:20).

The Pharisees are confronted with these claims of Jesus: that he has been sent by the Father to be the world's true Light, and their response to him is their response to the Father. Here is the heart of genuine witness even today: we witness to Jesus, not ourselves, and the response to our witness to Jesus is a response to God. This is our burden, it is weighty, and it requires measured words.

Keep in mind this passage is a back-and-forth of claims and challenges with responses and shifting of issues. The logic is not always easy to follow even when the drift is clear.

## RESPONDING TO UNBELIEVING JEWS/JUDEANS

The next section begins as did the former one, with a claim. Jesus claims he is going away—and that means they will not be able to find him and that they, as unbelievers, will "die in your sin"—and that means they "cannot" go where he is going. He is going to the Father (8:21). The sharpness of the boundaries has a rhetorical edge designed to prompt listeners to respond positively to Jesus.

John shifts the audience from unbelieving Pharisees to unbelieving Judeans, and the two are not the same. The former was a small (percentagewise) subgroup of the latter. This group of unbelieving Judeans/Jews[2] interprets Jesus' words as suicide (8:22), a rather common heroic act among Romans but not among Jews. In fact, among Jews it was a reprehensible, unforgiving sin. Their question is prompted because of the intense opposition to Jesus, which they infer he'd rather avoid by suicide.

Jesus responds deftly. Implying, yes, he will die but he turns death onto them by saying they will die in their sins, which means eternal death. They are "from below" and "of this world" because they do not know who he is or believe in him (8:23–24). Jesus must have grabbed their attention because they want to know who he is (8:25).[3] He reiterates that he and the Father are so close that his witness in the world is based in the Father's utter reliability (8:26). John inserts himself again with a comment that they had no idea "he was telling then about the Father" (8:27). He intentionally mystifies the Judean leaders.

"When you," he says to them, "have *lifted up the Son of Man*." They would know "Son of Man" from Ezekiel, from common Aramaic expressions here it means "a person," or from (what is most likely) Daniel 7. This statement may be clear, but it requires of the unbelieving Judeans to connect their opposition to Jesus to his death (by crucifixion), to Jesus being "lifted up" as Son of Man in that he was raised to the right hand of the Father, and, well, one has to think it was not that clear to anyone but Jesus.

The subject matter of this chapter is so serious it's hard to step back to see something painfully obvious and tragic. People have always diverted discussions about Jesus away from the "who is he?" and "therefore what does that mean for you?" to questions that distract from the truth and distort what Jesus said and did. He has just revealed to the unbelievers his relationship to the Father and to the glorious figure of Daniel 7. Instead of seeing the truth-claim and the personal revelations of Jesus' identity, they distract to the seductions of a Roman view of suicide and the befuddlements about who he may be. His explanations land on rocky surfaces, undoubtedly made rockier by his intentional mystifications.

Jesus reveals who he is by connecting himself to the divine plan as expressed in Daniel's Son of Man, but it takes—this is so Johannine—an eye of faith to see what he's pointing at. Many, John intrudes again, "believed in him" after these words (8:30). So Jesus now turns to the believing Jews with a brief response.

## RESPONDING TO BELIEVING JEWS/JUDEANS (8:31–32)

"Many," John informs us, "believed in him." Jesus, like a good teacher, coach, or parent, discerns they need a sustainable commitment to him. He wants them to *abide*, which means to be attentive to, absorbed by, and participating in "my teaching" then "you are really my disciples" (8:31). I don't like the NIV's "really" because the word is "truly," and truth is a major concept in John. "Really" blunts the power of "truly." This true abiding in Jesus—please notice this—leads to perceptions unavailable to the one who merely observes Jesus. Abiding in Jesus leads to knowing "the truth" that alone "will set you free" (8:32).

Both Jesus in John and Paul connect new birth, discipleship, and the Spirit of God to freedom. Freedom is not the ability to do what one wants and not to do what one does not want to do, which is the Western world's sense of "freedom." No, for Jesus, freedom is empowerment to know God's will, to believe in and become allegiant to Jesus, to love God and love others, and to be transformed from a world-shaped life to an abundant-life-shaped life.

## RESPONDING AGAIN TO UNBELIEVING JUDEANS (8:33–59)

By now readers of this Gospel know that what Jesus means and what people perceive are not the same. The *un*believing

Judeans overhear Jesus, hear the word "free" and think of physical, economic slavery (8:33). Jesus responds to that new audience with four connections:

(1) sin leads to slavery to sin,
(2) slaves have "no permanent place in the family" while a "son belongs to it forever,"
(3) Jesus is the Son, and
(4) if the Son "sets you free, you will be free indeed" (8:34–36).

Jesus' language is noticeably realistic, straight from their world of sons and slaves and slavery and liberation. As Kathleen Norris once said, "When God-talk is not of this world, it is a false language," and because God chose to become human in Jesus, "a spiritualized jargon that does not ground itself in the five senses should be anathema" (*Amazing Grace*, 211).

Jesus turns against them with sharp words. Yes, he says, you are Israelites in Abraham's line but "you are looking for a way to kill me" (8:37). Who asks this question in 8:33 (asked by "They") shifts from the believing to the unbelieving Judeans. They want to bring Jesus down because they "have no room for my word" (8:37). He now turns to an uber spiritual image: he knows the Father and they are from their father, who is the devil (8:38), who inspires lies, murder, and death (8:44).

They come right back with direct denial: their father is Abraham (8:39). The back-and-forth is sharp. Jesus now: if they were Abraham's true children, they would not be seeking to kill him, "a man who has told you the truth" (8:40). Abraham would never do that, and this proves they are "doing the works of your own father" (8:41; cf. 8:44). His opponents disagree by announcing they are not "illegitimate children."

They toss a slur at Jesus, legitimating themselves by saying their "only Father . . . is God himself" (8:41).

Jesus rebuts their argument as he did their claim about Abraham: If they were God's children, they would love the One whom God loves, the one and only Son, the one who is next to God, the one who participates in what God does, the Logos, the Life, the Light, the Lamb, the Messiah, the Son of Man. But they don't, and that disproves their claims. They simply don't belong to the God they claim or the ancestry they claim.

The unbelieving Jews match Jesus for his statement about the devil. Using classic slurs and stereotypes to demonstrate the absolute distinctions, they say Jesus is a "Samaritan and demon-possessed" (8:48). Denying their slurs Jesus once more connects himself to God the Father, that he has been sent by the Father and so they need to hear and obey his teachings (8:49–51). Jesus claims he can give eternal life, and they know Abraham never had such a power. Which means for them Jesus has just claimed to be greater than Abraham, which is preposterous for them. Their question dominates the entire dispute in John 8. Here is my translation of their words: "Who do you make yourself [to be]?" (8:53).

Jesus turns their opening question inside out: they sought to deconstruct Jesus by asserting his claims were unjustifiable self-claims. Jesus now says the true witness to him is the Father who "glorifies me" (8:54). Even Abraham longed to see Jesus!

Jesus has now gone too far. He's too young to have seen the patriarch.

Jesus will now go even farther: the entire dispute now spins down to one final saying: "Before Abraham was born, *I AM*" (8:58). This is a claim both to divinity and to pre-existence. He has either gone too far or they have failed to perceive God's revelation of the Logos. As a reminder, the

145

just-quoted line is another of the I Am statements. One set of I Am statements gives predicates, like I am X, like I am the "light of the world" (8:12; 9:5). Others are absolute or have no predicate. These sound like the great I am who I am of Exodus 3:14. John 8:58 is one of those absolutes. Jesus has said he Is the I Am. Either he is, or he isn't. There are only two options. He is either sent by God or not, and this entire passage is a battle of words about those options.

They now "knew" he had gone too far: "they picked up stones to stone him" for blasphemy. Just as in Nazareth at the outset of his ministry (Luke 4:30), he escaped, "slipping away from the temple guards" (John 8:59). The options are clear as he exits from the stage.

## QUESTIONS FOR REFLECTION AND APPLICATION

1. Have you ever heard passages such as this one used to express anti-Jewish sentiment? How does this section shed light on such uses of the text?

2. How does it impact your view of this dispute to see it as an intra-family disagreement, a debate within Judaism, a "family quarrel"?

3. What does it mean to abide in Jesus?

4. How do the translation notes in this study guide affect your understanding of the text? For example, the note that this passage should include "said" and not "challenged" or the fact that the ending of 8:25 is hard to translate.

5. What does Jesus mean when he talks about being free? In what areas of your life do you need Jesus' type of freedom?

## FOR FURTHER READING

Kathleen Norris, *Amazing Grace: A Vocabulary of Faith* (New York: Riverhead, 1998).

# JESUS HEALS
# A BLIND MAN

## *John 9:1–41*

**Special Note to the Reader:** Jesus performs the healing sign of a blind man being given sight. This long passage becomes a series of interrogations of the blind man about the One who healed him. Jesus is present in the opening scene and then not again until the last scene. The question again is "Who is Jesus?"

*¹ As he went along, he saw a man blind from birth. ² His disciples asked him, "Rabbi, who sinned, this man or his parents, that he was born blind?"*

*³ "Neither this man nor his parents sinned," said Jesus, "but this happened so that the works of God might be displayed in him. ⁴ As long as it is day, we must do the works of him who sent me. Night is coming, when no one can work. ⁵ While I am in the world, I am the light of the world."*

*⁶ After saying this, he spit on the ground, made some mud with the saliva, and put it on the man's eyes. ⁷ "Go," he told him, "wash in the Pool of Siloam" (this word means "Sent"). So the man went and washed, and came home seeing.*

## Neighbors and Observers

<sup>8</sup> *His neighbors and those who had formerly seen him begging asked, "Isn't this the same man who used to sit and beg?"* <sup>9</sup> *Some claimed that he was.*

*Others said, "No, he only looks like him."*

*But he himself insisted, "I am the man."*

<sup>10</sup> *"How then were your eyes opened?" they asked.*

<sup>11</sup> *He replied, "The man they call Jesus made some mud and put it on my eyes. He told me to go to Siloam and wash. So I went and washed, and then I could see."*

<sup>12</sup> *"Where is this man?" they asked him.*

*"I don't know," he said.*

## Pharisees and Blind Man

<sup>13</sup> *They brought to the Pharisees the man who had been blind.* <sup>14</sup> *Now the day on which Jesus had made the mud and opened the man's eyes was a Sabbath.* <sup>15</sup> *Therefore the Pharisees also asked him how he had received his sight. "He put mud on my eyes," the man replied, "and I washed, and now I see."*

<sup>16</sup> *Some of the Pharisees said, "This man is not from God, for he does not keep the Sabbath."*

*But others asked, "How can a sinner perform such signs?" So they were divided.*

<sup>17</sup> *Then they turned again to the blind man, "What have you to say about him? It was your eyes he opened."*

*The man replied, "He is a prophet."*

## Pharisees and Blind Man's Parents

<sup>18</sup> *They still did not believe that he had been blind and had received his sight until they sent for the man's parents.* <sup>19</sup> *"Is this your son?" they asked. "Is this the one you say was born blind? How is it that now he can see?"*

<sup>20</sup> *"We know he is our son," the parents answered, "and we*

know he was born blind. <sup>21</sup> But how he can see now, or who opened his eyes, we don't know. Ask him. He is of age; he will speak for himself." <sup>22</sup> His parents said this because they were afraid of the Jewish leaders, who already had decided that anyone who acknowledged that Jesus was the Messiah would be put out of the synagogue. <sup>23</sup> That was why his parents said, "He is of age; ask him."

## Pharisees and Blind Man Again

<sup>24</sup> A second time they summoned the man who had been blind. "Give glory to God by telling the truth," they said. "We know this man is a sinner."

<sup>25</sup> He replied, "Whether he is a sinner or not, I don't know. One thing I do know. I was blind but now I see!"

<sup>26</sup> Then they asked him, "What did he do to you? How did he open your eyes?"

<sup>27</sup> He answered, "I have told you already and you did not listen. Why do you want to hear it again? Do you want to become his disciples too?"

<sup>28</sup> Then they hurled insults at him and said, "You are this fellow's disciple! We are disciples of Moses! <sup>29</sup> We know that God spoke to Moses, but as for this fellow, we don't even know where he comes from."

<sup>30</sup> The man answered, "Now that is remarkable! You don't know where he comes from, yet he opened my eyes. <sup>31</sup> We know that God does not listen to sinners. He listens to the godly person who does his will. <sup>32</sup> Nobody has ever heard of opening the eyes of a man born blind. <sup>33</sup> If this man were not from God, he could do nothing."

<sup>34</sup> To this they replied, "You were steeped in sin at birth; how dare you lecture us!" And they threw him out.

## Jesus and Blind Man

<sup>35</sup> Jesus heard that they had thrown him out, and when he found him, he said, "Do you believe in the Son of Man?"

<sup>36</sup> *"Who is he, sir?" the man asked. "Tell me so that I may believe in him."*

<sup>37</sup> *Jesus said, "You have now seen him; in fact, he is the one speaking with you."*

<sup>38</sup> *Then the man said, "Lord, I believe," and he worshiped him.*

<sup>39</sup> *Jesus said, "For judgment I have come into this world, so that the blind will see and those who see will become blind."*

### Pharisees and Jesus

<sup>40</sup> *Some Pharisees who were with him heard him say this and asked, "What? Are we blind too?"*

<sup>41</sup> *Jesus said, "If you were blind, you would not be guilty of sin; but now that you claim you can see, your guilt remains.*

The back-and-forth dispute of the previous chapter morphs in this chapter into a sign. Healing the man born blind is the sixth sign in John (see, p. 103), and a sign is a public deed performed by Jesus that reveals who he is but requires faith in order to perceive. Yes, Jesus works wonders, but the wonders are not the point: he, the I Am, is. Isaiah prophesied more than once that when the kingdom came the blind would be able to see (Isaiah 29:18; 35:5; 42:7), and perhaps some observers would wonder if this healing fulfilled that prophecy. What they could not avoid wondering about was, "Who is this Jesus?"

This sign-miracle entails the beginning of some back-and-forths with the blind man. We learn who Jesus is in this passage through a series of interrogations of the blind man who becomes a witness to Jesus. As such, we learn too what it means to be a witness. In fact, as we read through this passage, we get the feel that the man is on trial. Many of us have experienced being on trial for our witness about Jesus.

I'm thinking of Jemar Tisby, whose wonderful book *The Color of Compromise* was both praised by many and attacked by others. Why? Because he witnessed, on the basis of his Christian faith, to the centuries long racist structures and systems in American society. Those systems, though created by people claiming to be Christians, were wildly inconsistent with the gospel that values all humans as made in God's image. Social media put him on trial.

## DISCIPLES ASK,
## JESUS ANSWERS AND HEALS

The question about the "blind man from birth" (John 9:1) by the disciples—"who sinned?"—is instinctively "biblical" because sin and sickness are connected in the Bible (Deuteronomy 5:9, for instance). But their question also bobs on the waters of curiosity and intellectual pretense while it fails pastorally. A blind man becomes for the disciples an object for theological curiosity. Jesus transforms their question into a sign. *Sin*, he reveals to them, *has nothing to do with this man's blindness*. No, "this happened so that the works of God might be displayed in him" (9:3). Perhaps your heart is pierced as mine is to think God purposed that man's blindness. Some, in fact, think it is better to translate not with "so that" but with "with the result that the works of God might be displayed." However we read that line, what is clear is that Jesus has a mission to do God's works because he is the Light of the world (9:4–5). His Light-ness is about to become sight-ness for a blind man. At the Tabernacles festival every day ended with lighting four large lampstands in the Court of Women. The hyperbole was that it gave light to the whole of Jerusalem. Good timing for Jesus.

Material realities, flesh and blood, bread and wine, and water embody the very presence of God so spit and mud become the medium of revelation. Jesus then tells the man to go wash. The water in the pool of Siloam at the southern edge of Jerusalem becomes a medium of revelation and redemption for this man (9:6–7).

The blind "man went and washed" and then magical words follow, and I translate: he "came [back] seeing" (9:7). Don't you just love that line? Not until that tactile watery wash was the man given sight. As a sign, his eyesight works at more than one level. Marianne Meye Thompson enters into the sign's meaning when she writes, "In order to judge rightly [who Jesus is], one must see rightly, and the narrative also raises a question: What does it take to see?" (Thompson, *John*, 204).

We are about to watch scenes unfold in which a blind man sees and seeing men do not.

## Neighbors and Observers Ask, Blind Man Witnesses

Miracles of any kind are by nature incomprehensible. Which is why we call them miracles, a term expressing that we have no explanation of what happened other than God. Those who knew the blind man personally and those who had seen him begging in Jerusalem could not comprehend whether the seeing man was the blind man they knew. A man suddenly given eyes may look different, so the healed man becomes a witness with "I am the man" (9:9). His words illustrate the core of what it means to witness: to speak about and act on the basis of one's experience. The healed man responds to their wondering how this can happen by pointing them to the one named Jesus.

The "they" who ask, that is the ones split over the identity of the healed man, ask "Where is this man?" who revealed to the blind man how to get healed. The seeing man has no idea where Jesus is. Which reminds us of the earlier healing in John 5 (cf. 5:13) and also sets us up for another set of back-and-forths, this time with the blind man becoming an accidental witness.

## PHARISEES ASK, BLIND MAN WITNESSES

The Pharisees' point is succinct and conventional: if Jesus healed you on a Sabbath, then Jesus can't be "from God" (9:16) because he would be violating Sabbath. They of course have a point, while the blind-man-who-now-sees perceives a different level. He must be thinking *Who but a man "from God" can do to me what Jesus did?* The Pharisees, however, ask a question that makes it possible for an answer that cuts into their own stance: "What do you have to say about him?" (9:17). The blind man's answer makes him a witness once again, now with growth in perception: "He is a prophet" (9:17). A witness is unafraid to speak of God after experiencing healing. Some call these "only God" moments.

## PHARISEES ASK, BLIND MAN'S PARENTS ANSWER

Sticking to their theological principles, the Pharisees think the healed man's words are insufficient. They choose to get his parents involved. They tell the truth: *Yes, he's our son; Yes, he was born blind.* A kind of "we don't know the whole story" is their stance because, as John informs us, "they were afraid of the Jewish [Judean] leaders" (9:22). So they shift the weight back on their son. John inserts a comment: any association with Jesus could lead to excommunication from the synagogue. The Greek term is *aposynagōgos*, which literally is "out-of-synagogue" (9:22). The parents' fear is rooted in the understandable desire for social belonging. One must say that most think anything approaching official excommunication from a synagogue because of faith in Jesus would not be practiced in the first century. If that is the case, either this term is less official—a kind of "you'll be in trouble"—or it could be anachronistic, that is, the use of a term at the time the Gospel was written, at which time it was more official, for the time of Jesus. I think it is less official language.

The blind man is unlike his parents because witnesses are unafraid of social pressure.

## PHARISEES ASK, BLIND MAN WITNESSES

The Pharisees turn to the healed man again, this time pressing the edge harder. First, they say give glory to God (not to Jesus) and, second, that Jesus, because he is reported to have done this on the Sabbath, is actually a "sinner" (9:24). The blind man's witness tersely tells his own truth: "Whether he is a sinner or not, I don't know. One thing I do know. I was blind but now I see!" (9:25). If you want to know what a witness is, this is it: a witness simply states one's own redemptive story.

That they want the seeing man to tell his story again annoys him, but he turns the situation against them: "Do you want to become his disciples, too?" (9:27). This leads to insults from those with power and to words that divide them from the man: "You are this fellow's disciple! We are disciples of Moses!" Like many an argument on Twitter and in the lunchroom, they claim biblical power in connecting themselves to the authoritative status of their theological, moral hero (9:28–29).

The healed man's witness moves to the next level in argumentation. He opens with an undeniable reality: "There is something stunning in this" (9:30; my translation). That is, a blind man now seeing stuns everyone into wondering Who and How. He proceeds to their own words: those known for knowing religious realities don't know the origins of Jesus' stunning work (9:30). Then he agrees with them, only to get them to reconsider their own point: *Yes, you are right. God does not listen to sinners, but God does listen to the "godly person who does his will"* (9:31). We are ready for him to say, "So, Jesus is godly and not a sinner," but he backs off. Instead, he makes a confession about who Jesus is: "If this man were not from God, he could do nothing" (9:32).

Truth has a way of unmasking pretensions and power, just as it has a way of undergirding abuse of one's powers. Instead of following the logic of this healed, theologically untrained man, they accuse him of an origin wholly in sin from birth and, with such a depraved, degraded status, they insult him as someone who presumes to teach them. "They threw him out" suggests excommunication from the socially unifying location: the synagogue.

As one who is involved as an advocate for victims, as an advisor, as one often in public discussions about accusations against pastors, I think I have a different angle on what occurs in this passage. Christians have far too often turned this dispute with Jesus over the healed man into a form of anti-Jewish if not anti-Semitic stereotypes. I see it as what happens when powerful men are challenged by unpowerful people. That is, when the veracity of their authority is put at risk, powerful leaders power up and gaslight their critics. In most cases those around the powerful people support the powerful and too often then attack, gaslight, and discredit the ones who accuse and who are in need of empathy and healing. The rhetoric of this passage, then, can be seen as typical reactions by those in power.

The healed man is on Jesus' side and that thread in this narrative will get bolder.

## JESUS ASKS,
## BLIND MAN WITNESSES

The healed man has witnessed to Jesus to neighbors, observers, Pharisees, and parents. Jesus finds the man and invites a commitment: "Do you believe in the Son of Man?" (9:35). Had Jesus said "me," the man surely would have said "Yes," but Jesus wants the healed man to perceive who he is. "You have now seen him," and I translate "the one speaking with you is that man" (9:37). Witnesses learn from Jesus new depths of who he is. So far Jesus has done it all, and the man has been a witness with gradual perception. Jesus wants more. He wants the man's relational trust.

Witness is not enough because what one *thinks* of Jesus is not enough. Faith requires more than right beliefs. The healed man believes and prostrates himself on the ground before Jesus. True faith acts on what one believes. Jesus then clarifies what "Son of Man" means. Daniel's Son of Man executed judgment for the Ancient of Days in Daniel 7, and here Jesus' coming into the world for "judgment" (9:39) entails erasing darkness and filling the void as the Light of the world (9:5), but it also means blinding unbelievers (9:39).

## PHARISEES ASK,
## JESUS WITNESSES

The episode ends with a twist. The Pharisees overheard the words about blindness and ask Jesus if he thinks they are blind too (9:40). Jesus' words twist to make a sharp turn into their hearts: "If you were blind, you would not be guilty of sin." This seems to let them off the hook, only to make the sharp turn: "but now that you claim you can see, your guilt remains [and thus, they are blind]" (9:41).

A witness lets Jesus do the talking.

## QUESTIONS FOR REFLECTION AND APPLICATION

1. What is the connection between physical sight and spiritual sight in this scene?

2. Why do you think some religious authorities opposed Jesus' healing miracles on the Sabbath instead of celebrating them?

3. What do you think of the interpretive possibility presented here that the Pharisees in question are combative because they are afraid of their authority and power being challenged?

4. Have you ever had the sensation of being "on trial" for your witness of Jesus? Or have you seen someone else interrogated for their witness?

5. Has your faith moved from right beliefs to acting on beliefs? In what ways do you want to keep acting out your faith?

# JESUS IS THE GOOD SHEPHERD

## *John 10:1–21*

¹ *"Very truly I tell you Pharisees, anyone who does not enter the sheep pen by the gate, but climbs in by some other way, is a thief and a robber.* ² *The one who enters by the gate is the shepherd of the sheep.* ³ *The gatekeeper opens the gate for him, and the sheep listen to his voice. He calls his own sheep by name and leads them out.* ⁴ *When he has brought out all his own, he goes on ahead of them, and his sheep follow him because they know his voice.* ⁵ *But they will never follow a stranger; in fact, they will run away from him because they do not recognize a stranger's voice."* ⁶ *Jesus used this figure of speech, but the Pharisees did not understand what he was telling them.*

⁷ *Therefore Jesus said again, "Very truly I tell you, I am the gate for the sheep.* ⁸ *All who have come before me are thieves and robbers, but the sheep have not listened to them.* ⁹ *I am the gate; whoever enters through me will be saved. They will come in and go out, and find pasture.* ¹⁰ *The thief comes only to steal and kill and destroy; I have come that they may have life, and have it to the full.*

¹¹ *"I am the good shepherd. The good shepherd lays down his life for the sheep.* ¹² *The hired hand is not the shepherd and does not own the sheep. So when he sees the wolf coming, he abandons the*

*sheep and runs away. Then the wolf attacks the flock and scatters it. [13] The man runs away because he is a hired hand and cares nothing for the sheep.*

*[14] "I am the good shepherd; I know my sheep and my sheep know me—[15] just as the Father knows me and I know the Father— and I lay down my life for the sheep. [16] I have other sheep that are not of this sheep pen. I must bring them also. They too will listen to my voice, and there shall be one flock and one shepherd. [17] The reason my Father loves me is that I lay down my life—only to take it up again. [18] No one takes it from me, but I lay it down of my own accord. I have authority to lay it down and authority to take it up again. This command I received from my Father."*

*[19] The Jews who heard these words were again divided. [20] Many of them said, "He is demon-possessed and raving mad. Why listen to him?"*

*[21] But others said, "These are not the sayings of a man possessed by a demon. Can a demon open the eyes of the blind?"*

John 10 flows out of John 9, the healing of the blind man, without interruption and, were it not for the chapter divisions, we'd think of one (very) long discourse. To take the conversation one step higher, we are given a parable or a proverb-like saying that has become one of the favorite parables in the history of the church—Jesus as the good shepherd (10:1–6).

What distinguishes the *tov* (good or excellent or beautiful) shepherd from the false or bad shepherd not only distinguishes Jesus from some of Jerusalem's powerful leaders but also provides for us marks for discerning good leaders and parents today. Imagine sheep, a courtyard of some sort, a gate, and a good shepherd as well as false shepherds who sneak in to steal the shepherd's sheep. Jesus uses this image to contrast his pastoral healing of the blind man and how the leaders in Jerusalem responded to the blind man, his parents, and to Jesus.

## MARKS OF
## FALSE TEACHERS

There is a right way and a wrong way to relate to people pastorally. Good shepherds nurture trust through loving, sensitive, and mentoring relationships. False teachers presume their authority and so barge into a person's life and, as someone "of the cloth" (or close to such persons), they violate the conscience of a person and disrespect boundaries. A spiritual relationship with someone is earned over time and becomes precious but, because the one benefiting from that relationship is vulnerable, a false teacher usurps the space and wounds. The aim of the false teacher is to capture someone for their own agenda, to enhance their own ego, to bolster their supporters, and to breed loyalty to the person on that platform. Bad shepherds make themselves the center of attention; in good shepherds, as Lesslie Newbigin once said to a group of pastors, "the life of the Good Shepherd is being lived" through them (Newbigin, *The Good Shepherd*, 17).

Jesus pins such a description on those who failed to care for the blind man. He calls such a person a "thief" and a "robber," two terms more or less describing the same action. Jesus degrades them when he says they are "hired hands" (10:12, 13), by which he means they work for the money not out of the loving care of the sheep, the calling, or the vocation. He clarifies the "hired hand" as the one who "cares nothing for the sheep." This expression is about the person himself or herself. One could phrase it as "there is not a care in the person about the sheep" (10:13). Such a person lacks character and is irreverent about the calling. His words are general enough to apply to many pastors in many places and times.

## MARKS OF THE GOOD SHEPHERD

Contrast such a person with Jesus, who was himself Character-in-Person and fully absorbed with his mission. This passage combines remarkable traits of character, and it's easy to miss so stay with me. Jesus simultaneously exudes loving care and powerful protection. He knows his sheep, they know him; yet, he's the gate that protects them. Like the ideal medieval knight, Jesus was "a work not of nature but of art" (C.S. Lewis, *Present Concerns*, 4). How so?

The shepherd (1) enters the gate rightfully, (2) the sheep listen to his voice, (3) the shepherd knows his sheep by name, and (4) the shepherd leads them, and they follow him. Even more, (5) he saves or rescues the sheep, (6) finds the places of food for his sheep, and thus (7) provides life "to the full" (10:10). His description of a good shepherd is not done. This good shepherd (8) "lays down his life for the sheep" (10:11; cf. 10:17–18). As Marianne Meye Thompson expresses the paradox, "the death of [this] shepherd is the very means by which his work of protecting the lives of the sheep is accomplished" (Thompson, *John*, 226). He does this because his death leads to resurrection (10:17). One more: (9) he's making all his sheep of all time and every location into "one" flock (10:16).

As such, Jesus is both "the gate for the sheep" (10:7; cf. Psalm 118:20) and the "good shepherd" (John 10:11, 14; cf. Ezekiel 34). These are three and four of the I Am Sayings of Jesus (see p. 103). That little parable Jesus tells in John 10:1–6, then, is an icon onto Who Jesus is. His loving care for his sheep reveals who he is: God's love incarnate. In fact, Jesus slides easily from his knowledge of his sheep to the Father's knowing him and his knowing of the Father (10:15). Don't miss this: the loving care of Jesus for the sheep and the love of the sheep for Jesus *participates in God's own self-knowing!* In knowing Jesus as our good shepherd, we know God, and God knows us, what one might describe as a radical mutual knowing. Does that not make your back tingle with joys of intimacy?

The actions of the good shepherd in this parable tilt toward the abstract and metaphorical, so let's turn to the novelist P.D. James, who, in *Death in Holy Orders*, sketches the realities of actual pastoral care. The pastor, James writes,

> . . . had returned from two hours of visiting long-term sick and housebound parishioners. As always he had tried conscientiously to meet their individual and predictable needs: blind Mrs. Oliver, who liked him to read a passage of scripture and pray with her; old Sam Possinger, who on every visit re-fought the Battle of Alamein; Mrs. Poley, caged in her Zimmer frame, avid for the latest parish gossip; Carl Lomas, who had never set foot in St. Botolph's but liked discussing theology and the defects of the Church of England. Mrs. Poley, with his help, had edged her way painfully into the kitchen and made tea, taking from the tin the gingerbread cake she had baked for him. He had unwisely praised it four years ago, on his first visit, and was now condemned to eat it weekly, finding it impossible to admit that he disliked gingerbread. But the tea, hot and strong, had been welcome and would save him the trouble of making it at home (p. 166).

When the metaphors turn into practice, they look a lot like what James describes here. Many have found George Bernanos's remarkable novel, *The Diary of a Country Priest*, to be one worthy model of a good shepherd. Metaphors put aside means idealisms too much be put aside. Jesus knew the rough side of being a good shepherd, too.

Jesus' teaching, all taking place at the Feast of Tabernacles (John 7:1–10:21), splits his audience once again (10:19–21). Some think he's "raving mad" and others that no one in league with evil can do what Jesus just did! One thing is very clear about Jesus: you must make up your mind and answer the question—Who is this man?

## QUESTIONS FOR REFLECTION AND APPLICATION

1. What are some differences between good pastoral shepherds and bad ones?

2. In what ways did Jesus exemplify a good shepherd?

3. How does Jesus as shepherd point us to God?

4. Have you ever been mistreated by a pastor who was supposed to care for you? Or have you seen others experience this violation? How did it impact your relationship with God and the church?

5. When have you experienced excellent pastoral care from a good shepherd? What was that like?

## FOR FURTHER READING

George Bernanos, *The Diary of a Country Priest: A Novel* (Cambridge: Da Capo Press, 2002).

P.D. James, *Death in Holy Orders* (New York: A.A. Knopf, 2001).

C.S. Lewis, *Present Concerns: Journalistic Essays* (ed. Walter Hooper; New York: HarperOne, 2017), 1–6. Originally published in 1947.

Lesslie Newbigin, *The Good Shepherd: Meditations on Christian Ministry in Today's World* (Grand Rapids: Wm. B. Eerdmans, 1977).

# JESUS ANSWERS
# HIS CRITICS

## *John 10:22–42*

### Are You the Messiah?

*22 Then came the Festival of Dedication [=Hanukkah] at Jerusalem. It was winter, 23 and Jesus was in the temple courts walking in Solomon's Colonnade. 24 The Jews who were there gathered around him, saying, "How long will you keep us in suspense? If you are the Messiah, tell us plainly."*

*25 Jesus answered, "I did tell you, but you do not believe. The works I do in my Father's name testify about me, 26 but you do not believe because you are not my sheep. 27 My sheep listen to my voice; I know them, and they follow me. 28 I give them eternal life, and they shall never perish; no one will snatch them out of my hand. 29 My Father, who has given them to me, is greater than all; no one can snatch them out of my Father's hand. 30 I and the Father are one."*

### Are You Claiming to Be God?

*31 Again his Jewish opponents picked up stones to stone him, 32 but Jesus said to them, "I have shown you many good works from the Father. For which of these do you stone me?"*

*33 "We are not stoning you for any good work," they replied, "but for blasphemy, because you, a mere man, claim to be God."*

34 *Jesus answered them, "Is it not written in your Law, 'I have said you are "gods" '? * 35 *If he called them 'gods,' to whom the word of God came—and Scripture cannot be set aside—* 36 *what about the one whom the Father set apart as his very own and sent into the world? Why then do you accuse me of blasphemy because I said, 'I am God's Son'?* 37 *Do not believe me unless I do the works of my Father.* 38 *But if I do them, even though you do not believe me, believe the works, that you may know and understand that the Father is in me, and I in the Father."* 39 *Again they tried to seize him, but he escaped their grasp.*

40 *Then Jesus went back across the Jordan to the place where John had been baptizing in the early days. There he stayed,* 41 *and many people came to him. They said, "Though John never performed a sign, all that John said about this man was true."* 42 *And in that place many believed in Jesus.*

Time and time again the issue for those watching and listening to Jesus was the identity of Jesus. The critics of Jesus, those who contest the origins of his astounding works, want him to own up to who he is by answering to their categories. In this passage they ask Jesus two basic questions, neither of which Jesus answers quite the way they want. (That's so like Jesus.) The most important question asked by the Gospel of John is, "Who is Jesus?" and the entire book sweeps us up into answering that question. Whatever answer we give stands us at the elbow in the fork in the path. If we say "Lord," we are to follow him. If we say "Messiah," we are to see him as the riddle of all history. If we say "God," we admit before all that God has become the Logos in history (John 1:14). Over and over the question is asked, and over and over we are summoned to give our answer.

This passage finishes off the back-and-forths of John's middle chapters, after which John begins to lead us into the last week of Jesus' earthly life. As the climax to chapters five through ten, the identity of Jesus emerges at its most intense level.

Only someone with an extraordinary self-awareness, call it Ego, could have forced this question on his audiences as often as Jesus did. His Ego matched his Identity. There are hints that his audiences suspect more than they let on by the questions they ask him. We can focus on two questions.

## ARE YOU THE MESSIAH?

Jesus' approach to questions asked is somewhat Socratic. At Hanukkah, a feast of renewed celebration of regaining control of the temple through the Maccabees, in the courts of the temple under shade, Jews/Judeans ask Jesus if he is the Messiah (10:22–24). Months have passed since Tabernacles but the same question about the same person arises. *Who does this man from Galilee think he is?* One detects pressure in their forming a circle around him and not a little exasperation. Their question is a kind of "How long will you hold our whole beings in the air about this?" Their second question asks for frankness on his part ("plainly").

The easiest answer is "Yes" or "No." But Jesus won't go there. He wants them to answer their own question, so he probes by claiming, "I did tell you, but you do not believe" (10:25). We might ask when he told them. Let's consider what's in the air about Jesus. Was *good shepherd* a messianic claim? Verse thirty-six perhaps answers their question with *God's Son*. This label for Jesus appeared in John's lengthy discussion at Tabernacles (8:36) but also the term was in the air around Jesus who often spoke of Son with Father (1:49; 3:16–18; 3:35–36; 5:19–23, 25–27; 6:40). In the Jewish world king, son of God, and Messiah overlap in meaning.

But these terms seem inadequate. Jesus is greater than king. In 10:30 Jesus will say, *"I and the Father are one."* He is a king unlike all other kings and a Son unlike all other sons of God. He and the Father mutually indwell one another. Father and Son are in concord in the mission to bring life. That the Father is "greater than all" (10:29) elevates Jesus' claim to oneness to the highest level. Hence, he is accused of "blasphemy" (10:33).

They fail to perceive who he is, so Jesus backs off to the obvious: *his works* (10:25). They reveal who Jesus is for those with eyes to see and a heart to comprehend. In other words, his works are signs to the one with faith. His words penetrate even deeper into the purposes of God when he says they don't believe because they are "not my sheep." Those who do are granted "eternal life" (10:26–29). Sight and insight are not the same, as Marianne Meye Thompson observes (Thompson, *John*, 232). His opponents see but lack insight; the believer sees and gains insight.

## ARE YOU CLAIMING TO BE GOD?

That Jesus claims he and the Father are one is for them the perfect storm of sin. They determine to take matters into their own hands and stone him (10:31) but Jesus shifts the conversation to his works. "Which of them deserves death?" he asks them. They turn the conversation back to his self-claims and now say he has a "claim to be God" (10:33). By the way, Hanukkah rededicated the temple after a pagan king, Antiochus Epiphanes, claimed to be equal with God.

In our passage's intense back-and-forth, we pull out for notice how often John uses irony: the opponents have just said what John said in 1:1! They perceive him to be blasphemous while articulating who he is (cf. 19:7). He sabotages their response by citing a line in a psalm (82:6). There the children of Israel are "gods" and "sons of the Most High" but they die (82:7). His logic is deadly: if all humans are "gods" then he is even more, and Jesus is the "god" who will grant eternal life (John 10:35–36, with 10:28). On first reading it's hard to spot all this indirection and irony, but when we slow down to read it carefully, we can see it.

So, Jesus summons them to respond to what they can see in his works (10:37–38). That is, if they will ponder them carefully with an eye of trust. Those works show two things: "that the Father is in me" and that "I [am] in the Father" (10:38). This man is God in the flesh. Father and Son, Face-to-Face.

Their attempt to seize him is foiled by his escape to the east of the Jordan where John the Baptist had baptized. Notice this too: in sketching Jesus' successful ministry beyond the Jordan, we encounter bold contrasts of unbelief in Jerusalem with belief by "many" in the hinterlands (10:40–42).

*Yes as God's Son, Yes as God's Son,* those are the answers to their questions. He has given them what they wanted, which is step one. He has identified himself. Step two is their response. Frederick Buechner once wrote that there is only one reason to take Jesus at his word for who he claims to be: if he can save. "If he is [who he says he is], he can. If he isn't, he can't. It may be that the only way in the world to find out is to give him the chance, whatever that involves. It may be just as simple and just as complicated as that" (Buechner, *Beyond Words,* 257). Faith opens curtains to the Light who is the Logos.

We could ask this question after every passage in this Gospel: Who do you think Jesus is? What does your answer mean for your life today?

## QUESTIONS FOR REFLECTION
## AND APPLICATION

1. What do you think it was like for the religious leaders and the everyday people trying to puzzle out who Jesus was? What questions would you have asked in their position?

2. How does John use irony as a literary device in this passage?

3. Why do you think the normal people believed in Jesus when many of the religious elites did not?

4. When you gave Jesus the chance to save you, what happened in your life?

5. How is this study so far reshaping your answer to the question: Who is Jesus?

### FOR FURTHER READING

Frederick Buechner, *Beyond Words: Daily Readings in the ABC's of Faith* (San Francisco: HarperSanFrancisco, 2004).

# JESUS RAISES
# LAZARUS

## *John 11:1–44*

### Lazarus Dies

*¹ Now a man named Lazarus was sick. He was from Bethany, the village of Mary and her sister Martha. ² (This Mary, whose brother Lazarus now lay sick, was the same one who poured perfume on the Lord and wiped his feet with her hair.) ³ So the sisters sent word to Jesus, "Lord, the one you love is sick."*

*⁴ When he heard this, Jesus said, "This sickness will not end in death. No, it is for God's glory so that God's Son may be glorified through it." ⁵ Now Jesus loved Martha and her sister and Lazarus. ⁶ So when he heard that Lazarus was sick, he stayed where he was two more days, ⁷ and then he said to his disciples, "Let us go back to Judea."*

*⁸ "But Rabbi," they said, "a short while ago the Jews there tried to stone you, and yet you are going back?"*

*⁹ Jesus answered, "Are there not twelve hours of daylight? Anyone who walks in the daytime will not stumble, for they see by this world's light. ¹⁰ It is when a person walks at night that they stumble, for they have no light."*

*¹¹ After he had said this, he went on to tell them, "Our friend Lazarus has fallen asleep; but I am going there to wake him up."*

¹² His disciples replied, "Lord, if he sleeps, he will get better." ¹³ Jesus had been speaking of his death, but his disciples thought he meant natural sleep.

¹⁴ So then he told them plainly, "Lazarus is dead, ¹⁵ and for your sake I am glad I was not there, so that you may believe. But let us go to him."

¹⁶ Then Thomas (also known as Didymus ) said to the rest of the disciples, "Let us also go, that we may die with him."

### Lazarus's Sisters

¹⁷ On his arrival, Jesus found that Lazarus had already been in the tomb for four days. ¹⁸ Now Bethany was less than two miles from Jerusalem, ¹⁹ and many Jews had come to Martha and Mary to comfort them in the loss of their brother. ²⁰ When Martha heard that Jesus was coming, she went out to meet him, but Mary stayed at home.

²¹ "Lord," Martha said to Jesus, "if you had been here, my brother would not have died. ²² But I know that even now God will give you whatever you ask."

²³ Jesus said to her, "Your brother will rise again."

²⁴ Martha answered, "I know he will rise again in the resurrection at the last day."

²⁵ Jesus said to her, "I am the resurrection and the life. The one who believes in me will live, even though they die; ²⁶ and whoever lives by believing in me will never die. Do you believe this?"

²⁷ "Yes, Lord," she replied, "I believe that you are the Messiah, the Son of God, who is to come into the world."

²⁸After she had said this, she went back and called her sister Mary aside. "The Teacher is here," she said, "and is asking for you." ²⁹ When Mary heard this, she got up quickly and went to him. ³⁰ Now Jesus had not yet entered the village, but was still at the place where Martha had met him. ³¹ When the Jews who had been with Mary in the house, comforting her, noticed how quickly she got up and went out, they followed her, supposing she was going to the tomb to mourn there.

³² *When Mary reached the place where Jesus was and saw him, she fell at his feet and said, "Lord, if you had been here, my brother would not have died."*

³³ *When Jesus saw her weeping, and the Jews who had come along with her also weeping, he was deeply moved in spirit and troubled.* ³⁴ *"Where have you laid him?" he asked.*

*"Come and see, Lord," they replied.*

³⁵ *Jesus wept.*

³⁶ *Then the Jews said, "See how he loved him!"*

³⁷ *But some of them said, "Could not he who opened the eyes of the blind man have kept this man from dying?"*

### Jesus Raises Lazarus

³⁸ *Jesus, once more deeply moved, came to the tomb. It was a cave with a stone laid across the entrance.* ³⁹ *"Take away the stone," he said.*

*"But, Lord," said Martha, the sister of the dead man, "by this time there is a bad odor, for he has been there four days."*

⁴⁰ *Then Jesus said, "Did I not tell you that if you believe, you will see the glory of God?"*

⁴¹ *So they took away the stone. Then Jesus looked up and said, "Father, I thank you that you have heard me.* ⁴² *I knew that you always hear me, but I said this for the benefit of the people standing here, that they may believe that you sent me."*

⁴³ *When he had said this, Jesus called in a loud voice, "Lazarus, come out!"* ⁴⁴ *The dead man came out, his hands and feet wrapped with strips of linen, and a cloth around his face.*

*Jesus said to them, "Take off the grave clothes and let him go."*

The best proof of who Jesus is can be seen in the lived theology of Jesus. His ideas turn words about ideas into living realities. His overt claims to grant eternal life are easier said than done. In this chapter Jesus *does eternal life,* and he does so to generate new life in the observers. David Ford rightly says chapter eleven in John is a "drama of encounters, relationships, passionate feelings, decisions, and actions" (Ford, *John*, 219, all italics in original). Yes, a drama, and that happens in other passages too (as we have noticed).

Seven strands weave together in this wonderful passage, but we will separate them so each can be seen for what it is. There are a number of characters involved too: Jesus, Lazarus, Mary, Martha, Jesus' disciples including Thomas, and Judean friends of the family. (A note about Mary in John 11:2 indicates that John thinks his readers already know what he will record in John 12:1–11.)

## DEATH

Mostly in Jerusalem and in connection with major festivals, Jesus performed miracles. In Jerusalem he healed at the pool of Bethesda (5:1–15), fed 5,000 up near the Sea of Galilee (6:1–15), and heals a blind man back in Jerusalem (9:1–12)—all along creating controversies—and in each act reveals himself as the Son of the Father who sent him to do the works of God. When God works, new life explodes. In the previous chapter (10:28), Jesus declares that he not only works miracles but grants *eternal* life.

The problem for such a claim is death, and the story about Lazarus turns life into the final word. The language of death in the chapter develops: first the man is sick (or weak; 11:1, 3), then he is asleep (11:11), and finally Jesus informs the disciples that Lazarus is dead (11:14, 17, 39). The one who grants eternal life now has an opportunity to make his life-granting powers into "lived" theology.

In describing death in this passage, the realities of loss, grief, exasperation, and death are not diminished. Instead, they are openly acknowledged, but life beyond death will get the final word.

177

## DELAY

Oddly, Jesus, knowing the sickness is unto death, intentionally delays a journey to Jesus' close friends. Jesus was informed of Lazarus' condition from a report sent by the sisters (11:3), but Jesus "stayed where he was two more days," and only then did he inform his disciples he wanted to return to Judea from Galilee (11:6–7). Because of this delay, at least according to the sisters, Lazarus died (11:21, 32) and, according to some of their friends, Jesus could have "kept this man from dying" (11:37). Jesus, however, says he was glad he delayed (11:15). John sketches for us a drama.

## LOVE

What makes this delay more intense is Jesus' love for Lazarus (11:3) and for Martha and Mary, whom he comforts (11:5, 31). Allen Dwight Callahan gives a lyrical turn to what happened: "Jesus loved Lazarus and his sisters. Martha and Mary loved their brother. And in love they all meet at the grave" (Callahan, "John," 199). Readers of this Gospel know of a person referred to as "the disciple whom Jesus loved" (13:23; 20:2–8; 21:7, 20) and, though some suggest that person is Lazarus, that suggestion seems unlikely to me. I think it's John.

Jesus was also so deeply moved or, better yet, he expressed disturbance or exasperation, the Greek having the sense of snorting. Snorting mixes together both love for Lazarus and anger at death. So moved was he that he wept over his friend's death (11:33, 38 and 11:35) and, when others see Jesus, they observe how much Jesus loved Lazarus (11:36). Weeping over the death of those we love participates in the grief of Jesus.

Why then did he intentionally delay, knowing what he knew and knowing how much he loved this family?

## UNVEILING

More than once, Jesus explains the delay. First, seemingly speaking to the sisters' messenger, "It is for God's glory so that God's Son may be glorified" (11:4). Second, he delayed "so that you [disciples] may believe" (11:15). One can reasonably infer that delay allowed Lazarus time to die and be good and dead, and it allowed Jesus to probe the faith of Martha when he said, "Your brother will rise again" (11:23). And then he also probed the faith of Mary by informing her that this delay occurred for God's glory (11:40). The final expression of the purpose of the delay involves Jesus' public prayer when he thanks the Father for hearing him, which he says he said aloud "for the benefit of people standing here" (11:42).

Following the last few chapters of controversies over Jesus' astounding healings, this delay creates drama for the act of acts as a sign of all signs. In this action Jesus will reveal who he is so people may believe. This is not a *proof* of who Jesus for he needs no proof. No, this is not a proof but a *pulling back of the veil* so others may see that God unleashes Life in Jesus.

## REVELATION

What one finds behind the veil is who he is. Yes, he is "Rabbi" (11:8), he is "Teacher" (11:28), but he's more than those labels. Martha's faith is honest and developing. Rodney Reeves sketches her honest faith in these words he attributes to her speaking to Jesus:

> You are faithful, but you let me down. You will never forsake us, but you left us hanging. You are good, but this is bad. You love us, but you weren't here to help us. You are life, but my brother is dead (Reeves, *Spirituality*, 41).

Martha is the one who confesses the true confession: "You are the Messiah, the Son of God, who is to come into the world" (11:27). That is the right confession but lived theology for a human is not just to say the right words or to think the right theology but to live consistently with those truths.

The truth comes from the lips of Jesus when he gives another of his "I Am" statements. To Martha Jesus revealed, "I am the resurrection and the life," and that the person who believes in Jesus "will live, even though they die" (11:25). This is the fifth I Am statement (see p. 103). The revelation is that Jesus is not only the one who turns water into wine, not only the one who can heal the paralyzed and blind, not only the one who can turn a plate of food into a picnic for thousands, not only the one who can stride upon the waters, but he is the Life that can turn dead bones into living ones and raise dead bodies from the grave. He not only grants life, *he is the Life that creates, sustains and raises into Life.* Affirming Jesus as the Resurrection at a grave empowers a person to participate in Jesus' own Life.

## SHALLOWS

Faith operates in the shadows, even at the superficial level, at times. Jesus wants us to move from the shallows into the deep. The shallows are on display in this text, and they are not descriptive of unbelievers but believers learning to deepen their faith in who Jesus is and what Jesus can accomplish. We catch glimpses of the revelation that forms in this chapter and along with those glimpses, what people see and say by way of their own forming of faith. The disciples, upon hearing Jesus say he wanted to return to Judea, express the danger that awaits Jesus in Judea. Jesus cuts through that one with they "have no light" (11:9–10). The disciples want the Lord of Life to avoid Judea out of fear of death when the one entering into that darkness will bring the Light of Life and conquer all Death.

Jesus informed the disciples that Lazarus had "fallen asleep" and that he would go to him to wake him up (11:12). The disciples hear "sleep" and think that's good as rest can lead to healing (11:13). They heard "natural sleep" when Jesus meant death, so he tells them Lazarus has died. They will go to him so Jesus can probe and deepen their faith (11:14–15).

Thomas, who will doubt Jesus after the resurrection, is rarin' to go to Jerusalem and expresses his courage to head to Judea even if it means death with Jesus (11:16). He does not show at the crucifixion scene later. Crickets.

When Jesus informs Martha that her brother will rise again, Martha connects such a moment with the end of time general resurrection (11:23–24), but Jesus is about to raise her brother in the here and now. Both of the sisters had a futuristic faith in the resurrection but had no perception that Jesus had the powers to raise in the present (11:21, 32). When Jesus arrives at the tomb Martha didn't want the stone rolled from the opening into the tomb/cave because of the stench of a decomposing body (11:39). The One who can raise a dead body surely is a stench-remover too.

One shallow perception after another weaves through the drama of Jesus' raising Lazarus.

## DEAD MAN WALKING

The one who heals is about to do an uber-healing. His words were loud for all to hear: "Lazarus, come out!" (11:43). As the sheep know the voice of their shepherd, so Lazarus knows the voice of the Lord of Life (Quast, *John*, 85). Saying you can give eternal life and even claiming you are the Resurrection and the Life are easier to say than do. Jesus now does eternal life. His theology becomes lived theology when "the dead man came out, his hands and feet wrapped with strips of linen, and a cloth around his face" (11:44). Jesus liberates his friend from death and informs those around the tomb to "take off the grave cloths and let him go." The last word for this man is not death but life. It is perhaps worth observing that this is a resuscitation of a dead man more than the kind of resurrection we see with Jesus. His grave clothes were not left behind as was the case with Jesus. Instead, they had to unwrap the man so his former body could live some more. The dust-to-dust demand had been snapped for a season.

Imagine that!

What kind of person walks up to a tomb, has the stone rolled away, and summons a dead man to get up and get on with it? And what kind of man can make that happen? Answering those questions are why John wrote this Gospel. Which is why what comes next comes next.

## QUESTIONS FOR REFLECTION AND APPLICATION

1. What does it mean that Jesus "does eternal life" in this story about Lazarus?

2. Note Martha's confession of who Jesus is, her answer to John's ongoing question. Who does she say that he is, and what is the significance of that revelation?

3. Jesus not only heals Lazarus, but he also liberates him from death. What does liberation mean in the ministry of Jesus?

4. How do Jesus' emotions in this scene impact you? What emotional expressions do you observe in him?

5. What does Jesus' whole-hearted entrance into grief here speak to you? How can this help you in your own griefs?

# RESPONSES TO JESUS DIVIDES PEOPLE

## John 11:45–54

⁴⁵ *Therefore many of the Jews who had come to visit Mary, and had seen what Jesus did, believed in him.* ⁴⁶ *But some of them went to the Pharisees and told them what Jesus had done.*

⁴⁷ *Then the chief priests and the Pharisees called a meeting of the Sanhedrin. "What are we accomplishing?" they asked. "Here is this man performing many signs.* ⁴⁸ *If we let him go on like this, everyone will believe in him, and then the Romans will come and take away both our temple and our nation."*

⁴⁹ *Then one of them, named Caiaphas, who was high priest that year, spoke up, "You know nothing at all!* ⁵⁰ *You do not realize that it is better for you that one man die for the people than that the whole nation perish."*

⁵¹*He did not say this on his own, but as high priest that year he prophesied that Jesus would die for the Jewish nation,* ⁵² *and not only for that nation but also for the scattered children of God, to bring them together and make them one.*

⁵³ *So from that day on they plotted to take his life.* ⁵⁴ *Therefore*

*Jesus no longer moved about publicly among the people of Judea. Instead he withdrew to a region near the wilderness, to a village called Ephraim, where he stayed with his disciples.*

Tragic words about the aftermath of the stunning resuscitation of Lazarus open verse forty-six: "But some." John tells us that "many of the Jews [Judeans] . . . had seen what Jesus did" and "believed in him" (11:45). Their faith, their allegiance, their orientation in life was directed at and from their relationship with Jesus. *But some* did not believe, did not surrender their lives, could not accept the revelation of who Jesus was in the very act of summoning a dead man from a tomb, and so they report him to authorities in Jerusalem, the Pharisees (11:46). Which led to a conclave with the Sanhedrin, a term John uses for the more official gathering of the leading authorities in Jerusalem.

Jesus divides. Or, put differently, responses to Jesus divide people.

From the opening page of this Gospel to the end we watch Jesus divide the audiences who hear him and see him. "His own did not receive him," John told us at 1:11. So it was (and so it is today), and what happens is a discussion with some debate and some different views tossed into the mix. People want to explain Jesus, they want to explain the undeniable influence of the church (even today), they want to explain the church's decline, and they want to explain why some leaders are so charismatic and crowd-attracting.

## SPECULATION

The NIV's "accomplishing" squeezes a simple verb into a precise meaning. It is best to leave the question the leaders ask with "What *are we doing?*" (11:47). They realize his gifts and attractiveness with "If we let him go on like this" and speculate, first, that "everyone will believe in him" and they will lose ideological power and, second, that—because of the unrest that will be created by so many following Jesus—the "Romans" will have to destroy the temple (better, "our place," which could also mean Jerusalem) and nation to calm things down (11:48). They speculate rebellion, riots, and a coup.

Exaggeration and hyperbole always gain ears, especially when it is all folded into apocalyptic images. Politicians attempt to shift a public with apocalyptic fear. That is, *if you don't vote for me our red-white-and-blue democracy will collapse into fascism.*

## PRAGMATICS

In many conclaves someone will think more pragmatically. A high priest, Caiaphas offers a minority opinion on the case. Let Jesus be the scapegoat for all this tension, let his death soothe the populace. If he is put down, the furor will go away, and Rome will leave us alone. A scapegoat pacifies angry actors and creates a shallow peace. Jesus is now trapped between the ruthless power of Rome and the pragmatics of politics in Jerusalem.

What Caiaphas didn't know was that "he did not say this on his own" (11:51). That is, God spoke through him of what would happen or perhaps what he said took a different life later: Jesus would die as a scapegoat "for the [NIV adds "Jewish"] nation" but that unjust death would bring redemption also "for the scattered children of God" and it would "bring them together and make them one" (11:52; cf. 10:16; 17:20–26). John is pointing either to the regathering of the twelve tribes (Jeremiah 31–33) or to gentile conversions–or perhaps both. Marianne Thompson's words probe the way John operates: "while the council intends that Jesus should die instead of the people, by their unwitting collusion, he dies for them" (Thompson, *John*, 253).

## WITHDRAWAL

The conclave seems to break up without resolution. The tension was high and any attempts by Jesus to continue with his ministry in Jerusalem or Bethany was likely to lead to his arrest. John informs us (his readers) that the plot was on to take Jesus down (11:53).

But Jesus' time was not yet so John shifts his attention to Jesus who chooses to stay away from his public, bold presence in Judea. Instead, he travels to Ephraim near the Judean wilderness, that arid, rocky area northeast of Jerusalem (11:54). (Ephraim could be Ophrah, near Bethel.) He "stayed with" may indicate that Jesus withdrew *to wait* for the next major festival, and our next chapter's first verse has Jesus back in Jerusalem for Passover (12:1).

People then and now want to explain the attraction called Jesus. One can only explain him right by seeing in him God's Sign, and one can only see the Sign well if one believes in him and, like Mary, anoints Jesus' feet (12:1–11).

## QUESTIONS FOR REFLECTION AND APPLICATION

1. What is the difference between "Jesus divides" and "responses to Jesus dividing people"?

2. How does Jesus become trapped between Jewish leaders and Roman leaders?

3. What foreshadowing are you beginning to see for Jesus' eventual death?

4. Note how John seems to center action in Jesus' life around the major religious festivals. Why do you think that is?

5. How have you seen differing views on Jesus divide people in your life?

# JESUS PERFUMED BY MARY

## John 11:55–12:11

⁵⁵ When it was almost time for the Jewish Passover, many went up from the country to Jerusalem for their ceremonial cleansing before the Passover. ⁵⁶ They kept looking for Jesus, and as they stood in the temple courts they asked one another, "What do you think? Isn't he coming to the festival at all?" ⁵⁷ But the chief priests and the Pharisees had given orders that anyone who found out where Jesus was should report it so that they might arrest him.

¹²:¹ Six days before the Passover, Jesus came to Bethany, where Lazarus lived, whom Jesus had raised from the dead. ² Here a dinner was given in Jesus' honor. Martha served, while Lazarus was among those reclining at the table with him. ³ Then Mary took about a pint of pure nard, an expensive perfume; she poured it on Jesus' feet and wiped his feet with her hair. And the house was filled with the fragrance of the perfume.

⁴ But one of his disciples, Judas Iscariot, who was later to betray him, objected, ⁵ "Why wasn't this perfume sold and the money given to the poor? It was worth a year's wages." ⁶ He did not say this because he cared about the poor but because he was a thief; as keeper of the money bag, he used to help himself to what was put into it.

⁷ "Leave her alone," Jesus replied. "It was intended that she should save this perfume for the day of my burial. ⁸ You will always have the poor among you, but you will not always have me."

⁹ Meanwhile a large crowd of Jews found out that Jesus was there and came, not only because of him but also to see Lazarus, whom he had raised from the dead. ¹⁰ So the chief priests made plans to kill Lazarus as well, ¹¹ for on account of him many of the Jews were going over to Jesus and believing in him.

The Gospel of John should be published like a novel by Marilynne Robinson—without chapters. John's Gospel unfolds and moves onward with hints backward and forward, with scenes developing the previous ones. Chapter divisions break apart the originally seamless story about Jesus. Gospels, remember, tell the story of Jesus. They are not about us but about Jesus. Not all of it is pretty and happy.

Christians are rightly absorbed with the atoning power of Jesus' death. Our confession is that he died for our sins. His atoning death, however, easily morphs into abstractions, into a timeless event, into a transaction, and into a theological claim. Even into a meal symbolizing his death called Eucharist, which means thanksgiving! The realities are that he was betrayed by an intimate, arrested and brutalized, tried and unjustly condemned, crucified to the point of suffocation, punctured with a spear, removed from the cross, and placed in a tomb. Mary's perfuming of the body of Jesus in our passage anticipates these brutal realities. Of course, she has no idea of such lurid details.

The foreshadowing of the death of Jesus, flowing noticeably from Jesus' raising of Lazarus from among the dead, looms over this entire passage. At least three elements are involved in Jesus' knowledge of his own death and John's presentation. First, Jesus knew the trouble he was in with the authorities, and that his behaviors and words could lead to death. That our last passage ended with an inner circle plot to kill him, that he withdrew, and that he returned surely made Jesus aware that he was poking his head into a lion's mouth called Rome at work in Jerusalem. Second, Jesus knew his life was in the Father's hand, that his life was designed through a death to conquer death for believers, and that his death was inching closer day by day. Third, Jesus' own witness to himself, not to mention that of others, aggravated leaders because terms used for him ushered him into the front row seats of power in Jerusalem, including the king's throne. It's all here in this passage.

## THE LEADERS PLOT JESUS' DEATH

Jesus customarily attended the major Jewish festivals, which meant he went "up" to Jerusalem three times per year. Passover was about to arrive, and most pilgrims arrived "before the Passover" so they could immerse in purification pools or undergo some ritual washing—all so they could enter into the temple pure. Hundreds of purification pools dotted the path from the southern tip of the City of David up to the temple's southern entrance at the Gates of Huldah. Passover was a week-long event (as the Gospels also show in Holy Week from the triumphal entry to Easter). The "chief priests and the Pharisees" ordered those who would be among the pilgrims to nab Jesus if anyone spotted him. Caiaphas's advice to permit Jesus to be the scapegoat evidently convinced the council to concentrate only on Jesus (11:49–50). Meanwhile Jesus is not to be found.

## MARY ANTICIPATES JESUS' DEATH

But he arrives early for Passover and is staying with his friends Mary, Martha, and an uber joyous Lazarus just east of Jerusalem in Bethany (which means "house of the poor"). They host a party for Jesus, which is the least they could do. Martha serves, Lazarus reclines (as the beloved disciple does; 13:23–25), and John shifts our attention away from the resuscitated one to Mary. That well-known strong contrast between Martha and Mary in Luke 10:38–42 disappears in John. All three people exemplify intimacy and adoration of Jesus. Martha is more prominent in chapter eleven, Mary in chapter twelve.

In the House of the Poor, Mary has saved up "a pint of pure nard, an expensive perfume" (12:3). In an extravagant gesture of gratitude and generous reciprocation, Mary "poured it on Jesus' feet and wiped his feet with her hair" and the home became dense with the fragrance, which is a world apart from the stench of Lazarus' body in the tomb. She anoints Jesus' feet (not his head), and in chapter thirteen Jesus will wash the feet of his disciples. Mary uses neither oil (anointing) nor water but perfume. This turns the washing of his feet into an over-the-top purification. She readies his body for the tomb.

Judas, not in tune with Jesus, with Mary, with Martha, or with Lazarus, balks at the expense and pulls out his charity card, saying the nard could have been sold and the funds used for the offering customarily given to the poor after the Passover meal. John opens and peeks into the envelope to tell us Judas wanted to swipe the funds (12:4–6).

## JESUS PREDICTS JESUS' DEATH

Jesus pushes back by saying God prompted Mary to save this perfume for the "day of my burial" (12:7). Jesus' next words are not insensitive to the poor. Instead, when he says "the poor you will always have with you" he wants to inform those listening that ranking significance matters. He is more important at this moment because he's about to be arrested and crucified. He predicts his death to those in the house by predicting his burial. A burial placed a corpse in a cave that could be sealed until it was sufficiently decomposed to be buried in the ground. The traditional site of Jesus' entombment is now encased in an extravagantly ornate church in Jerusalem called The Church of the Holy Sepulchre which millions of Christians enter and line up, sometimes for hours, to express their faith in Jesus.

## THE LEADERS PLOT LAZARUS' DEATH

Bethany is a short walk up over the rocky hills east of Jerusalem, so it can be no surprise the leaders of Jerusalem catch wind of where Jesus is staying. Some of the "large crowd" were willing to inform them (12:9–10). Now that people were absorbed with a man raised from the dead, the leaders have their eyes on arresting Lazarus and putting him down, too. The problem with Jesus remained the same: he attracted many to become allegiant to himself as Lord, as Son of God, as Messiah, as Savior. Summoning Lazarus from the tomb made the allegiance more problematic.

For John, the public ministry of Jesus comes to an end here. From the next passage on we enter the tragic ending of Jesus' life and the glories of what he will accomplishing through his death and resurrection.

## QUESTIONS FOR REFLECTION AND APPLICATION

1. At this point in his story, what do you think Jesus understood about his coming death?

2. How does John's presentation of Martha's hosting and service in this section differ from Luke's presentation of her hosting work in Luke 10?

3. What do you think Mary understood about the significance of her sacrifice here?

4. Which character do you most relate to in this scene? Why?

5. Have you ever made a costly sacrifice for Jesus? What prompted your act of allegiance?

# JESUS ENTERS JERUSALEM

## John 12:12–19

<sup></sup>

¹² *The next day the great crowd that had come for the festival heard that Jesus was on his way to Jerusalem.* ¹³ *They took palm branches and went out to meet him, shouting,*

> *"Hosanna!"*
> *"Blessed is he who comes in the name of the Lord!"*
> *"Blessed is the king of Israel!"*

¹⁴ *Jesus found a young donkey and sat on it, as it is written:*

> ¹⁵ *"Do not be afraid, Daughter Zion;*
> *see, your king is coming,*
> *seated on a donkey's colt."*

¹⁶ *At first his disciples did not understand all this. Only after Jesus was glorified did they realize that these things had been written about him and that these things had been done to him.*

¹⁷ *Now the crowd that was with him when he called Lazarus from the tomb and raised him from the dead continued to spread the word.* ¹⁸ *Many people, because they had heard that he had performed this sign, went out to meet him.* ¹⁹ *So the Pharisees said to one another, "See, this is getting us nowhere. Look how the whole world has gone after him!"*

Departing from Bethany, Jesus makes his way to Jerusalem from the east. His entry into Jerusalem, usually called the "triumphal" entry, was a staged prophetic symbolic action that provoked—once again—various responses.

## PRAISE

Perhaps John exaggerates in saying the "great crowd" at Jerusalem for Passover acclaim him king by waving (date) palm branches as he passes by. Perhaps, but not only has John already used "great crowd" (12:9), the Synoptic Gospels too recognize a sizable crowd welcoming Jesus (Matthew 22:8). Luke labels this crowd disciples (19:37). Hyperbole aside, Jesus' following was noticeable and that's probably all that was intended by John. An event celebrating liberation from slavery, which is what Passover was, and now acclaiming someone a king in terms used for God's return to Zion, surely created challenges for the local establishment ever concerned about riots and rebellions.

The crowd's spontaneous acclamations quote from the Passover Hallel Psalms (113–118). The words "Hosanna" and "Blessed is he who comes in the name of the Lord!" are from Psalm 118, a psalm celebrating the victory of God over Israel's enemies. The word "Hosanna" literally means "God save us" but it had acquired the sense of "Praise God!" by the time of Jesus. That psalm instructed the worshipers to join God's entry into the temple with "boughs in hand" (118:27). John adds to the words from Psalm 118 words that may have come from Zephaniah 3:15 about the "King of Israel," an expression of Nathanael's in chapter one (John 1:49).

The scene is dramatic. The leaders are concerned about Jesus, they have moles in the crowds, Jesus arrives from Bethany with friends, and now he approaches Jerusalem with his followers declaring that he is the arriving King of Israel, a label John likes (18:33; 19:19–22). As Marianne Thompson rightly shifts topics, "What is at stake is not whether Jesus is king, but how he will assume and exercise his sovereignty" (Thompson, *John*, 265). Just how Jesus does this is about to unfold.

## PROVOCATION

The other Gospels tell us more about the entry than does John, but two features stand out in John, one unexpressed. The unexpressed point is that Jesus enters, not where the political leaders of Rome stage their parades and entries into Jerusalem. They entered from the west or from the north in great pageantry, but Jesus enters through what is called the Beautiful (or Golden) Gate that led into the temple area (now blocked off).

More significantly, Jesus entered on a small donkey while the Roman military powers entered Jerusalem on steeds and armor. John quotes Zechariah 9:9 to connect Jesus' action to Scripture. Zechariah stated that God's redemption involved the removal of "warhorses from Jerusalem" (9:10) because God "will proclaim peace to the nations" and his kingdom "will extend from sea to sea . . . to the ends of the earth" (9:10). Jesus enters Jerusalem as the world's true Lord. Strikingly and missed by no one, he enters the holy city on a donkey, an act that embodies his approach to kingship and kingdom. His rule is not by way of military victory or raw power but by way of humility and service. His entry subverts Rome's type of entry. Even more, his entry subverts the agents of Rome running Jerusalem.

Put together we must say Jesus' entry is a deliberate, staged provocation of the way of Rome that was shaping the way of Jerusalem.

## PERCEPTIONS

It is not uncommon for us to realize the depth of some event after much time, sometimes years. The quotation from Zechariah is not jostling for attention in the minds of the disciples as they walk alongside Jesus. No one is muttering to another, *Hey, blokes, this is just what Zechariah said.* No, only after the crucifixion do they remember and comprehend what happened that Passover (John 12:16; see 15:20; 16:4).

At the moment, however, the crowds (of disciples) continue their acclamations so clearly that more decide to join the parade (12:18) as the Pharisees perceive that the passive approach of Caiaphas somehow is promoting the growth of the Jesus movement (12:19).

## QUESTIONS FOR REFLECTION AND APPLICATION

1. The Passover celebration marked the liberation of God's people from slavery in Egypt. What metaphorical significance is there to the deaths and resurrections of Lazarus and Jesus happening around this festival?

2. How do Jesus' choices for his entrance subvert Roman cultural norms and people's expectations?

3. What does Jesus forecast about God's kingdom with these choices?

4. Read Zechariah 9:9–17 and Zephaniah 3. What do you think the disciples later perceived of what Jesus had done by riding into Jerusalem on a donkey?

5. What is your feeling while reading this passage? What anticipation are you sensing for the next stage of the story?

# JESUS PREDICTS HIS DEATH

## *John 12:20–36*

[20] Now there were some Greeks among those who went up to worship at the festival. [21] They came to Philip, who was from Bethsaida in Galilee, with a request. "Sir," they said, "we would like to see Jesus." [22] Philip went to tell Andrew; Andrew and Philip in turn told Jesus.

[23] Jesus replied, "The hour has come for the Son of Man to be glorified. [24] Very truly I tell you, unless a kernel of wheat falls to the ground and dies, it remains only a single seed. But if it dies, it produces many seeds. [25] Anyone who loves their life will lose it, while anyone who hates their life in this world will keep it for eternal life. [26] Whoever serves me must follow me; and where I am, my servant also will be. My Father will honor the one who serves me.

[27] "Now my soul is troubled, and what shall I say? 'Father, save me from this hour'? No, it was for this very reason I came to this hour. [28] Father, glorify your name!" Then a voice came from heaven, "I have glorified it, and will glorify it again." [29] The crowd that was there and heard it said it had thundered; others said an angel had spoken to him.

[30] Jesus said, "This voice was for your benefit, not mine. [31] Now is the time for judgment on this world; now the prince of this world

*will be driven out. ³² And I, when I am lifted up from the earth, will draw all people to myself." ³³ He said this to show the kind of death he was going to die.*

*³⁴ The crowd spoke up, "We have heard from the Law that the Messiah will remain forever, so how can you say, 'The Son of Man must be lifted up'? Who is this 'Son of Man'?"*

*³⁵ Then Jesus told them, "You are going to have the light just a little while longer. Walk while you have the light, before darkness overtakes you. Whoever walks in the dark does not know where they are going. ³⁶ Believe in the light while you have the light, so that you may become children of light." When he had finished speaking, Jesus left and hid himself from them.*

What has become commonplace assumption for Christians was hardly that in the first century, even for Jesus. I speak of the inclusion of gentiles in the one people of God. The first century Jesus movement was entirely Jewish until the gospel missions of Peter and Paul, which we read about in the Book of Acts. Jesus was a Galilean and so were the apostles. Jesus' words and teachings and way of living were entirely Jewish, as was that of the apostles and disciples around him. So, when we read in John 12 that some "Greeks" (or "Hellenes," which indicates Greek-speaking) approached the Galilean apostle Philip and requested a meeting with Jesus, John wanted to get our attention. He got it. The problem is that we don't know that the Greeks even got to meet Jesus. John finishes this little cameo with "Andrew and Philip in turn told Jesus" that the Greeks wanted to see him (12:21). Scene shift.

## A SURPRISING CONNECTION

Which launches Jesus' prediction of his own death. Is the inquiry of some Greek-speaking Passover worshipers connected to Jesus' death somehow? They inform Jesus the Greeks want to meet him and Jesus "replied" (12:23) by predicting his death! Jesus has come to gather not only Galileans and Judeans but also Greek-speaking Jews, and perhaps they are part of the scattered people of God (7:35; 10:16; 11:52; 12:32; 17:20–26). Now that such persons have inquired of Jesus the time is ripe for him to begin speaking more openly about his (inevitable, unjust, and redemptive) death. These Greeks anticipate the global mission of the gospel, which cannot occur until the "Son of Man" is "glorified" (12:23). Jesus's imminent death spawns at least the following convictions.

## THE TIME FOR DEATH

Not only is Jesus' death inevitable because of a swelling opposition to him but his death is part of God's plan for Jesus. Jesus' words in our passage have that sense of divine plan: that hour that had not yet come (2:4) is now "the hour [that] has come" (12:23) and "it was for this very reason I came to this hour" (12:27). But his mission is not some doomed-to-death life. Kevin Quast states this provocatively when he wrote "his entire ministry to this point has meaning only in light of his death and resurrection" and the "cross is the reason for the incarnation" (Quast, *John*, 90, 91).

## A FERTILE DEATH

Jesus plays with an image. As a kernel that is planted dies and then produces many seeds, as anyone who has ever held a stalk of wheat or barley knows from experience, so Jesus' death will produce life in abundance for many. His fertile-life death provides a vision for following him: grasping one's life crushes that life but giving one's life ("hates their life") leads to "eternal life" (12:25). Which leads Jesus to use another image, "servant." To serve Jesus means walking toward the cross of his death, but with the consciousness that the "Father will honor" that way of life (12:26).

Jesus connects serving him with the promise of being with Jesus "where I am." Jesus puts it this way: "where I am, my servant also will be" (12:26). Where is Jesus? In a crucifixion called glorification, which means serving Jesus will lead to being honored by his Father (12:26). Which is why Eugene Peterson once preached about the cross in terms that turn the world upside down: "His death, a willed and sacrificial death, was an offering for the death-dealing sins of the world, a death that conquered death. It was the death of death" (Peterson, *As Kingfishers Catch Fire*, 257).

## A Glorifying Death

Though his inner being is fraught with tension ("Now my soul is troubled"; 12:27), Jesus knows death is "the very reason" for his life! So, Jesus turns to the Father with "glorify your name!" (12:28), and the Father affirms the Son by affirming the answer to the prayer. The sound of the Father's voice was unclear to those around Jesus as some thought it was thunder and others an angel's voice. John's Gospel, as we have already said, connects the crucifixion with the Son's glorification. To call the humiliating crucifixion "glorification" is a resurrection perspective that subverts the powers of Rome, the prince of this world, and death. In the crucifixion of Jesus, we gain the truest vision of who God is and what God is like. In that crucifixion the Son lovingly trusts the Father all the way down (and then up). Death, the destiny of all of us, does not have the final word because the cross turns death into glorification. There's more to consider.

## A Conquering Death

One of the great themes of the Bible is the battle between good and evil, between God and the evil one (cf. 8:44; 13:2, 27; 14:30; 16:11). In this passage Jesus announces "the time for judgment on this world" is "now," and that the "prince of this world will be driven out" (12:31). The theme is prominent in the Gospels, from the temptation to the exorcisms to this conquering of the enemy on the cross. This theme, however, is ignored in evangelism today because the gospel has been reduced to one God and one person. The Bible's gospel is captured by cosmic redemption and the establishment of world peace, justice, and love. Hence the Book of Revelation tells the story of God's defeat of the evil powers so that the New Jerusalem can flourish.

Pause now to think of what comes to your mind when you hear of Jesus speaking of his death. Is it not true that we think of our sins being forgiven so we can be made right with God and spend eternity in heaven? Not one hint of such a theme is present in this very explicit set of statements by Jesus. Our gospel is not big enough because our cross is not big enough. The cross as presented by John conquers the evil one and sin and systemic evil and death.

## A Mission Death

Furthermore, the crucifixion/glorification of Jesus launches a gospel mission to the whole world (12:32). His words are that he will "draw all people to myself." John clarifies that Jesus' words "when I am lifted up" is a veiled prophecy of crucifixion (12:33). The crowd is left wondering by both "Son of Man" and "lifted up" as Jesus moves on to an invitation, and all these convictions are at work in Jesus' understanding of his death.

## A Decision-Shaping Death

He's about to die; it's time for those who see him and hear him to decide. Jesus uses the images of "light" and "darkness," as well as "walking" as a metaphor for "believing." I wonder what you think of this story told by the former Supreme Court Justice, Antonin Scalia:

> A friend of mine once told me of his experience in returning to a boys' boarding school in England—a monastery school—that he had attended many years ago. Most of his teachers were gone, but one elderly brother was still there, the headmaster of the place. After speaking with him at some length about old times, he asked the brother how the school was faring today. "Oh, I think we are preparing our boys quite well." he said. "And what are you preparing them for?" my friend asked. A puzzled look came over the old face, as though he was surprised by a question that had such an obvious answer. "Why," he said, "for death." (Scalia, *Scalia Speaks*, 80–81)

## Questions for Reflection and Application

1. What do you think is the connection between the asked-for meeting between the Greek-speakers and Jesus and Jesus' prediction of his death?

2. How does John show the power in paradox of humiliation leading to glorification?

3. Read Isaiah 52:13–53:12 and compare what is said about the death of the Servant with how Jesus talks about his death in John 12:20–36.

4. How do these themes about Jesus' death (fertile, glorifying, conquering, mission, decision-shaping) compare and contrast with ways you have previously learned or thought about Jesus' death?

5. Which theme is most personally significant to you? Why?

## FOR FURTHER READING

Eugene Peterson, *As Kingfishers Catch Fire: A Conversation on the Ways of God Formed by the Words of God* (Colorado Springs: WaterBrook, 2017).

Antonin Scalia, ed. Christopher J. Scalia and Edward Whelan, *Scalia Speaks: Reflections on Law, Faith, and Life Well Lived* (New York: Crown Forum, 2017).

# JESUS EXPLAINS FAITH

## *John 12:37–50*

### John's Observations about Faith

³⁷ Even after Jesus had performed so many signs in their presence, they still would not believe in him. ³⁸ This was to fulfill the word of Isaiah the prophet:

> "Lord, who has believed our message
> and to whom has the arm of the Lord been revealed?"

³⁹ For this reason they could not believe, because, as Isaiah says elsewhere:

> ⁴⁰ "He has blinded their eyes
> and hardened their hearts,
> so they can neither see with their eyes,
> nor understand with their hearts,
> nor turn—and I would heal them."

⁴¹ Isaiah said this because he saw Jesus' glory and spoke about him.

⁴² Yet at the same time many even among the leaders believed

*in him. But because of the Pharisees they would not openly ac-
knowledge their faith for fear they would be put out of the synagogue; ⁴³ for they loved human praise more than praise from God.*

### Jesus' Observations about Faith

*⁴⁴ Then Jesus cried out, "Whoever believes in me does not believe in
me only, but in the one who sent me. ⁴⁵ The one who looks at me is
seeing the one who sent me. ⁴⁶ I have come into the world as a light,
so that no one who believes in me should stay in darkness.*

*⁴⁷ "If anyone hears my words but does not keep them, I do not
judge that person. For I did not come to judge the world, but to save
the world. ⁴⁸ There is a judge for the one who rejects me and does
not accept my words; the very words I have spoken will condemn
them at the last day. ⁴⁹ For I did not speak on my own, but the
Father who sent me commanded me to say all that I have spoken.
⁵⁰ I know that his command leads to eternal life. So whatever I say
is just what the Father has told me to say."*

John's Gospel was written so people would believe in Jesus
as God's Son and Messiah (20:30–31). In the closing section of John 12, which draws the public ministry of Jesus
to a close, we are treated both to John's observations about
unbelief in spite of the "many signs" Jesus had done "in their
presence" and to Jesus' own observations about faith. There
are two complementary approaches to faith in this passage.
But each expresses the cry of Jesus for his generation to trust
him as God's Agent of Light in this world.

Faith can be confusing at times. Something Barbara
Brown Taylor once wrote can clear out the smoke:

> While it may seem more respectable to approach faith
> as an intellectual exercise or more satisfying to approach
> it as an emotional one, our relationship to God is not
> simply a matter of what we think or how we feel. It is

more comprehensive than that, and more profound. It is
a full-bodied relationship in which mind and heart, spirit
and flesh, are converted to a new way of experiencing
and responding to the world. It is the surrender of one
set of images and the acceptance of another. It is a matter
of learning to see the world, each other, and ourselves as
God sees us, and to live as if God's reality were the only
one that mattered (Taylor, *The Preaching Life*, 44).

With those words dancing in our bodies, especially "as if
God's reality were the only one that mattered," we move now
to the closing of John's twelfth chapter.

## BELIEVING ACCORDING TO JOHN

One can begin to believe in Jesus because of the "signs" but
it's not enough. Those who had seen many of the signs chose
not to believe in Jesus in spite of the signs. For many first
century Jesus-believers the unbelieving response to Jesus
by their contemporaries confounded them. John begins to
explain that lack of faith by working with two passages from
Isaiah, the first from 53:1 and the second from 6:10.

First, Isaiah's experience of his contemporaries not
trusting his prophetic words anticipates how the leaders
of Jerusalem respond to Jesus' mighty signs (John 12:38).
Isaiah extolled the glories of the "good news" that "Your God
reigns!" (52:7) because God will redeem Israel, but when
God's Messiah enters Jerusalem, the leaders do not embrace
the Messiah. They reject him.

Second, John appeals to a correspondence between
divine purpose and human response in John 12:39–41 by
turning all the way back in his Bible to Isaiah 6. There the
prophet Isaiah was given a vision of "the Lord, high and
exalted, seated on a throne" surrounded by "seraphim" and,

after confessing his own unworthiness to glimpse the throne room of God, he is sent to tell the people of God—notice that—their response would be dull and inadequate until "the cities lie ruined" (because of exile). But he turns at the end of Isaiah 6 to announce there will still be life in the stumps that remain. Their condition of unbelief would end with belief.

In citing this passage from Isaiah John explains (1) the unbelief of the leaders as divine discipline but also (2) that their unbelief is temporary. Kevin Quast sums it up perfectly: "God intends persistent unbelief to lead to decisive judgment, consequent repentance, and ultimate deliverance" (Quast, *John*, 92). Too many forget the context of Isaiah 6 and see here a brutally unfair god. The Father of Jesus, however, would never hold someone responsible for unbelief if he both determined and caused unbelief. Never. John is here suggesting the unbelief of these leaders will someday be turned into faith.

In fact, "many even among the leaders believed in him" (12:42), indicating another dimension of faith: humans remain responsible. Sadly, John continues, these leaders who do believe in Jesus would not declare their allegiance to Jesus because of the social pressure put on them by the "Pharisees"—and John says they "loved human praise more than praise from God" (12:43). Perhaps we need to give some grace by remembering that faith is a journey, and they were just beginning.

## BELIEVING ACCORDING TO JESUS

Believing, if you remember from the first passage we discussed (pp. 7–9), combines elements of discernment, decision, dependence, and obedience. Here one element is emphasized and there another, but each says something true about faith. At the end of our passage Jesus turns the entirety of faith in a new direction, and it should stun anyone who imagines themselves standing in Jerusalem listening to Jesus. Jesus, in fact, "cried out"—an expression of exasperation and pathos flowing from the depths of his heart.

Believing in Jesus means believing in the Father (12:44) but then he goes radical: "The one observing me observes the One who sent me" (12:45, my translation). Jesus, to switch categories, is himself the Sign of all signs, and the one who gazes at him sees the Father. That is an astounding claim, worthy in fact of being blasphemous were it not true. Jesus embodies God (cf. 1:14). Such faith requires keeping, or obeying, the words of Jesus (12:44). Bonhoeffer said this well: "Faith is only faith in deeds of obedience" (Bonhoeffer, *Discipleship*, 64).

Faith for Jesus is believing in the Father by believing in Jesus: he is the "Light" who can lead people out of the "darkness" (12:46). So much is faith through the revelation of Jesus that he says he does not judge those who reject him. He did not come to judge but to save (12:47) because God's mission flows from love (3:16–17). No, his "words" will do that (12:48), which also shows that humans are held responsible for their response. We might pause and wonder if this isn't a bit of sleight of hand. Aren't his words an extension of Jesus? Hold on a second. Not entirely. Jesus pins his words on the Father who gave them to him (12:49–50). Jesus' teachings are the Father's teachings, and he is the Father's Agent.

To believe in Jesus is to believe in the Father. It is a faith-in-the-Father faith in Jesus. If we fail to balance Father and Son, we commit what David Ford calls "Jesusolatry" (Ford, *John*, 249). If we fail in the other direction, we commit "Fatherolatry."

## QUESTIONS FOR REFLECTION
## AND APPLICATION

1. How does John explain people's unbelief in Jesus?

2. What does John indicate about the future possibility of these unbelievers turning to belief?

3. What elements make up believing?

4. How does your understanding of Jesus shape your understanding of the Father?

5. Consider the Bonhoeffer quote: "Faith is only faith in deeds of obedience." What are your acts of obedience that show your faith?

## FOR FURTHER READING

Dietrich Bonhoeffer, *Discipleship* (Dietrich Bonhoeffer Works 4; Minneapolis: Fortress, 2001). [Formerly called *The Cost of Discipleship*.]
Barbara Brown Taylor, *The Preaching Life* (Lanham, Md.: Cowley, 1992).

# JESUS EXHIBITS SERVICE

## John 13:1–20

¹ It was just before the Passover Festival. Jesus knew that the hour had come for him to leave this world and go to the Father. Having loved his own who were in the world, he loved them to the end.

**Jesus Washing Feet**

² The evening meal was in progress, and the devil had already prompted Judas, the son of Simon Iscariot, to betray Jesus. ³ Jesus knew that the Father had put all things under his power, and that he had come from God and was returning to God; ⁴ so he got up from the meal, took off his outer clothing, and wrapped a towel around his waist. ⁵ After that, he poured water into a basin and began to wash his disciples' feet, drying them with the towel that was wrapped around him.

**Jesus and Peter**

⁶ He came to Simon Peter, who said to him, "Lord, are you going to wash my feet?"

⁷ Jesus replied, "You do not realize now what I am doing, but later you will understand."

⁸ "No," said Peter, "you shall never wash my feet."

Jesus answered, "Unless I wash you, you have no part with me."

⁹ "Then, Lord," Simon Peter replied, "not just my feet but my hands and my head as well!"

¹⁰ Jesus answered, "Those who have had a bath need only to wash their feet; their whole body is clean. And you are clean, though not every one of you." ¹¹ For he knew who was going to betray him, and that was why he said not every one was clean.

### Jesus the Example and More

¹² When he had finished washing their feet, he put on his clothes and returned to his place. "Do you understand what I have done for you?" he asked them. ¹³ "You call me 'Teacher' and 'Lord,' and rightly so, for that is what I am. ¹⁴ Now that I, your Lord and Teacher, have washed your feet, you also should wash one another's feet. ¹⁵ I have set you an example that you should do as I have done for you. ¹⁶ Very truly I tell you, no servant is greater than his master, nor is a messenger greater than the one who sent him. ¹⁷ Now that you know these things, you will be blessed if you do them.

¹⁸ "I am not referring to all of you; I know those I have chosen. But this is to fulfill this passage of Scripture: 'He who shared my bread has turned against me.' ¹⁹ "I am telling you now before it happens, so that when it does happen you will believe that I am who I am. ²⁰ Very truly I tell you, whoever accepts anyone I send accepts me; and whoever accepts me accepts the one who sent me."

The #1 most effective practice in education and formation is "Be the example." Tweet that. Facebook that. TikTok that. The most effective form of learning is to observe the example and then attempt to repeat it on your own until you can be the example. Jesus said it: "I have set you an example," or he has *demonstrated and exhibited his teaching in his actions,* and he did so "that you should do as I have done for you" (13:15). He serves in order to nurture a culture of service, but there's more to our passage than moral example.

## EXHIBITING SERVICE

"Show me, don't tell me" is a lesson one learns in a Creative Writing Class, so novelists like John Steinbeck, instead of telling us that greedy capitalism exploits the poor, narrates a novella called *The Pearl* about Kino, Juana, and Coyotito. Their baby Coyotito, bitten by a scorpion, needs medical attention and, to complicate matters, Kino has found in the ocean the pearl of the world of inestimable value. The entire community seems then to be against him, rather than for the son's recovery, because of what the pearl can become in money. The priest wants a donation, the doctor seems to treat the child in order to get money, the buyers are in cahoots to keep the price low, and on and on. The story exhibits greed and its consequences.

Steinbeck's story, like the action of Jesus, accomplishes far more than what a moral proposition achieves. Jesus, though "Lord and Teacher," does what either a person did for herself or, more likely, what was done by an ordinary domestic servant. His action achieves more than instructing them to serve one another. He washed their feet and then dried their feet with the towel around his waist (13:4–5). Noticeably, he did this *not upon their entry* into the reserved room but *at the meal itself*, which makes the action stand out all the more. Even more noticeably, he was their Lord acting outside what they considered to be his role. Never mind, his role will be radically redefined in the last week anyway. Taken together, the disciples had to be stunned by what Jesus did.

So stunned Peter blurts out a question about whether or not Jesus was going to wash his feet. When Jesus says he was, Peter says he would never permit Jesus to do that. (Peter had not yet grasped the upside-down nature of the mission of Jesus.) Jesus' words go where Peter has not yet gone: "Unless I wash you, you have no part with me" (13:8), or "you have no share with me," and Peter, never lacking a response, then says "wash not just my feet but my hands and my head as well" (13:9). After affirming that Peter only needs his feet washed, the exhibition turns into explanation.

## EXPLAINING THE DEMONSTRATIONS

Jesus, ever the good teacher, ensures the disciples see through the action into its meaning, treating the event as a kind of sign. First, he explains the event as a *washing* that makes a person fit to be "with" Jesus in a redemptive, eternal sense (13:5, 8–10). The footwashing then anticipates the cross and resurrection and empowerment by the Spirit. Second, he explains the footwashing as an embodiment of serving one another in a way that equalizes everyone (13:14–17). Though their Teacher and Lord, Jesus serves his disciples. Disciples, regardless of their or the others' perceived "rank," are to serve one another. The act of washing and the act of receiving the washing become sacraments of participation in who Jesus is and what he provides, just as it unites believers to one another. They are the (foot)washed.

Footwashing has been controversial at times. Some believe we should *do as Jesus did even today* (cf. 1 Timothy 5:10), and others think doing as Jesus did is to practice *comparable acts of service for one another* (again, regardless of perceived rank). Many find footwashing to be a wondrous act of love for one another while others find it wildly out of place or mildly quaint. Jesus and his band of followers wore sandals and walked rocky, dusty paths. Their feet and ankles were therefore dirty, and washing was a way of freshening up as one entered a home. We do our best to find forms of hospitality as our way of doing what Jesus did. It's like a pastor showing up to mow your lawn, or your supervisor staying after to sort through your mess for you, or like countless mothers running home at their lunch hour, grabbing something a school child forgot, dropping it off at the school's front office, and making it back to work in time to begin the afternoon. Lunch still in the fridge.

Status denied in acts of loving service re-embody footwashing.

## WATCHING IS NOT ENOUGH

John will not let his readers forget that a betrayer was on the loose at this event. In three different parts of this brief narrative John mentions Judas. The most ominous of his descriptions is the first, and here is my translation: "the Accuser already having tossed into the heart that Judas, [son of] Simon the Dagger Man, would betray him." The Accuser, or the devil, had already seized some of Judas' heart. Jesus knows this and so he said at the supper, "you [plural] are clean, *though not every one of you*" (13:10–11). Moments later he revealed to them that the betrayal was to "fulfill" a specific passage in Scripture (Psalm 41:9).

Judas watched Jesus as the others had. He saw Jesus' loving act of service. He heard what Jesus said. Judas chose not to serve Jesus but to serve up Jesus, and he chose not to deny himself as the others did but to aggrandize his financial status. Seeing an example doesn't turn a person into a doer of the practice. One must believe in it and do it, habitually, before the character is properly formed.

## ANCHORING THE EXPLANATION

Again, Jesus teaches by example, but he also explains, and I want to draw our attention to three anchors of Jesus' explanation. First, Jesus knew his mission on earth to save and to judge sin was about over, but he also knew he would return to the Father from whence he was sent (13:1, 3). John's first chapter informed us that Jesus was the "Lamb of God" (1:29). Second, his mission and action were prompted by his until-the-end-of-life and his completion-of-his-mission love (13:2). John writes in 13:1 "he loved them to the end [*telos*]" and the verbal form of that word is what Jesus utters from the cross ("it is finished"; 19:30). The theme of love runs straight through this Gospel (cf. 3:16; 3:35; 11:5). His embodied act of footwashing gives the disciples a paradigm of love for others (13:35). Third, he knew the response of those who saw him and heard his explanations was, as we have seen already in John, a response to the One who sent him, that is, God the Father (13:20).

Now read each of the points above in light of each of these three anchors: Jesus washed their feet because it was his mission to clean sinners; Jesus washed feet because he loved them; and Jesus washed feet to prompt a God-shaped response to him.

As he did, so are we to do. Beginning with those at the (perceived) top of the heap. This final meal is not just Eucharist, which John does not record as the other Gospels do, but a lesson in mutual service. Serving others can be personally transformative in the one who serves. Francis of Assisi, it is said, was converted (at least in part) when he experienced the power of footwashing. His biographer, Augustine Thompson, tells the story of Francis washing the feet of a leper:

> As Francis showed mercy to these outcasts, he came to experience God's own gift of mercy to himself. As he cleaned the lepers' bodies, dressed their wounds, and treated them as human beings, not as refuse to be fled from in horror, his perceptions changed. What before

was ugly and repulsive now caused him delight and joy, not only spiritually, but also viscerally and physically. Francis's aesthetic sense, so central to his personality, had been transformed, even inverted. The startled veteran sensed himself, by God's grace and no power of his own, remade into a different man. Just as suddenly, the sins that had been tormenting him seemed to melt away, and Francis experienced a kind of spiritual rebirth and healing. Not long after this encounter, later accounts tell us, perhaps in allegory, that Francis was walking down a road and met one of these same lepers. He embraced the man in his arms and kissed him. Francis's spiritual nightmare was over; he had found peace (Thompson, *Francis of Assisi*, 17).

The perfect example can become the practitioner's virtue.

## QUESTIONS FOR REFLECTION AND APPLICATION

1. How much impact do you think Jesus' example of service by washing feet had on the disciples compared to his previous teachings about service?

2. In what ways does John show that the foot washing was not just an example but was also a sign?

3. What are the three anchors of Jesus' explanation of this act?

4. Have you ever been part of a footwashing experience in a church context? What was that like for you?

5. How do you interpret and apply Jesus' example of foot-washing in your life today? Do you think Christians should literally wash each other's feet or do you think this is accomplished in spirit by other acts of service and hospitality?

## FOR FURTHER READING

John Steinbeck, *The Pearl* (New York: Penguin, 2002).

Augustine Thompson, *Francis of Assisi: A New Biography* (Cornell: Cornell University Press, 2012).

# JESUS AND JUDAS

## John 13:21–30

*²¹ After he had said this, Jesus was troubled in spirit and testified, "Very truly I tell you, one of you is going to betray me."*

*²² His disciples stared at one another, at a loss to know which of them he meant. ²³ One of them, the disciple whom Jesus loved, was reclining next to him. ²⁴ Simon Peter motioned to this disciple and said, "Ask him which one he means."*

*²⁵ Leaning back against Jesus, he asked him, "Lord, who is it?"*

*²⁶ Jesus answered, "It is the one to whom I will give this piece of bread when I have dipped it in the dish." Then, dipping the piece of bread, he gave it to Judas, the son of Simon Iscariot. ²⁷ As soon as Judas took the bread, Satan entered into him.*

*So Jesus told him, "What you are about to do, do quickly."*

*²⁸ But no one at the meal understood why Jesus said this to him. ²⁹ Since Judas had charge of the money, some thought Jesus was telling him to buy what was needed for the festival, or to give something to the poor. ³⁰ As soon as Judas had taken the bread, he went out. And it was night.*

Some stories in the Bible are told because they are true, not because they are comforting. I don't like the story about Abraham lying about his wife Sarah, the story of Moses murdering a man, about David raping Bathsheba, and

I don't like the one about Solomon's multitudinous marriages. David Lamb, with his characteristic wit, candor, and wisdom, wrote a book about some of these stories called *Prostitutes and Polygamists: A Look at Love, Old Testament Style.* These stories, and there are many more, are at times embarrassing while at other times we ask, *Why is this in the Bible? Do we need this story in our Bibles? What will the kids think?*

The same with the betrayal of Jesus by Judas. It's a bit too easy for us to counter our intuitions by saying, *Well, it was all part of God's plan.* It is one thing to think God turned nightmare into Easter, but it is another to brush off the horrors of betrayal, a betrayal that led to a brutal, public crucifixion, by claiming this is how God works in the world. No, by all means, we must learn to see the betrayal as a diabolical act perpetrated by a greedy man who sold the Lord of Life, the Lamb of God, the Son of God, the Bread of Life—just start listing the attributes of Jesus in this Gospel—for money.

Betrayal assaults the heart and soul of one who trusts. Painful disagreements and group-dividing decisions do not rise to the level of betrayals. Betrayals suddenly erase intimacies and love and collapse the foundations of relationships. Betrayals destroy the moral fibers of trust. One should never dismiss a betrayal by minimizing the act or the wounds. Betrayals require emotional strength to face, to endure, and to process. Betrayals may be forgiven but regaining trust requires time. Here is an abstract of a technical study of the psychological impact of betrayal:

> Betrayal is the sense of being harmed by the intentional actions or omissions of a trusted person. The most common forms of betrayal are harmful disclosures of confidential information, disloyalty, infidelity, dishonesty. They can be traumatic and cause considerable distress. The effects of betrayal include shock, loss and

grief, morbid pre-occupation, damaged self-esteem, self-doubting, anger. Not infrequently they produce life-altering changes. The effects of a catastrophic betrayal are most relevant for anxiety disorders, and OCD and PTSD in particular. Betrayal can cause mental contamination, and the betrayer commonly becomes a source of contamination (S. Rachman, "Betrayal: A Psychological Analysis").

Betrayal today is betrayal then, so this modern analysis describes the betrayal by Judas. Jesus was betrayed but so too were the other eleven and the various circles of Jesus' followers, not least his mother and brothers. They all *felt* betrayed. Betrayal violates love, so we should notice the first verse of this chapter: "Having loved his own who were in the world, he loved them to the end" (13:1).

## JESUS' AGITATION

Jesus had just washed the feet of his betrayer and the impending betrayal forms one emotional strain of why he "was troubled in spirit" (13:21). John has described Jesus' visible emotions before (John 11:3, 5, 33, 36; and 12:27). The term points us at the feeling of inner turbulence, chaos, disorder, confusion, and agitation. Think of your washing machine's agitation cycle and what happens to the water: that's comparable to what happened to Jesus' feelings. He knew what Judas would do, he knew when he would do it, but this is the moment when his knowledge became feeling.

## JESUS' ACTION

Next to Jesus is "the disciple whom Jesus loved," who is probably John. The language used for him, that he "was reclining next

225

to him," is the same language used for the Logos's relationship to the Father (1:18). Peter gestured to that disciple and asked him to ask Jesus to identify the betrayer (13:21–25). Jesus privately identifies him by an action: "the one to whom I give this bread when I have dipped it in the dish" (13:25). He then gave the piece of bread to Judas. The stage scene evokes darkness, lightning, and thunder: "As soon as Judas took the bread, Satan entered into him" (13:27; cf. 13:2). Human responsibility remains as Satanic force enters. Evil prefers the human agent.

But Jesus is greater, and he has and will have the last word.

## JESUS' COMMAND

It was the hour. Judas was the instrument.

Jesus tells Judas, "What you are about to do, do quickly" (13:27). The privacy of knowledge is matched by the privacy of Jesus' words to Judas—some at the table thought Judas had left to perform a customary Passover act of generosity for the poor (13:28–30). Allen Dwight Callahan says it well: "now he who single-handedly held the funds in common would single-handedly betray and endanger the common good" (Callahan, "John," 203).

John, writing that it was "night," places the act of Judas in the realm of darkness as the darkness sees to put out the Light of all lights.

## QUESTIONS FOR REFLECTION AND APPLICATION

1. What are the impacts of betrayal on a victim?

2. How do you think Jesus' love for Judas intensified the impact of Judas' betrayal?

3. What impact do you think Judas' betrayal had on the other disciples and followers?

4. What do you see as the balance between human responsibility and satanic responsibility when humans do horrible acts like betraying a friend?

5. Have you even been betrayed by someone you trusted? Have you ever been the betrayer? How does this scene affect you?

## FOR FURTHER READING

David T. Lamb, *Prostitutes and Polygamists: A Look at Love, Old Testament Style* (Grand Rapids: Zondervan, 2015).

S. Rachman, "Betrayal: A Psychological Analysis," *Behaviour Research and Therapy* 48.4 (April, 2010): 304–11. @ doi: 10.1016/j.brat.2009.12 .002. Epub 2009 Dec 24. PMID: 20035927.

# JESUS PREDICTS PETER'S DENIALS

## *John 13:31–38*

31 *When he was gone, Jesus said, "Now the Son of Man is glorified and God is glorified in him.* 32 *If God is glorified in him, God will glorify the Son in himself, and will glorify him at once.*

33 *"My children, I will be with you only a little longer. You will look for me, and just as I told the Jews, so I tell you now: Where I am going, you cannot come.*

34 *"A new command I give you: Love one another. As I have loved you, so you must love one another.* 35 *By this everyone will know that you are my disciples, if you love one another."*

36 *Simon Peter asked him, "Lord, where are you going?"*

*Jesus replied, "Where I am going, you cannot follow now, but you will follow later."*

37 *Peter asked, "Lord, why can't I follow you now? I will lay down my life for you."*

38 *Then Jesus answered, "Will you really lay down your life for me? Very truly I tell you, before the rooster crows, you will disown me three times!*

Alongside Jesus knowing and privately telling one or two of his followers about the betrayal by Judas, Jesus also predicted another tragedy of the last supper: that Peter, one of the closest of the disciples and for many the first among equals, would deny relationship with Jesus that very night three times. Denying Jesus builds the underground passage for a betrayal, but the two are not the same.

Two events that must be narrated because they happened: Jesus foreknows Judas's betrayal and Peter's denial. Nothing pretty there. Are we willing to tell the stories of our lives, our church, our community, and our nation "warts and all"? Or would we prefer to erase the bad moments so we can tell only the good ones? The latter is called hagiography, the former is called history. Israel told the stories of its heroes and nation, warts and all. In fact, one holiday in the Jewish calendar is called *Yom Kippur*, the Day of Atonement. That holiday, like our Lent, summons the covenant people to review the year and confess their sins. Every year. Because Israel cares about history and eschews hagiography. The Gospel writers learned how to write their histories by reading Israel's history. They told these stories because they were part of the story.

If one assumes the traditional sites in modern Jerusalem approximate the real locations, this is what happened:

---

In upper Jerusalem at the last supper Jesus predicts betrayal and denials.

At least a 10–20-minute walk down beyond the temple, into the Kidron Valley, and up a short distance to the garden of Gethsemane.

The betrayal in the garden.

Jesus taken under custody is escorted back to the upper city to Caiaphas's house.

Jesus on trial; Peter in the courtyard; Peter denies Jesus and hears the rooster crow.

---

On top of a hill at the traditional site of Caiaphas's palace is Church of St. Peter in Gallicantu, or Church of the Rooster Crow. Its roof has a golden rooster on the top of a cross.

## TIME

With that narrative all about to unfold before us, Jesus, having sent Judas on his evil mission, declares to those remaining at the table that Father and Son of Man will now be glorified, which is code language in John for the paradox of the cross (13:31–32). The complexity of the crucifixion reveals the depth of the Father's love for the Son, the Son for the Father, and those who embrace that cross express their love for the Son and the Father. The time coming to its end means also his time with the disciples is over, and he will return to the Father (13:33).

231

What do you do when you know this is the last time you will be with your closest friends? Jesus gives them a special mark.

## LOVE

Jesus gives them a "new command" to "love one another" and tells them that when they learn to live in love "everyone will know that you are my disciples" (13:34–35). Love is a rugged, affective commitment to another person to be present with the person, to be an advocate for the person, and to grow together as followers of Jesus (McKnight, *Pastor Paul*, 41–48). Jesus has just demonstrated this kind of love in the footwashing.

The centrality of love stands tall here, just as does the noticeability of love by those who are watching. Jesus urges his followers to become people known for their love of one another, the kind of love that makes others stand up and take notice of something new and distinct. What is new here is not the words themselves, as they are found in Leviticus 19:18, but their connection to Jesus as the one virtue that embodies the very life of Jesus among his followers (recall John 13:1). (The word "Maundy" in Maundy Thursday comes from this command (*mandatum*) to his disciples.)

What gets smushed down below the sight line is that Jesus said this *in the midst of announcing his betrayal by one of the followers and predicting a denial by a leading follower.* Judas has launched the last hours with his followers, Jesus knows he will return to his Father, and he knows Peter will deny him, and his words for his followers are not rebukes or warnings but the love command. The distinctive practice of the Christian, which is what Jesus gave his disciples at the very end, was to love one another as he loved them.

The summons of Jesus to be marked by love may not make sense at times, and perhaps more often than that. There is a doggedness, however, about love for Jesus that summons us to love even our enemies. There is a kind of resistance in love that breaks down barriers. Love like that takes risks. This is why Peter Groves, in his essay on "Love Enacted–Redemption and the Cross," said these words:

> Love makes no sense. It is unsettling, undermining, deconstructive. It turns our world upside down, challenges all our preconceptions, invites us to reconsider the whole of our lives now that love has arrived on the scene. The absurdity of Christianity is not just that the love that makes no sense is the truth that we find in Jesus of Nazareth. The real absurdity of Christianity is the claim that that love is what we are talking about when we are talking about God himself. God is love, and love makes no sense (Groves, "Love Enacted," 10–11).

## PETER

Peter evidently failed to hear the love command and, as will happen again in the very next chapter, prefers to know where in the world Jesus is going that they cannot be with him (13:36). So Jesus repeats what he has just said: they cannot go where he is going (13:33 and 13:36). Peter, who has just had pushback for swelling his chest about his desire to be washed, now says he's got the courage to face the enemies in the powers in Jerusalem and "will lay down" his life (13:37). Jesus predicts that night Peter will deny Jesus three times "before the rooster crows" (13:38).

## QUESTIONS FOR REFLECTION
## AND APPLICATION

1. What is the difference between hagiography and history? Why do the Gospel writers include the difficult and ugly stories?

2. How is "love" defined here?

3. What do you think enabled Jesus to teach about love and to command love even in the midst of betrayal?

4. What are the stories in the Bible that you would prefer not to read? How do you feel about their inclusion in Scripture?

5. Who is the hardest person you have ever had to love? How can Jesus' example and teaching here help you love your enemies and obey in faith?

## FOR FURTHER READING

Peter Groves, "Love Enacted–Redemption and the Cross," in Jennifer Strawbridge and others, *Love Makes No Sense: An Invitation to Christian Theology* (London: SCM, 2019).

# JESUS COMFORTS

## *John 14:1–14*

¹ "Do not let your hearts be troubled. You believe in God; believe also in me. ² My Father's house has many rooms; if that were not so, would I have told you that I am going there to prepare a place for you? ³ And if I go and prepare a place for you, I will come back and take you to be with me that you also may be where I am. ⁴ You know the way to the place where I am going."

⁵ Thomas said to him, "Lord, we don't know where you are going, so how can we know the way?"

⁶ Jesus answered, "I am the way and the truth and the life. No one comes to the Father except through me. ⁷ If you really know me, you will know my Father as well. From now on, you do know him and have seen him."

⁸ Philip said, "Lord, show us the Father and that will be enough for us."

⁹ Jesus answered: "Don't you know me, Philip, even after I have been among you such a long time? Anyone who has seen me has seen the Father. How can you say, 'Show us the Father'? ¹⁰ Don't you believe that I am in the Father, and that the Father is in me? The words I say to you I do not speak on my own authority. Rather, it is the Father, living in me, who is doing his work. ¹¹ Believe me when I say that I am in the Father and the Father is in me; or at

*least believe on the evidence of the works themselves. [12] Very truly I tell you, whoever believes in me will do the works I have been doing, and they will do even greater things than these, because I am going to the Father. [13] And I will do whatever you ask in my name, so that the Father may be glorified in the Son. [14] You may ask me for anything in my name, and I will do it."*

Jesus is about to depart (13:1, 3, 33, 36; 14:2–4). Peter's question in 13:36, "where are you going?" was not given enough of an answer so Jesus returns to the question and—true to form—provokes even more questions! In our passage Jesus answers questions by Thomas and Philip. The evening's events spun the disciples into the chaos of emotional agitation. Jesus pastorally comforts them with four words that have comforted millions of Christians since.

## FIRST WORD OF COMFORT: PRESENCE

The Galilean disciples of Jesus, now gathered far from home with Jesus in Jerusalem, now swarmed by trepidations of what could occur to Jesus and to them for their association with him, and now pondering their commitment to Jesus in light of these dangers, are "troubled" (14:1). Their faces revealed their consternation. The word used here is the same word used for Jesus about the impact of Lazarus's death (11:33), about his own prospect of imminent suffering and death (12:27), and about the knowledge one of his own would betray him (13:21). He looks them in the eye knowing all this—what is going on and what is about to happen to him—and urges them not to be disoriented. What will happen will not be the final word. Easter will be the final word.

So Jesus steps in to tell them their final destiny. Because they trust God and Jesus, he tells them that the "Father's house has many rooms" (14:2). He's leaving to get their rooms ready. A room prepared for them requires that they somehow get there, but Jesus is leaving–so he tells them he will return for them and then usher them to their rooms (14:3). Most think this is the Second Coming.

He will take them there not to escape life or death or hell but "that you also may be where I am" (14:3). Rooms are not the point either, as if a hotel room like one in the Grand Hotel on Mackinac Island in upper Michigan is the point. No, the point of it all is *to be with Jesus eternally*. It is reasonable to think Jesus is talking about heaven here even if it is not as clear as most of us have assumed. Let's assume we are accurate in our judgment. Heaven is about being with God and with Jesus, filled to the top as we will be with the Spirit. The Revelation's final vision is a New Jerusalem and a New Heaven and a New Earth, but the biggest idea of all is not "new" but God dwelling with God's people in a place where there is no longer a need for a temple "because the Lord God Almighty and the Lamb are its temple" (Revelation 21:22). God's glory will be its "light" and the Lamb is its "lamp" (21:23). The "many rooms" Jesus mentions in John 14 would then be about being with Jesus (14:3) just as the New Jerusalem is about the presence of God.

Having said that there is an alternative, and it is not easy to decide between the two interpretations: John 14:23 will say to those who love his teachings that "My Father will love them, *and we will come to them and make our home with them.*" Does this perhaps suggest that he's referring to God's dwelling with us in the Spirit in the here and now and not in some distant future? In that verse Jesus uses "make our home with them" and that word "home" is the same as the "rooms" of 14:2. So maybe after all 14:1–4 is not about heaven but about heaven's presence coming to us in the here and now.

## Second Word of Comfort: *Way*

What surprises the disciples in the midst of their chaos is Jesus' word that they "know the way" (14:4), for they seem to think they don't. Thomas's question represents the others (14:5). The question is about Where but Jesus shifts the question to Who. He clarifies that the where question is not a tunnel away from Jerusalem and not a rapture into the skies and not some vision that transports them to heaven, but a person: "I am the way and the truth and the life" (14:6). This, the sixth of the I Am Statements (see p. 103), turns a very simple term—path, way—into a person and union with that person. The words that follow "way" can be read as two more predicates: way and truth and life. Or one can combine them in various ways: "I am the true and living Way." The Greek simply creates three predicates, each influencing the others so that by the time we are at their end we gain a fuller disclosure of what kind of Way Jesus is: a Way that is the true Way, and a Way that brings true Life, and a Life that is the true Way.

Thomas gets his answer. It's not what he wanted, but it's better than he wanted. The mystery about Jesus' going—where, how, and how can he join him—is over. The answer is Jesus. Which is why Jesus said, "believe also in me" (14:1). Jesus strengthens his "I am" statement when he makes an exclusive claim: "No one comes to the Father except through me" (14:6). The claim either borders on the blasphemous or reveals the heart of final rest in the presence of God. It is the ultimate Christian claim: Jesus is God's appointed Agent of redemption, and there is redemption in no other (cf. Acts 4:12).

## Third Word of Comfort: *In*

The rest of our passage answers Philip's question by exploring one word, the word "in." Jesus once again claims to reveal the

Father so clearly that those who see Jesus see the Father, that those who know Jesus know the Father, and that those who believe in the Father believe in Jesus. He can say this because "I am *in* the Father and the Father is *in* me" (14:11). That means that everything he utters—as the Logos (1:1, 14)—is an utterance from the Father (14:10).

## FOURTH WORD OF COMFORT: *GREATER*

The disciples basked in surrounding Jesus when he was teaching, preaching, healing, confounding, debating, and doing signs. They, let's put it frankly, basked in his glory. Now they wonder what they will do. They've given up everything for him. Jesus comforts that emotional worry too (14:12–14).

His comforting word is that allegiant trust in Jesus will yield "greater" works than Jesus even did (14:12). Yes, I did not quote him wrong, and we are not reading John wrong. Because of Jesus' departure to the Father, he will become their Agent with the Father (cf. Hebrews 2:14–18; 4:14–16), from which location Jesus will provide the powers of grace. Powers unleashed "in my [Jesus's] name" will lead to the Son being glorified (John 14:13). Jesus, to comfort them with rhetoric that surely has a hint of hyperbole in it, says "You may ask me for anything in my name, and I will do it" (14:13). There are two approaches to this: one contends that if we have enough faith, we can get what we want, which has only proven no one has had enough faith not to die or to get something they really wanted, and the other approach sees this as an incitement to trust by exaggerating the benefits. Perhaps the best word about these two promises has been stated by David Ford: "Daring prayer and daring action are two sides of the same coin" (Ford, *John*, 270).

## QUESTIONS FOR REFLECTION
## AND APPLICATION

1. How does Jesus explain the future hope to his disciples through the concept of presence?

2. How does Jesus answer Thomas with a re-directed answer, as discussed in a previous section?

3. What comfort can the disciples find in Jesus' promise that they will do greater works than him?

4. In what ways has God comforted you when you have faced uncertain futures?

5. How could you follow Jesus' example here to offer comfort to others?

# JESUS PROMISES

## John 14:15–31

[15] "If you love me, keep my commands. [16] And I will ask the Father, and he will give you another advocate to help you and be with you forever—[17] the Spirit of truth. The world cannot accept him, because it neither sees him nor knows him. But you know him, for he lives with you and will be in you. [18] I will not leave you as orphans; I will come to you. [19] Before long, the world will not see me anymore, but you will see me. Because I live, you also will live. [20] On that day you will realize that I am in my Father, and you are in me, and I am in you. [21] Whoever has my commands and keeps them is the one who loves me. The one who loves me will be loved by my Father, and I too will love them and show myself to them."

[22] Then Judas (not Judas Iscariot) said, "But, Lord, why do you intend to show yourself to us and not to the world?"

[23] Jesus replied, "Anyone who loves me will obey my teaching. My Father will love them, and we will come to them and make our home with them. [24] Anyone who does not love me will not obey my teaching. These words you hear are not my own; they belong to the Father who sent me.

²⁵ "All this I have spoken while still with you. ²⁶ But the Advocate, the Holy Spirit, whom the Father will send in my name, will teach you all things and will remind you of everything I have said to you. ²⁷ Peace I leave with you; my peace I give you. I do not give to you as the world gives. Do not let your hearts be troubled and do not be afraid.

²⁸ "You heard me say, 'I am going away and I am coming back to you.' If you loved me, you would be glad that I am going to the Father, for the Father is greater than I. ²⁹ I have told you now before it happens, so that when it does happen you will believe. ³⁰ I will not say much more to you, for the prince of this world is coming. He has no hold over me, ³¹ but he comes so that the world may learn that I love the Father and do exactly what my Father has commanded me.

"Come now; let us leave.

The last supper was a long evening. John's thirteenth through the seventeenth chapters shift tides and currents but one can wonder if these chapters point back only to the last supper. Notice that the last line in the passage above says, "Come now; let us leave." Perhaps chapters fifteen to seventeen occurred on the path or at Gethsemane.

Jesus' own discussions shift from those grievous predictions about Judas and Peter to the imminent reality that he will return to the Father, which leaves the disciples gapemouthed about what they will do in his absence. Jesus fills that absence in our passage with the promise of the Holy Spirit's personal presence in nothing less than a special presence of illumination. In fact, there are six promises in our passage that are variations on the same theme, the presence of the Spirit. Jesus does something here no human has done, does, or ever will do. He promises that after his death, he will increase his presence among them! What would you promise others if you could make it happen? We get to see what Jesus thinks his disciples need most, and it can be reduced to one word: Spirit.

## THE SPIRIT TO GUIDE THEM

Loving Jesus entails observing Jesus' commands (14:15), but to do that Jesus knows they need God's gracious power. Which leads to one of the most astounding revelations of the last supper: "I will ask the Father, and he will give you another advocate to help you[1] and be with you forever–the Spirit of truth" (14:16–17). One presumes the other advocate is Jesus, who is now advocating for us in the Father's presence. The new advocate is the Spirit, and the word for "advocate" is *paraklētos*, a term describing someone called to stand with or alongside a person as a mediator or intercessor who can offer support, wisdom, and empowerment. Noticeably, this term points to the gifts of illumination and revelation. There is no suggestion of legal defense or advocacy in the use of this term in this Gospel. The Spirit carries on the ministry of the Father and the Son (notice 5:37 and 15:26–27; 13:31–32 and 16:14). Thompson rightly observes that what the Father does the Son also does, but what the Father does the Spirit does, too (Thompson, *John*, 320).

Jesus informs his followers about two dimensions of this Spirit-advocate: first, that the "world cannot accept" the Spirit [see note 7 below] but this is because "it neither sees" the Spirit nor does it "know" the Spirit (14:17). The second dimension affirms the disciples as personally indwellt by the Spirit: "you know" the Spirit that "lives with you and will be in you" (14:17) from the moment Jesus makes that gift available to them. (Traditionally, at Pentecost but notice "John's Pentecost" in 20:21–23.)

## JESUS' PRESENCE TO
## INDWELL THEM

Which means Jesus is not abandoning the disciples as "orphans" but he "will come to them" (14:18). The Spirit's presence as illuminator and the presence of Jesus in them are indistinguishable at times, as they are here, but they are not identical. Having said that, we simply have to assume that both the Spirit and Jesus are present with us. Notice this: because Jesus asks the Father to send them the Spirit *Jesus will be with them through the Spirit's presence* and thus they will "see" Jesus (14:19). Which now clicks to a new level: "you will realize that I am in my Father, and you are in me, and I am in you" (14:20). Here we have the essential teaching of the abiding presence of the Son in the Father and that same kind of abiding presence of the disciples in Jesus and Jesus in the disciples. This is nothing less than some kind of mutual indwelling. Again, all to emphasize that, *Yes,* Jesus is going to the Father, *but he will be with them as will the Spirit, and they will see and know him intimately as present.*

If you were to ask the disciples which they preferred, don't you think they would have preferred the embodied presence of Jesus over the disembodied presence of Jesus?

## GOD'S LOVE TO INHABIT THEM

Alongside the presence of God in the Spirit and Jesus in them, Jesus promises the disciples the reality of a life of love. Again, observing Jesus' teachings expresses love for Jesus and those who love Jesus' teachings, because he teaches what the Father reveals to him, are loved by the Father and, because that love is given to the Son, Jesus will also love them and will "show myself to them" (14:21). Jesus' words here are like some weaving of

a Celtic cross or of a mutual inter-twining relationship: Father, Son, Spirit, disciples—all woven together in the Father's love. Jesus explains this even more (14:22–24).

To respond affirmatively to the teachings of Jesus is to enter into the weaving of the love of the Father, Son, and Spirit. To reject those teachings tears the threads in the weaving.

## SPIRIT'S MEMORY TO INSTRUCT THEM

The Spirit-sent-by-Jesus, the Illuminator, will enhance the memory of the disciples by teaching and reminding them in a special way of what Jesus taught when he was in their midst (14:26). Many have believed this Spirit-prompted remembering enabled the disciples to write the words now in our Gospels. The Spirit in our passage gives the disciples *perception of the significance of Jesus*, who gives the capacity to see through the works of Jesus as signs of who he is. Hence, the Spirit teaches the church through the teaching, preaching, and prophetic gifts in the church, and the message of the Spirit's revealing gift is the centrality of Jesus (15:26; 16:14). The first mention of the Spirit as the Paraclete, or Illuminator, speaks of the Spirit "of truth" (14:17).

## JESUS' PEACE TO COMFORT THEM

Instead of "troubled hearts" (14:1), Jesus now can offer them "peace." Because his departure is replaced and enhanced by the interweaving of the Spirit's empowering presence with

Jesus' indwelling presence, and with the Father's love surrounding presence, Jesus offers them the tranquility of God's blessed peace (14:27). Not just peace but "my peace" and it is a peace unlike that of the world. As such, this peace is both inner peace and peace between one another.

## FATHER'S KNOWLEDGE TO PREPARE THEM

Our chapter and passage ends with Jesus promising inside knowledge to the disciples. He had told them about Judas before but now he tells them the inside knowledge pertains to his going to the Father, who is "greater" than Jesus (14:28). But he enhances that going-to-the-Father knowledge: his departure involves the "prince of this world" will be unleashed in some way. But with a real twist to it: the evil one's presence enables believers to perceive that "I love the Father and do exactly what my Father has commanded me" (14:31). Instead of grasping control of the current situation in Jerusalem, Jesus surrenders to the plan of the Father: crucifixion, resurrection, and the gift of the Spirit.

## QUESTIONS FOR REFLECTION AND APPLICATION

1. What does Jesus promise the Spirit will do for the disciples?

2. How does Jesus explain that his ongoing presence with them will work?

3. In what ways will all three persons of the Trinity be with the disciples in the future?

4. Have you ever experienced a beloved teacher or mentor moving or passing away? What did they leave for you to help you?

5. How do Jesus' promises to his followers then empower and enable you in your life-in-Christ today?

# JESUS IS THE VINE

## John 15:1–17

*1 "I am the true vine [vineyard], and my Father is the gardener. 2 He cuts off every branch [vine] in me that bears no fruit, while every branch [vine] that does bear fruit he prunes so that it will be even more fruitful. 3 You are already clean because of the word I have spoken to you. 4 Remain in me, as I also remain in you. No branch [vine] can bear fruit by itself; it must remain in the vine. Neither can you bear fruit unless you remain in me.*

*5 "I am the vine; you are the branches [vines]. If you remain in me and I in you, you will bear much fruit; apart from me you can do nothing. 6 If you do not remain in me, you are like a branch [vine] that is thrown away and withers; such branches [vines] are picked up, thrown into the fire and burned. 7 If you remain in me and my words remain in you, ask whatever you wish, and it will be done for you. 8 This is to my Father's glory, that you bear much fruit, showing yourselves to be my disciples.*

*9 "As the Father has loved me, so have I loved you. Now remain in my love. 10 If you keep my commands, you will remain in my love, just as I have kept my Father's commands and remain in his love. 11 I have told you this so that my joy may be in you and that your joy may be complete. 12 My command is this: Love each other as I have loved you. 13 Greater love has no one than this: to lay down one's life for one's friends.* <sup>14</sup> *You are my friends if you do what I command.* <sup>15</sup> *I no longer call you servants, because a servant does not know his master's business. Instead, I have called you friends, for everything that I learned from my Father I have made known to you.* <sup>16</sup> *You did not choose me, but I chose you and appointed you so that you might go and bear fruit—fruit that will last—and so that whatever you ask in my name the Father will give you.* <sup>17</sup> *This is my command: Love each other.*

Many of us wonder what Jesus meant when he promised the disciples they would do *even greater works than he did* (14:12). We also wonder how. Clearly the indwelling of the Spirit is part of our answer. Notice, though, that Jesus shifts from "works" to "fruit" in chapter fifteen. We are empowered to expand the work of Jesus in our world by abiding or remaining in Jesus, and so producing works and fruit.

Let's remember the context as we read this passage together.

The last supper now over, Jesus and the disciples seem to have left the upper room. We can't be sure for it is not until 18:1 that they cross the Kidron Valley, on the east edge of Jerusalem and the temple mount. Jesus has just promised the Spirit-Illuminator to his disciples who guides, indwells, and instructs the disciples. Parallel to the Spirit's indwelling Jesus now instructs the disciples to abide in him as the vine or, better yet, as the vineyard. It is the last night with his disciples alone, and Jesus instructs them about what is most important for life ahead.

## THE SOURCE

Twice in this passage Jesus makes "I am" statements. It is the seventh and final I Am statement. "I am the true vine" (as he is "the way and the *truth* and the life"; 14:6) and "I am the vine" (15:1, 5). Is it vine or vineyard? Recent research has shown that the word translated "vine" (*ampelos*) more likely means the whole vineyard while the word usually translated "branch" (*klēma*) refers to the "vine" (Caragounis). The vineyard is cultivated by the vintner to produce vines that produce grapes, consumed as grapes or wine. Jesus' Father is the farmer, a generic term, and if one farms grapes, one is a vinedresser, which makes the Father a kingdom viticulturist! The "vine" is woody and grows from the soil upwards, is held up by poles and ropes, and extends outward for exposure to sun so it can produce branches and leaves for grapes. Jesus is the vineyard, and his disciples are the vines that produce fruit.

The word "vineyard" has a history in the Bible, where it is used frequently enough for Israel as can be read in Isaiah 5:1–10 and 27:2–6 (cf. Jeremiah 2:21; Ezekiel 15:1–5; Psalm 80:8–16). Jesus used this term, too, in the parable of the vineyard (Mark 12:1–12). That parable, told during the last week, uses vine and vineyard much as it was used in the prophets. In John 15 Jesus turns the vineyard image for Israel into an image for himself. Jesus instructs his followers that he alone is the source for their sustenance. Jesus depicts himself as the fulfillment of Israel as the vineyard in which vines are cultivated by the Father. Which is why Jesus shapes his words to emphasize their need to remain.

## THE CONNECTION

The magical word here is "remain" (NIV) or what others translate as "abide" (NRSV). The Greek word is *menō*, and it occurs 33x in the Gospel of John and 11x in this chapter alone. They are to receive and absorb and be sustained by energies passing through the vine. The word *menō* can mean inhabit, dwell, stay, remain, linger, continue, stand fast, hang on, and wait. The sense in our passage is to stay connected, to remain in relationship with Jesus, to be faithful to the Lord, to depend on the vinedresser's nurture, and to draw on the vine's energies. As in the last passage, there is a sense of being woven together. In John's larger picture abiding is a dimension of faith or believing with the sense of ongoing trust and dependence. At times it can be the intimate prayer and conversation life with Jesus, it can become at times mystical and even ecstatic, but we are not to restrict it to the private life.

In our passage we are to abide or remain in Jesus' love (15:9), in obeying Jesus' commands (15:10), and in loving one another (15:12). The innovative term in this passage is that those who so abide in, love, and obey Jesus are his "friends" (15:14, 15). Abiding and friendship are synonyms here. All of these terms, and other terms connected to believing (see pp. 7–9) that could be added, are at work in the term "abide." It is both profoundly personal as one's relationship to Jesus and at the same time clearly group-shaped because the ones abiding in Jesus abide together in loving one another and Jesus. The vines abide alongside one another in the vineyard.

We abide when we pray together, when we read Scripture, when we meet together, when we worship together, when we partake of the Lord's supper together, and when we share life with one another. Both alone and together we abide. Yet, Jesus warns twice in this passage that vines and branches that choose not to abide in Jesus will wither away, then be lifted up and out by the vintner, and eventually tossed out of the vineyard into the fire (15:2, 6). The vintner, then, lifts out the bad vines (or "lifts away"; *airō*) and prunes (or "cleanses"; *kathairō*) good vines.

## The Results

To stick with the image at work in this passage, grapes grow through connection with the branch and vine (and soil, water, and sun) and through the vinedresser pruning the vines of his vineyard. The word "grape" is not used in the passage. Instead, we get "fruit" and "much fruit." What kind of fruit then does Jesus have in mind? Put different, what are the results in real life for those who abide in Jesus and his love?

I suggest the (1) works-greater-than-Jesus' of 14:12 get new skin in this passage as grapes or fruit. In addition to fruit, which is used 8x in this passage, Jesus describes the results of abiding as:

(2) prayers being answered (15:7, 16),

(3) glorifying the Father (15:8),

(4) a witness to their being Jesus' disciples (15:8),

(5) an abundant joy (15:11),

and above all, (6) love for Jesus, for the Father, and for one another (15:9, 10, 12–14, 17).

These are Jesus' intended results for his followers. Though the imagery gets lots of attention in the passage, Jesus summons his followers to expand his ministry to others, to pray, to glorify God in all they do, to become witnesses to Jesus, and to find pleasure in God, that is, to be maximally joyful. Notice, too, that they are not summoned to bear fruit but to abide, and in that abiding they bear these fruits. The work is God's gracious empowerment.

## QUESTIONS FOR REFLECTION
## AND APPLICATION

1. What is the significance of Jesus' shift from speaking about works to speaking about fruit?

2. How does the discussion about translating vineyard vocabulary help you understand these verses better?

3. What does John mean with his use of remain/abide?

4. What have been your experiences of abiding with others in unity in the church, as vines working together in a vineyard? Have you ever had the sensation of being a valued part of a whole, or have you felt isolated and left outside?

5. Of the "fruit" listed at the end of this section, which ones do you observe in your life? Which do you want to cultivate further?

## FOR FURTHER READING

Chris Caragounis, "'Abide in Me': The New Mode of Relationship between Jesus and His Followers as a Basis for Christian Ethics (John 15)," in Jan G. van der Watt and Ruben Zimmermann, eds., *Rethinking the Ethics of John: "Implicit Ethics" in the Johannine Writings* (Tübingen: Mohr Siebeck, 2012), 250–263.

# JESUS WARNS ABOUT THE WORLD'S HATRED

## John 15:18–16:15

¹⁸ *"If the world hates you, keep in mind that it hated me first.* ¹⁹ *If you belonged to the world, it would love you as its own. As it is, you do not belong to the world, but I have chosen you out of the world. That is why the world hates you.* ²⁰ *Remember what I told you: 'A servant is not greater than his master.' If they persecuted me, they will persecute you also. If they obeyed my teaching, they will obey yours also.* ²¹ *They will treat you this way because of my name, for they do not know the one who sent me.* ²² *If I had not come and spoken to them, they would not be guilty of sin; but now they have no excuse for their sin.* ²³ *Whoever hates me hates my Father as well.* ²⁴ *If I had not done among them the works no one else did, they would not be guilty of sin. As it is, they have seen, and yet they have hated both me and my Father.* ²⁵ *But this is to fulfill what is written in their Law: 'They hated me without reason.'*

²⁶ *"When the Advocate comes, whom I will send to you from the Father—the Spirit of truth who goes out from the Father—he will testify about me.* ²⁷ *And you also must testify, for you have been with me from the beginning.*

16:1 *"All this I have told you so that you will not fall away.* *2 They will put you out of the synagogue; in fact, the time is coming when anyone who kills you will think they are offering a service to God. 3 They will do such things because they have not known the Father or me. 4 I have told you this, so that when their time comes you will remember that I warned you about them. I did not tell you this from the beginning because I was with you, 5 but now I am going to him who sent me. None of you asks me, 'Where are you going?' 6 Rather, you are filled with grief because I have said these things. 7 But very truly I tell you, it is for your good that I am going away. Unless I go away, the Advocate will not come to you; but if I go, I will send him to you. 8 When he comes, he will prove the world to be in the wrong about sin and righteousness and judgment: 9 about sin, because people do not believe in me; 10 about righteousness, because I am going to the Father, where you can see me no longer; 11 and about judgment, because the prince of this world now stands condemned.*

*12 "I have much more to say to you, more than you can now bear. 13 But when he, the Spirit of truth, comes, he will guide you into all the truth. He will not speak on his own; he will speak only what he hears, and he will tell you what is yet to come. 14 He will glorify me because it is from me that he will receive what he will make known to you. 15 All that belongs to the Father is mine. That is why I said the Spirit will receive from me what he will make known to you."*

What do you do when you realize that your neighbors, or your fellow workers, or your family, or your community do not like that you are a follower of Jesus? To use Jesus' words, when the world hates you because you are one of his disciples? The temptations are to withdraw and hide, to strike back with snark and social media blasts, to plot a rebellion, to write vendettas against those who don't like you, to write fake emails or invent fraudulent social media accounts, and there are more temptations and you can fill this list out.

What did Jesus instruct his followers to do when they became enemies of others? You might be surprised, but the surprise only comes when we grip how the opposition, that is, "world," is.

## WORLD

The word "world" is a big one in John (and in Paul), and its meaning is quite different than what we find in our dictionaries. In the Gospel of John *world is a moral, cosmic term for systemic rebellion against God and against all God's agents in this world*. The world God loves and to whom the Father has sent the Son (3:16) is the same world that has turned against Father, Son, and Spirit and now is in rebellion along with the prince of this world, Satan. With the world, think of this spectrum of ideas: created, loved, rebellion, systemic, opposition.

The world's hatred is aimed at a unified set of names: Father, Son, believers. In this Gospel there are two teams; the battle then is cosmic. The world hates Jesus' followers because they do not belong to the world (15:18–19). Not to worry, the world hates Jesus and the Father (15:18, 20, 21, 23; 16:3). The world's hatred in our passage shows up in two ways, both extreme acts of social punishment. First, the world's agents kick some of the believers out of the synagogue, which was the social, cultural, economic, and spiritual center of the community (16:2), and second, they may well do to the believers what they will do to Jesus—namely, kill (16:2). In other words, one should not think hatred means an explosion of pent-up anger so much as actions of suppression. This Father-and-Son hating world is guilty of its sinful rebellion because it has heard the words of Jesus (15:22) and has observed his mighty works (15:24). Their hatred then is without excuse. Jesus wants his followers to be ready for the world (16:4–5).

Words like hatred and assigning massive blocks of people to the doom of "world" deserves our respect but also our care in learning how to understand and use such terms. This is prophetic rhetoric; an either-or world, one in which you are either for us or against us, is characteristic of prophets, and John seems to have imbibed this form of expression more than the other Gospels. We should reserve language like this for very rare settings, and only when the language will not have long-term impacts on either of the assigned groups.

What to do then when the world hates you?

It must be added here that our passage is not addressing abusive situations—like emotional, psychological, sexual, pastoral, or power abuse. When people call out church leaders for perpetuating or covering up abuse, that is not an example of the world hating the church. Rather it's an example of people longing to see God's justice done. Instead, the topic at hand is opposition to followers of Jesus as followers of Jesus. In the former situations we pursue justice and healing and healing and justice. In the latter we rely on God's Spirit to damage the world's ways by bringing Spirit-born illumination and redemption.

## RELY ON THE SPIRIT

As in chapter fourteen, Jesus turns to the Spirit of God as God's response to the world's hatred. The disciples grieve over Jesus' declaration that he is going to the Father (16:5–6). Jesus says his departure is "good" for them, or it is to their advantage. How so? The Spirit will come and be comprehensively present with all disciples, in all places, for all times, and at times in dramatically noticeable ways. Have you ever

been seized by the Spirit, consciously or not, when you said
or did something that, when you looked back on it, you knew
was God's Spirit at work? Jesus predicted it. Right here in
this passage. Perhaps we can clarify. To be "seized" by the
Spirit is to be directed to say or do something unplanned. In
such circumstances one realizes only later that God shifted
our minds or our mouths to accomplish what God wanted
in that situation.

The Spirit is sent by Jesus (16:7) in order to witness to
Jesus (15:26) and to glorify Jesus (16:14). The sent-Spirit,
the Illuminator, will guide the disciples "into all truth" that
he gets from the Son who gets it from the Father (16:13–15).
The Father has primacy in revelation, reveals through the
Son, and the Spirit pierces the human mind, heart, and will.
The Spirit is not on its own; the Spirit is a messenger of Jesus
who has been sent by the Father. Yet, the witness of the Spirit
is one with the Father's truth. If you have found yourself
twisting in circles to take words in, welcome to the Gospel
of John! Think again of that Irish cross.

We dare not reduce the Spirit's witness to the inner life
of contemplation. Rather, the Spirit's witness turns Jesus'
own followers into witnesses (15:27). Jesus says, "And you
also must testify, for you have been with me from the beginning." These words will take on fresh power when one turns
to the Book of Acts to see the launching of the mission of
the apostles from that Pentecost Spirit's initiative (Acts 2).
So, Jesus urges them to remain faithful and not to fall away
(John 16:1).

The Spirit as the Illuminator is on mission to prove the
world wrong about sin and righteousness and judgment (16:8).
Jesus' explanations require some nuancing and even then, one
may wonder if one has grasped all he is telling us. The Spirit
convicts of sin, but sin here finds its fundamental shape in
"because people do not believe in me" (16:9; look at 8:21, 34;

9:41; 15:22–24). That is the fundamental sin for Jesus. The Spirit convicts of "righteousness" because Jesus is proven right in his words and works by being raised by the Father (16:10). And the Spirit convicts of "judgment" "because the prince of this world now stands condemned" (16:11), which means the death and resurrection of Jesus not only remedy the sin problem, but they also are a cosmic defeat of the powers at work to establish the world's rebellion against the united bloc: Father, Son, Spirit, believers.

Instead of withdrawing, retaliating, or rebelling, believers are swarmed with words by Jesus about the empowerment and power of the Spirit at work in them and through them to defeat the world in this life and into the next.

## QUESTIONS FOR REFLECTION AND APPLICATION

1. How does John use the word "world"?

2. Who does the world hate, and why?

3. What are some of the functions of the Spirit as Illuminator?

4. What examples have you seen of the Spirit's work in your life, just as Jesus promised?

5. What do you think are the differences between situations where the world is showing their hatred of God and God's people versus situations where the world is rightly holding God's people accountable for not acting like Jesus? How would you discern between the two?

# JESUS PREDICTS THE FUTURE

## John 16:16–33

[16] Jesus went on to say, "In a little while you will see me no more, and then after a little while you will see me."

[17] At this, some of his disciples said to one another, "What does he mean by saying, 'In a little while you will see me no more, and then after a little while you will see me,' and 'Because I am going to the Father'?" [18] They kept asking, "What does he mean by 'a little while'? We don't understand what he is saying."

[19] Jesus saw that they wanted to ask him about this, so he said to them, "Are you asking one another what I meant when I said, 'In a little while you will see me no more, and then after a little while you will see me'? [20] Very truly I tell you, you will weep and mourn while the world rejoices. You will grieve, but your grief will turn to joy. [21] A woman giving birth to a child has pain because her time has come; but when her baby is born she forgets the anguish because of her joy that a child is born into the world. [22] So with you: Now is your time of grief, but I will see you again and you will rejoice, and no one will take away your joy. [23] In that

*day you will no longer ask me anything. Very truly I tell you, my Father will give you whatever you ask in my name. ²⁴ Until now you have not asked for anything in my name. Ask and you will receive, and your joy will be complete.*

²⁵ *"Though I have been speaking figuratively, a time is coming when I will no longer use this kind of language but will tell you plainly about my Father. ²⁶ In that day you will ask in my name. I am not saying that I will ask the Father on your behalf. ²⁷ No, the Father himself loves you because you have loved me and have believed that I came from God. ²⁸ I came from the Father and entered the world; now I am leaving the world and going back to the Father."*

²⁹ *Then Jesus' disciples said, "Now you are speaking clearly and without figures of speech. ³⁰ Now we can see that you know all things and that you do not even need to have anyone ask you questions. This makes us believe that you came from God."*

³¹ *"Do you now believe?" Jesus replied. ³² "A time is coming and in fact has come when you will be scattered, each to your own home. You will leave me all alone. Yet I am not alone, for my Father is with me.*

³³ *"I have told you these things, so that in me you may have peace. In this world you will have trouble. But take heart! I have overcome the world."*

It's one thing to know the future in detail. It's another to know the future in images that don't register with clarity. Complicate that with Jesus saying many of these things over and over in these chapters. We have been reading about Jesus' saying he is going to the Father matched with the disciples' wondering what in the world he means. But, finally, in this passage the disciples—it's been quite a night with more than one shocking, confusing revelation—the disciples will walk into the light on what he means (16:29–30).

Let's do what we can to make sense of their gradual perception of Jesus' predictions, and maybe take a look at our own gradual perceptions in the journey of faith.

## Show Some Sympathy

We should sympathize with them. What would you think if (1) you were convinced Jesus was the Messiah, (2) you believed Israel's Messiah would establish God's rule and kingdom, (3) you had spent three years or so with Jesus utterly impressed and overwhelmed with his goodness, baffled at times, but still 100% committed, and (4) he said he was "going away" or "going to the Father," which sure sounds like death or some kind of whisking away, and (5) you wondered what does that mean for the kingdom Jesus was establishing? Add to this that you absolutely loved being with and near him. The timeline Jesus was using made no sense to them, either from the Bible they had come to know or from the kingdom vision dancing in their minds and hopes. So their confusion and disappointment are understandable.

## Start with His Timeline

The secret sauce of Jesus' predictions begins with the ingredients of verse twenty-eight. It's a timeline of sorts: "I came from the Father and entered the world; now I am leaving the world and going back to the Father." If you mix verse sixteen with the ingredients you get the full timeline: "In a little while you will see me no more, and then after a little while you will see me." So here it is, and it is a basic Christian eschatology (with the zany Christian speculations absent):

Jesus with the Father
→ Sent to the World
→ Sent two times "little while" (crucifixion,
resurrection)
→ Returns to Father (ascension)
→ Comes back to the disciples (second
coming)
→ All go to the Father forever

Jesus, however, chooses to reveal his essential timeline "figuratively," or in images or metaphors (16:25). Which means the disciples don't catch it all, and they are consternated over his words (16:17–19), fastening their attention on one expression "in a little while." John probably works with some double meaning here. At one level, the first "little while" is Friday night and Saturday (burial), and the second "little while" is seeing him again after the resurrection. David Ford calls this "the most important 'little while' in history" (Ford, *John*, 318). Yet, there's also another two "little while's" in the period between his ascension and his second coming! That's just like John.

The disciples were confused so Jesus changes the subject. Which is just like Jesus.

## FIRST, GRIEF.
## THEN, JOY AND PEACE.

Jesus instructs his disciples somewhere between the upper room and before they crossed the Kidron Valley that they were about to enter into a period during which they would "weep and mourn . . . and grieve" (16:20, 22). In fact, he tells them "*now* is your time of grief" (16:22). The work of the evil one through Judas was underway. Within hours their expectations would crash into Roman soldiers, a trial of sorts, a verdict against Jesus, a crucifixion, and a burial. That history was now unrolling as they walked down toward the Kidron Valley.

Jesus now turns to their "When?" and "How long?" questions to say it will last a "little while," like a mother's birth pains (16:21). John doesn't write words without thinking. He wants them (and us) to perceive the grief of separation from Jesus as pains giving birth to the kind of joy that will make them (and us) forget the pain. "Now" is the time of grieving and giving birth, and that image is used in the prophets as Israel's labor pains in birthing redemption (Isaiah 26:17; 66:7–19). Now is also a time of abandoning Jesus at Gethsemane—he says this figuratively—at his most crucial hour. They will leave him "alone," but he will not be alone because the Father will be with him (16:31–32). He faces the cruelties of abuse, the pains of beatings, the injustices of false accusations, the trauma of betrayal, and the terrors of death for others all alone. Yet not alone. He and the Father, in the Spirit. That kind of alone. (I'm sure they needed the Illuminator present with them both to remember all these words and to discern their meaning. We need the same Illuminator.)

In that alone-ness Jesus launches redemption through a death for others and a resurrection for new life, finished off by an ascension to the right hand of the Father, from which "location" he sends them the Spirit for the followers to guide, instruct, and empower them until the return.

Just before Jesus spoke about their scattering, the disciples informed Jesus that his words were finally clear, that they perceived that he knows "all things" and that "this makes us believe you came from God" (16:29–30). Every time I read that little paragraph I say, "What????!" I thought they already believed he was from God and that he knew all things, even if they only here seem to grasp his teachings about the future. Faith, in John's Gospel, is not a once-and-over but a life-long movement from unfaith to faith, from blindness to sight, and from fear to faithfulness. No wonder Jesus responds with "Do you now believe?" (16:31). He knows more than they do. They are not yet there. In the now their faith is not yet complete, but someday it will be.

Grief giving way to abundant joy, that's one theme on Jesus' timeline. As S.M. Lockridge once famously preached, "It's Friday, but Sunday's coming"* so Jesus reveals to his followers that their weeping, mourning, and grieving over his sudden seizure and crucifixion, followed by his resurrection and ascension and return, will morph from sadness into great joy (16:22–24). "In that day" they will, and here we get a theme we've already seen, experience the receipt of the desires of the heart—answers to their longing and prayers (16:23–24; cf. 14:13–14). All of which will be done "in my name" (16:23, 24, 26). In that day they will have peace "in" Jesus in the midst of knowing "trouble" in "this world" (16:33). One more time Jesus explains that he is telling them all these things so they will know, so they will have a worldview that can comprehend what is going on, so they can be at peace.

## QUESTIONS FOR REFLECTION AND APPLICATION

1. What do you feel for the disciples when you try to put yourself in their shoes?

---

* S.M. Lockridge, https://www.youtube.com/watch?v=QS2wPotScZY&ab _channel=CarpenterMissions

2. How does the timeline here help you make sense of eschatology?

3. What is the impact of John's metaphor of birth pains? How does that help the disciples understand what this "little while" of waiting and pain will be like?

4. Why do you think the disciples were still coming to understand who Jesus was in new ways, even after all their time with him?

5. Where do you need hope for resurrection in your life?

# JESUS' DESIRE FOR THE CHURCH

## John 17:1–25

*¹ After Jesus said this, he looked toward heaven and prayed:*

### Prayer for Glorification
*"Father, the hour has come. Glorify your Son, that your Son may glorify you. ² For you granted him authority over all people that he might give eternal life to all those you have given him. ³ Now this is eternal life: that they know you, the only true God, and Jesus Christ, whom you have sent. ⁴ I have brought you glory on earth by finishing the work you gave me to do. ⁵ And now, Father, glorify me in your presence with the glory I had with you before the world began.*

### Prayer for Disciples
### For Their Protection
*⁶ "I have revealed you to those whom you gave me out of the world. They were yours; you gave them to me and they have obeyed your word. ⁷ Now they know that everything you have given me comes from you. ⁸ For I gave them the words you gave me and they accepted them. They knew with certainty that I came from you, and they believed that you sent me. ⁹ I pray for them. I am not praying for the world, but for those you have given me, for they are yours.*

*10 All I have is yours, and all you have is mine. And glory has come to me through them. 11 I will remain in the world no longer, but they are still in the world, and I am coming to you. Holy Father, protect them by the power of your name, the name you gave me, so that they may be one as we are one. 12 While I was with them, I protected them and kept them safe by that name you gave me. None has been lost except the one doomed to destruction so that Scripture would be fulfilled.*

## For Their Devotion

*13 "I am coming to you now, but I say these things while I am still in the world, so that they may have the full measure of my joy within them. 14 I have given them your word and the world has hated them, for they are not of the world any more than I am of the world. 15 My prayer is not that you take them out of the world but that you protect them from the evil one. 16 They are not of the world, even as I am not of it. 17 Sanctify them by the truth; your word is truth. 18 As you sent me into the world, I have sent them into the world. 19 For them I sanctify myself, that they too may be truly sanctified.*

## For Their Unity

*20 "My prayer is not for them alone. I pray also for those who will believe in me through their message, 21 that all of them may be one, Father, just as you are in me and I am in you. May they also be in us so that the world may believe that you have sent me. 22 I have given them the glory that you gave me, that they may be one as we are one—23 I in them and you in me—so that they may be brought to complete unity. Then the world will know that you sent me and have loved them even as you have loved me.*

## For Their Presence

*24 "Father, I want those you have given me to be with me where I am, and to see my glory, the glory you have given me because you loved me before the creation of the world.*

### For Their Love

[25] *"Righteous Father, though the world does not know you, I know you, and they know that you have sent me.* [26] *I have made you known to them, and will continue to make you known in order that the love you have for me may be in them and that I myself may be in them."*

Jesus has now finished teaching his disciples. It's worth pausing just to take that observation in. John 13–16 contains his final words for his followers (according to this Gospel).

Done teaching them, he prays for them. One typical posture for prayer begins by lifting one's eyes to heaven as Jesus does here (17:1; see also 11:41–42). In this prayer Jesus expresses his long-term desires for his church, and so this prayer can be read as our marching orders. As such, it contains six marks about the church. As such, it also reveals what Jesus *continues* to pray for his church (cf. Hebrews 2:14–18; 4:14–16).

I have held off until now to use a new term for John's style. His style is "rondo," that is, when principal themes and terms are repeated frequently in fresh contexts. John's rondo style revolves around principal terms like Father and Son or love and light, faith and obedience, and there are more. In this prayer of John 17 Jesus in essence turns those favorite themes into prayer requests. If we are not careful to read slowly, we will discover we are skipping lines because of repetitions. (Raise your hand if you have done this.) John's rondo style invites us, not to skip, but to pause to listen and to remember previous uses of these terms so we can move forward. What I know is that writing about John's Gospel requires repeating John's repetitions, and one wonders at times if what one is writing has not already been said. (Yes, it has.)

## THAT THE CROSS MAY GLORIFY GOD

The anticipated "hour" has arrived (17:1; see 2:4; 5:28; 8:20; 12:23, 27; 13:1). The hideousness of a brutal crucifixion—public, nude bodies, humiliation, suffering, suffocation—somehow in John's Gospel glorifies Jesus and therefore glorifies the Father. How so? At the cross, and by that we mean as well his resurrection and ascension, God's glory is on display. Jesus formerly had glory "before the world began" (17:5, 24; cf. 12:41), in his incarnation God's glory is displayed (1:14), his death is a glorification (13:31; 17:1) his exaltation is a glorification (3:14; 8:28; 12:32–36), and he will return to the Father's glory.

The church must not turn its face from the cross as merely a display of brutal violence and injustice. In the cross, God's glory is displayed as one who has come to earth, become human, and endured suffering for the sake of others—to bring redemption, to launch the kingdom, to usher in the age of the Spirit. One of the marks of Christian orthodoxy is redemption accomplished in the cross. Historic cathedrals in Europe are in the shape of a cross and Christian living is often called cruciform living.

Through the cross Jesus brings "eternal life" to those whom the Father has given to him (17:2), and this eternal life is to know the Father and the Son, and to know the Son truly is to know the crucified Son (17:3). Jesus' request then is for the Father to glorify the Son because the Son has now completed the Father's mission for him.

## THAT THE CHURCH BE WATCHED BY THE FATHER

Those who know the Father through the Son, who have heard Jesus pass on the Father's truth, who have accepted that message, who understand who Jesus is as God's Son, and who obey the Son are the ones who comprise the church (17:6–8). They will remain in the world that rejects Father and Son (17:9–11), and Jesus prays for their protection in that world (17:11). Jesus has protected them but now he asks the Father to protect them (17:12). Even more, he prays the Father will protect them from the "evil one" (17:15) as they are surrounded by the world (17:13–14). His prayer is not for their escape but for their protection (17:15).

Protection here translates *tēreō*, which can mean "keep" or "grip" or "watch over" or "look after" or "take care of" or "keep a close eye on." Think of parents hovering over their children learning to walk on a busy sidewalk near a busy street or running alongside a child learning to ride a bike, or a parent inspecting and asking questions about a budding child's choice of friends, or a therapist listening in order to guide a client in life-shaping decisions . . . and we could go on. Those are the ideas associated with our term. An example. Perhaps you've seen a raptor—hawk, eagle, owl—spreading its wings over something it has caught to feed its young and to ward off other raptors from robbing its catch. That is called "mantling," and Jesus wants the Father to "mantle" believers.

The Father is mantling over you right now.

## THAT THE CHURCH BE DEVOTED TO GOD

Jesus prays "Sanctify them by the truth" (17:17). This religious-sounding word, "sanctify," has acquired a fair number of toxic accretions over the years, things like smoking, movie attendance, or participation in politics. The term should be set loose from its accretions and seen for what it meant then. God alone is holy, and all that enters into the presence of God must be holy. To be holy something must be "holy-fied" or "sanctified." Which means those humans or materials are made fit by God for God's holy presence, and they become *devoted to the presence of God* and therefore withdrawn from the contaminating powers of the world. To sanctify is to devote or dedicate to God for God's mission.

Jesus wants his disciples to be devoted "by the truth" (about him, about God, about the Spirit, about the gospel) so they are fit for the mission of being "sent into the world" as Jesus was himself sent (17:17–18). As Jesus sanctified, or devoted himself to the Father's mission for the Son, so he wants them to be devoted (17:19). These two devotions are similar but not identical.

## THAT THE CHURCH LIVE INTO ITS UNITY

The disciples would be joined by other believers. The disciples were to become witnesses to bring in other believers. The worldwide growth of the church—past, present, future—confirms that prediction of Jesus. Like Peter and Paul, those early Christians formed the very ones Jesus said who "will believe in me through their message" (17:20).

Jesus prayed then and prays (even more) now "that all of them may be one" "just as you are in me and I am in you. May they also be in us" (17:21; cf. 10:16). This unity, this oneness, becomes active because of mutual indwelling or of participation in Christ and Christ in us. Unity in the church is grounded in the unity and love of Father and Son, and thus it is not an achievement of plots and plans and politics but a transcendent reality beyond our plans. We are one *because God is one* and because Jesus, who alone knows the Father, prayed for that unity. *We are to live into a unity that already exists.*

The impact of the church's global and local unity provokes the "world," that rebellious system, to "believe that you [Father] have sent me" (17:21). A unified set of believers becomes a force that challenges the world's system and draws people to Jesus. But Jesus continues his thought by saying that unity promotes knowledge in the world that the Father loves the people of Jesus and Jesus (17:23). Whether it is accurate or not, many today sense church fissures and factions and a lack of church fusion. What is accurate is that church factions resist the ongoing prayers of our great high priest, Jesus.

## THAT THE CHURCH WILL BE WITH JESUS

God's love is a love made real by presence—in the Garden of Eden, in the smoking pot with Abram/Abraham, in the pillar of cloud and fire in the wilderness wanderings, in the glory present in the temple, in the gift of God with us, Immanuel, the Incarnate One, in the presence of the Spirit with us—and in the final New Jerusalem's presence of God. Love entails being present with the one loved, which is why Jesus reassures his "disciples of his presence in spite of his absence" (Thompson, *John*, 358).

Hence, Jesus prays that "those you [Father] have given me" will "be with me where I am" (17:24). In the last supper according to the Gospel of Mark, Jesus said he would "not drink again from the fruit of the vine until that day when I drink it anew in the kingdom of God" (Mark 14:25). John's Gospel expresses that very same hope in Jesus' prayer that someday he will be reunited with his "friends" (cf. John 17:24; 15:14). When they are reunited, they will see Jesus' original before-all-creation glory. One could suggest they caught a glimpse of that at the transfiguration (Mark 9:2–13).

## THAT THE CHURCH
## COMPREHENDS GOD'S LOVE

Jesus' last lines of his prayer for the disciples addresses God as "Righteous" Father (17:25), a term that expresses the rightness and justice of the Father. Here Jesus contrasts what he and the disciples know of the Father that the world does not know. Jesus has made the Father known to the disciples but he will *continue* to make the Father known, presumably through the power of the Paraclete who will guide them into all truth (17:26). This knowledge is not intellectualism nor is it reducible to theological mastery. Rather, true knowledge of the Father and the Son is to be loved by God in such a way that God's love is "in them" because Jesus himself is "in them" (17:26). True knowledge of another person is love, and love of another person forms true knowledge.

Think of it this way: Jesus' mission invites humans into the love that he, the Son, and God, the Father, know. Participation in God's triune love forms the heart of the mission.

Think of it also this way: if this is how Jesus prays, it's how we can pray too. Some have said this is the true Lord's prayer, but I see no reason to get into a competition between Jesus' two famous prayers. In this prayer we learn what Jesus most desires and so we learn proper Christian desire. Perhaps we learn whether we desire what Jesus desires. As Marilynne Robinson says through one of her characters, In "prayer, you know, you open up your thoughts, and then you can get a clear look at them . . . . Prayer is a discipline in truthfulness, in honesty" (Robinson, *Home*, 132). May we participate in the honest prayer of Jesus.

These are Jesus' prayers for his disciples then, and they are his prayers for you and me today. I'm sure the disciples needed these prayers, but we need them even more.

May God have mercy!

## QUESTIONS FOR REFLECTION
## AND APPLICATION

1. To what extent does it change your view of Jesus' prayer here to think of it as his prayer for the disciples that concludes his years of teaching them?

2. What does "rondo" mean in terms of John's style?

3. What kind of protection does Jesus pray over his disciples?

4. Do you think the disciples had any idea how large the church would grow someday? How might that knowledge have impacted their understanding of Jesus' prayers for future unity?

5. As you read Jesus' prayer and think of it as a prayer for YOU, how does that affect you?

## FOR FURTHER READING

Marilynne Robinson, *Home* (New York: Farrar, Straus, and Giroux, 2008).

# JESUS AND THE
# CLASH OF POWERS

## *John 18:1–14*

*¹ When he had finished praying, Jesus left with his disciples and crossed the Kidron Valley. On the other side there was a garden, and he and his disciples went into it.*

*² Now Judas, who betrayed him, knew the place, because Jesus had often met there with his disciples. ³ So Judas came to the garden, guiding a detachment of soldiers and some officials from the chief priests and the Pharisees. They were carrying torches, lanterns and weapons.*

*⁴ Jesus, knowing all that was going to happen to him, went out and asked them, "Who is it you want?"*

*⁵ "Jesus of Nazareth," they replied.*

*"I am he," Jesus said. (And Judas the traitor was standing there with them.)*

*⁶ When Jesus said, "I am he," they drew back and fell to the ground.*

*⁷ Again he asked them, "Who is it you want?"*

*"Jesus of Nazareth," they said.*

*⁸ Jesus answered, "I told you that I am he. If you are looking for me, then let these men go." ⁹ This happened so that the words he had spoken would be fulfilled: "I have not lost one of those you gave me."*

*¹⁰ Then Simon Peter, who had a sword, drew it and struck the high priest's servant, cutting off his right ear. (The servant's name was Malchus.)*

*¹¹ Jesus commanded Peter, "Put your sword away! Shall I not drink the cup the Father has given me?"*

*¹² Then the detachment of soldiers with its commander and the Jewish officials arrested Jesus. They bound him ¹³ and brought him first to Annas, who was the father-in-law of Caiaphas, the high priest that year. ¹⁴ Caiaphas was the one who had advised the Jewish leaders that it would be good if one man died for the people.*

Turning from John 17 to 18, from that famous prayer of Jesus to his infamous arrest, is a journey from the sublime to the unjust. Only the attractiveness and explosiveness of Jesus' mission explains why this Galilean would be arrested under the cover of night. Sadly, only a failing disciple could guide Jerusalem's powers to the location of Jesus at this time of night. Only a God who turns a Galilean into the Messiah and a crucifixion into resurrection could transform this tragedy into a victory.

## GETHSEMANE

On the eastern edge of city of Jerusalem is a wall running north and south. Below that wall is a valley called Kidron. On the other side of the valley is the Mount of Olives, and on the lower side of the Mount of Olives is a garden called "Gethsemane," which means "oil press." The NIV's translation "garden" can be more precise with "orchard" or "grove." Jesus customarily met with his disciples, probably for conversations and prayers, in Gethsemane.

Jesus was betrayed in one of his most intimate, private, favorite locations.

## CLASH OF POWERS

John describes the betrayal and arrest of Jesus and the resistance of Peter as a clash of powers. One must learn to sympathize with the powers of Rome on display here to comprehend the death of Jesus accurately. He was a danger, they were on edge, the people thought Jesus was special, their thoughts turned to Messiah and Messiah meant king, and king meant *coup d'état*, and a *coup* meant Rome had to sweep in with its might and end the resistance. The crucifixion was an unjust death of a just man, but the powers of Rome and Jerusalem did what they thought they had to do.

Such a confusion of intentions formed into the "hour" in which God would be glorified. Yes, it was unjust, but God's plan is at work, and Jesus is faithful to the Father's mission.

Rome's might is the first power as John describes it: "a detachment [*speira*] of soldiers" along with some servants of the Jewish leaders (18:3). The *speira* was a cohort, which could refer to a military unit of as many as 500 or more, but in this case, it most likely refers to a military contingent sent to arrest Jesus. They were armed. There were more personnel than were needed. Think of a half dozen armed police surrounding a single man pulled over in a suburb with lights flashing. Now we encounter Rome and those aligned with Rome: the high priests (not the Pharisees). Politics tends not to improve a person's character, and the alignment of the priests with the Roman powers proves the point.

Second power: Jesus. Read it carefully—Jesus is in control here, he orchestrates the events at times. He is giving his life voluntarily (10:18). Instead of the contingent searching for him, Jesus comes out to meet them, thereby protecting his followers. He asks who they want, they say Jesus, Jesus says "I am" (as in CEB, not "I am he" as in the NIV and NRSV). Only the association of that language with "I am who I am" in

Exodus 3:14 and Isaiah 43:10, 13, 25, and the I Am statements in John, explains why "they drew back and fell to the ground" (John 18:6). John describes a theophany, a manifestation of God, one that overpowers humans in the presence of God. Divine power continues as Jesus asks again, they answer the same again, and he repeats that he is the "I am," but this time Jesus asks them to "let these men go" (18:8). John inserts his own voice, writing "This happened," that is, Jesus' saying "let these men go," so that "I have not lost one of those you gave me" from a previous passage (6:39; 10:28) would come to pass.

Peter aligns himself, ironically, with the first power when he pulls out a blade, a dagger, and cuts off the ear of "the high priest's" slave (18:10). (Somehow John knows the servant's name: Malchus. Most named persons in John are or become disciples.) Jesus rebukes Peter, revealing Peter's alignment with the ways of Roman might, and affirming that the way of Jesus is to "drink the cup the Father has given me" (18:11). Bible readers know of the prayer Jesus has just uttered in this very orchard that is found in the other Gospels (Mark 14:35–36). He has chosen to drain that cup of suffering for the redemption of his followers.

## CUSTODY

The first power wins on this occasion. They arrest Jesus and they haul him before Annas, father-in-law of Caiaphas the high priest, for a preliminary hearing and a decision about what to do with Jesus. It was Passover week. The city was chock full of festivities and visitors. Rome and Jerusalem were concerned about riots, disturbances, and revolutions. Group think, mob violence, breakouts–any of this and more were possible.

John's irony comes to the surface again when he reminds us, his readers, that Caiaphas "had advised the Jewish leaders

that it would be good if one man"—not a group of suspects—
"died for the people" (18:14; cf. 11:46–53).

Indeed.

## QUESTIONS FOR REFLECTION AND APPLICATION

1. How does it intensify your understanding of Judas'
   betrayal to realize he betrayed Jesus in a private, special
   place where they had shared friendship and spiritual
   connection?

2. In what ways does this scene play out as a clash of
   powers?

3. How does Peter align himself with the way of Rome?

4. Note that most of John's named characters "are or become disciples." If Malchus, the man Peter attacked, became a disciple later, how do you think he interacted with Peter later?

5. Have you been tempted to fight violence with violence, even over your Christian principles and convictions? How does this scene help you rethink those tendencies?

# JESUS IS COURAGEOUS

## John 18:15–27

[15] Simon Peter and another disciple were following Jesus. Because this disciple was known to the high priest, he went with Jesus into the high priest's courtyard, [16] but Peter had to wait outside at the door. The other disciple, who was known to the high priest, came back, spoke to the servant girl on duty there and brought Peter in.

[17] "You aren't one of this man's disciples too, are you?" she asked Peter.

He replied, "I am not."

[18] It was cold, and the servants and officials stood around a fire they had made to keep warm. Peter also was standing with them, warming himself.

[19] Meanwhile, the high priest questioned Jesus about his disciples and his teaching.

[20] "I have spoken openly to the world," Jesus replied. "I always taught in synagogues or at the temple, where all the Jews come together. I said nothing in secret. [21] Why question me? Ask those who heard me. Surely they know what I said."

[22] When Jesus said this, one of the officials nearby slapped him in the face. "Is this the way you answer the high priest?" he demanded.

[23] *"If I said something wrong,"* Jesus replied, *"testify as to what is wrong. But if I spoke the truth, why did you strike me?"* [24] Then Annas sent him bound to Caiaphas the high priest.

[25] *Meanwhile, Simon Peter was still standing there warming himself. So they asked him, "You aren't one of his disciples too, are you?"*

*He denied it, saying, "I am not."*

[26] *One of the high priest's servants, a relative of the man whose ear Peter had cut off, challenged him, "Didn't I see you with him in the garden?"* [27] *Again Peter denied it, and at that moment a rooster began to crow.*

A t the last supper Jesus predicted a betrayal and three denials (13:18–38). Judas has betrayed Jesus to the powers (18:1–14), and now Peter will deny Jesus (18:15–27). John weaves the story of Judas and Peter together so we can see the challenges of allegiance and then ponder humans under severe stress.

People walk away for a variety of reasons. Today many leave the church because they are *scandalized* by science and faith discussions, the hypocrisy of Christians and especially of well-known pastors, by so much of the church's preoccupation with institutions and systems and reputations while ignoring justice, compassion for the marginalized, spiritual trauma, and even care for their own. Many such persons don't leave their commitment to Jesus but they are scandalized, and we should distinguish scandalization from completely leaving the faith. At the core of walking away from the faith one often, though not always, finds a desire for independence, or personal autonomy, accompanied frequently by a desire for various forms of indulgence. At the top of the heap of indulgences is sexual pleasure (McKnight, Ondrey, *Finding Faith, Losing Faith*, 7–64).

Judas fits at the top of the heap with greed, but Peter fits in another category: social pressure mixed with the fear of persecution. The pressures of persecution have a history of turning Christians away from Jesus. When you watch from a distance your Lord's trial and observe around him the powers of Jerusalem sanctioned by the powers of Rome, you realize you could be next. Peter did, and Peter denied Jesus three times in the space of a few minutes. Some denials prompt persons to become like Judas while other denials are momentary failures in faith from which a person repents and turns back to faithful witness, which is the story of Peter.

The tragic nature of this scene is that Jesus, in the heat of heats, remains true to the Father's mission for him, while Peter, at a distance, finks out. Those two elements shape this passage, and they are arranged in a clever order: Peter's unfaithfulness (18:15–18), Jesus' faithfulness (18:19–24), Peter's unfaithfulness (18:25–27). We start with Jesus and then combine the two sections about Peter.

## JESUS REMAINS FAITHFUL

The exchange strikes me as testy, I don't know about you. The (former) high priest, Annas, queries Jesus—notice this— "about his disciples." This suggests a boisterous and potentially volatile crowd has captured Annas's attention. Then he queries Jesus about his "teaching" (18:19). He responds abruptly, a kind of *Sir, there's nothing secretive or furtive about what I have been doing. I spoke in synagogues and in the temple. Lots of people heard me. Ask them.* Jesus appeals rather subtly to confirming witnesses.

One of the high priest's retainers smacks Jesus in the face to humiliate him socially. He thinks Jesus has been rude to a high priest. Jesus does not back down and challenges the official with an either-or: *If what I have said, either just now or in my public teaching, is wrong, prove me wrong. If you can't, then striking me was unjust.*

The scene ends abruptly: "Annas sent him bound to Caiaphas" the "high priest" who succeeded Annas (18:24).

## PETER BECOMES UNFAITHFUL

The closer Peter got to Jesus and the high priest the more volatile Peter became. The closer he got to Jesus the more his earlier audacious claim ("I will lay down my life for you") disappears (13:37). Peter is with "another disciple," traditionally the disciple whom Jesus loved, probably John. The other disciple knew the high priest so he can go inside where the hearing occurs while Peter remains outside. But the other disciple decides to fetch Peter, who is warming himself with others over a fire, and the disciple speaks to a female servant who then queries Peter with "You aren't one of this man's disciples, too, are you?" (18:17). Peter: "I am not." A cold lie. A denial.

Still standing there, in spite of the offer to go inside, "they" ask him if he's a disciple. Peter: "I am not." A second cold lie. A denial.

A slave (not as in the NIV a "servant") of the high priest who was "a relative of the man whose ear Peter had cut off— word traveled fast on this one—"challenged Peter" with "Didn't I see you with him in the garden?" (18:26). Peter denies association with Jesus for a third time. Jesus said "I am" three times in the garden, and now Peter says "I am not" three times (the third implied).

As Jesus predicted at 13:38, the "rooster began to crow" (18:27).

Jesus had informed Annas that he had witnesses, but his primary witness has just denied any knowledge of Jesus. Peter's denials exacerbated Jesus' situation.

The wrapping of Peter's unfaithfulness around the faithful courage and frankness of Jesus highlights Jesus and exposes Peter's failures. Jesus dies for faithfulness, Peter survives due to his unfaithfulness. Jesus is the witness, Peter is not. The story's reading tells it all. It's sad. I'm glad there's a good ending (20–21).

## QUESTIONS FOR REFLECTION AND APPLICATION

1. How does Jesus' faithfulness contrast with Peter's unfaithfulness?

2. What strategies does Jesus use in his interrogation?

3. How does Peter make Jesus' situation worse?

4. Have you seen people walk away from faith, or have you been tempted to do that yourself? What are the reasons you have observed?

5. Have you ever denied your connection with Jesus? In what ways do you relate to Peter's story here?

## FOR FURTHER READING

Scot McKnight, Hauna Ondrey, *Finding Faith, Losing Faith* (Waco, Texas: Baylor University Press, 2008).

# JESUS SENTENCED TO CRUCIFIXION

## *John 18:28–19:16*

[28] Then the Jewish leaders took Jesus from Caiaphas to the palace of the Roman governor. By now it was early morning, and to avoid ceremonial uncleanness they did not enter the palace, because they wanted to be able to eat the Passover. [29] So Pilate came out to them and asked, "What charges are you bringing against this man?"

[30] "If he were not a criminal," they replied, "we would not have handed him over to you."

[31] Pilate said, "Take him yourselves and judge him by your own law."

"But we have no right to execute anyone," they objected.

[32] This took place to fulfill what Jesus had said about the kind of death he was going to die.

[33] Pilate then went back inside the palace, summoned Jesus and asked him, "Are you the king of the Jews?"

[34] "Is that your own idea," Jesus asked, "or did others talk to you about me?"

[35] "Am I a Jew?" Pilate replied. "Your own people and chief priests handed you over to me. What is it you have done?"

*36 Jesus said, "My kingdom is not of this world. If it were, my servants would fight to prevent my arrest by the Jewish leaders. But now my kingdom is from another place."*

*37 "You are a king, then!" said Pilate.*

*Jesus answered, "You say that I am a king. In fact, the reason I was born and came into the world is to testify to the truth. Everyone on the side of truth listens to me."*

*38 "What is truth?" retorted Pilate. With this he went out again to the Jews gathered there and said, "I find no basis for a charge against him. 39 But it is your custom for me to release to you one prisoner at the time of the Passover. Do you want me to release 'the king of the Jews'?"*

*40 They shouted back, "No, not him! Give us Barabbas!" Now Barabbas had taken part in an uprising.*

*19:1 Then Pilate took Jesus and had him flogged. 2 The soldiers twisted together a crown of thorns and put it on his head. They clothed him in a purple robe 3 and went up to him again and again, saying, "Hail, king of the Jews!" And they slapped him in the face.*

*4 Once more Pilate came out and said to the Jews gathered there, "Look, I am bringing him out to you to let you know that I find no basis for a charge against him." 5 When Jesus came out wearing the crown of thorns and the purple robe, Pilate said to them, "Here is the man!"*

*6 As soon as the chief priests and their officials saw him, they shouted, "Crucify! Crucify!"*

*But Pilate answered, "You take him and crucify him. As for me, I find no basis for a charge against him."*

*7 The Jewish leaders insisted, "We have a law, and according to that law he must die, because he claimed to be the Son of God."*

*8 When Pilate heard this, he was even more afraid, 9 and he went back inside the palace. "Where do you come from?" he asked Jesus, but Jesus gave him no answer. 10 "Do you refuse to speak to me?" Pilate said. "Don't you realize I have power either to free you or to crucify you?"*

*[11] Jesus answered, "You would have no power over me if it were not given to you from above. Therefore the one who handed me over to you is guilty of a greater sin."*

*[12] From then on, Pilate tried to set Jesus free, but the Jewish leaders kept shouting, "If you let this man go, you are no friend of Caesar. Anyone who claims to be a king opposes Caesar."*

*[13] When Pilate heard this, he brought Jesus out and sat down on the judge's seat at a place known as the Stone Pavement (which in Aramaic is Gabbatha). [14] It was the day of Preparation of the Passover; it was about noon.*

*"Here is your king," Pilate said to the Jews.*

*[15] But they shouted, "Take him away! Take him away! Crucify him!"*

*"Shall I crucify your king?" Pilate asked.*

*"We have no king but Caesar," the chief priests answered.*

*[16] Finally Pilate handed him over to them to be crucified.*

*So the soldiers took charge of Jesus.*

For years I have experienced a subtle dissatisfaction with homilies and sermons during Good Friday services. Not that the preachers haven't worked hard at their sermons, for they have. It's that someone, instead of showing you a video clip of a profound event straight through, interrupts it every two minutes for explanations and stories.

My disappointment comes from this: the text does it all. Leave it alone. A good slow reading of the various Good Friday Gospel texts, including the one above, with proper pauses and change of voices, and somehow indicating all the movements from inside (Rome's powers) to outside (Judean powers) in the text, puts in our minds and imaginations the realities we need to consider. Instead of explaining it, we best read it well by performing the text.

So, here I am at this spot in our study guide needing to offer commentary on a text that, when read well, does all that needs done. What I want to offer instead are observations that can help us read the text more meaningfully.

## INTERROGATION

Questions from Pilate (governor from 26–37 CE) in the "palace" (18:28)[1] meet subversive answers by Jesus: that's what we get in this passage (18:33–40; 19:8–11). The tension between the questions and Jesus' answers can frustrate the reader expecting straightforward answers. Here they are, with the important observation that Pilate, a Rome-based authority, has and will have the last word.

> Pilate: "Are you the king of the Jews?"
> Jesus: "Is that your own idea or did others talk to you about me?"
> Jesus: "My kingdom is not of this world. If it were, my servants would fight to prevent my arrest by the Jewish leaders. But now my kingdom is from another place."
> Pilate: "You are a king, then!"
> Jesus: "You say that I am a king. In fact, the reason I was born and came into the world is to testify to the truth. Everyone on the side of truth listens to me."
> Pilate: "What is truth?"

Then in 19:8–11 we get much the same, though this time there's some silence by Jesus.

> Pilate: "Where do you come from?"
> Jesus: No answer.

Pilate: "Do you refuse to speak to me? Don't you realize
  I have power either to free you or to crucify you?"
Jesus: "You would have no power over me if it were not
  given to you from above. Therefore the one who
  handed me over to you is guilty of a greater sin."

Jesus subverts the questions of Pilate with answers that
shift to the transcendent realities of the kingdom of God.
His answers and non-answer escape the charge of being the
king of Israel. And he will not give Yes or No to the questions
because what is happening is in the hands of his Father. Jesus,
not Pilate and not the Judean leaders, controls the scenes. In
this interrogation there appears to be utterly no nervousness
on Jesus' part, which contrasts with nearly everyone who has
ever been examined or interrogated with a death penalty as
a possible outcome.

## INJUSTICE

Christians affirm two truths about this trial and its sentence:
that Jesus died for our sins and that God controlled the process. This complicates things for Christians when they think
harder about it. Did God engineer acts of injustice against
Jesus? Such an engineering would make God complicit in
evil, and that won't do. So we need to admit the agency of
humans, which God surrounds with design and overwhelms
with redemption. At work here is the complicity of Roman
powers and Judean authorities, but the sovereign is God.

Jesus was innocent. His opponents fostered an injustice.
Pilate didn't have the courage to do the right thing at the
right time, so he too became an agent of injustice. Sin sent
Jesus to the cross to disestablish sin. We dare not shirk from
seeing the injustices of this scene (and the crucifixion), nor
should we slink away from seeing these injustices as mirrors

of injustices in our world. God therefore enters into the injustices of the world in order to bring justice.

---

## Location of the Action: Inside (Rome) and Outside (Judean Leaders)

Outside (18:29–32)          Outside (19:4–7)
Inside (18:33–38a)          Inside (19:8–12)
Outside (18:33b–40)         Outside (19:13–16)
Inside (19:1–3)

---

Notice that four different times Pilate says he has found no legal offense committed by Jesus, and as a Roman "judge" here he must follow the laws. Pilate's first expression of this appears in 18:38 ("I find no basis for a charge against him"; see too at 19:4, 6) and at the fourth one we read that "Pilate tried to set Jesus free" (19:12). The Judean leaders think Jesus is a criminal (18:29–30), they think he's worthy of death under Roman law for political claims and subversion, they know only a Roman authority can execute someone for that (18:31), and their accusation concerns capital punishment for his claim to be "Son of God," which is a political claim to be king (19:7). Pilate offers them an alternative: he appeals to a Passover custom to release a prisoner but, instead of Jesus, they want Barabbas (means "Son of the father"; 18:39–40). The unjust flogging of Jesus, which shredded the body, was ordered by Pilate (19:1), while others mock Jesus' kingly rule and kingdom (19:2–3).

The angered crowd, sensing Pilate was not persuaded by their accusations, shifts the argument to friendship and to loyalty to Caesar. The charge of disloyalty against Pilate would have doomed his authority and probably his life (19:12), and it is this accusation that sticks for Pilate. He hands Jesus over to be crucified (19:13–16). That decision completes that "trial's" stream of injustices.

## IRONY

At several places in this passage ironies break through the surface. In reading tone can do wonders to indicate irony. Our passage opens with "to avoid ceremonial uncleanness they did not enter the palace" (18:28). The one who will make clean is put to death by those who want to be clean. Pilate does all he can do to get Jesus to admit he claims to be king of Israel, but the king of Israel will not use that language while Pilate does (18:33, 37–38). The irony deepens when the soldiers make a "crown of thorns," dress Jesus in the royal color, and then mock him with false acclamations (19:2–3).

The Judean leaders believe Jesus has committed a capital offense for calling himself "Son of God," which is the very expression Jesus uses over and over for himself (19:7). For that, they say, Jesus "must die" and indeed he must—by divine plan. Pilate then presents Jesus with "Here is your king" and asks them "Shall I crucify your king?" (19:14–15). His kingdom is "not of this world" (18:36), but he is king, and he has a kingdom.

Ironies abound and they tend to bring a smile of perception to the one hearing them, but in these cases the ironies turn tragic, however true. For the unbeliever, the accusations ring true; for the believer they ring tragically true.

## IMPLICATIONS

One of the astounding features of all four Gospels is the absence of explicit theology in describing the sentence and crucifixion of Jesus. The "atonement" theology at work

occurs with one scene standing next to another or antici-
pating another. In our passage several factors anticipate an
interpretation of the crucifixion, and they have to do with
Passover.

It is the day of preparation, which is not the Day of
Passover on which they ate the lamb. In this Gospel Jesus
dies near to the time the Passover lambs are sacrificed in the
temple. So all the language about "preparation" (18:28; 19:14;
and 19:31) forms into an interpretation of the death of Jesus.
He is the Passover lamb whose blood is smeared on the door
of a believer's heart and who therefore protects the believer
from God's judgment on sin.

Another indication of the redemptive implication of
Jesus' death is found in John 18:31–32. The leaders say they
have no right to "execute," and that term leads John to speak
of the "kind of death" Jesus would have as he had predicted:
namely, execution by crucifixion. And one more indicator
comes from what Jesus says about his kingdom: it "is not of
this world" because it is "from another place" (18:36). His
kingdom is not political, earthly, or the result of war. His
kingdom will explode into its significance after the crucifixion and resurrection.

## QUESTIONS FOR REFLECTION
## AND APPLICATION

1. As you read the text of the passage slowly, what stands
   out to you? What observations do you make?

2. In what ways does Jesus control the scene, even while the authorities think they are in control?

3. How do the various responsibilities for Jesus' death play out here? What is the balance between God's plan, Judas's betrayal, the crowd's demand, and the role of the Jewish and Roman authorities?

4. What is your theological understanding of Jesus' crucifixion?

5. After reading the commentary, go back and read the Gospel passage again. What nuances do you notice in the second reading?

# JESUS CRUCIFIED
# AND BURIED

## *John 19:16–42*

*So the soldiers took charge of Jesus.*

*[17] Carrying his own cross, he went out to the place of the Skull (which in Aramaic is called Golgotha). [18] There they crucified him, and with him two others—one on each side and Jesus in the middle.*

*[19] Pilate had a notice prepared and fastened to the cross. It read: JESUS OF NAZARETH, THE KING OF THE JEWS. [20] Many of the Jews read this sign, for the place where Jesus was crucified was near the city, and the sign was written in Aramaic, Latin and Greek. [21] The chief priests of the Jews protested to Pilate, "Do not write 'The King of the Jews,' but that this man claimed to be king of the Jews."*

*[22] Pilate answered, "What I have written, I have written."*

*[23] When the soldiers crucified Jesus, they took his clothes, dividing them into four shares, one for each of them, with the undergarment remaining. This garment was seamless, woven in one piece from top to bottom.*

*[24] "Let's not tear it," they said to one another. "Let's decide by lot who will get it."*

*This happened that the scripture might be fulfilled that said,*

*"They divided my clothes among them and cast lots for my garment."*

*So this is what the soldiers did.*

25 *Near the cross of Jesus stood his mother, his mother's sister, Mary the wife of Clopas, and Mary Magdalene.* 26 *When Jesus saw his mother there, and the disciple whom he loved standing nearby, he said to her, "Woman, here is your son,"* 27 *and to the disciple, "Here is your mother." From that time on, this disciple took her into his home.*

28 *Later, knowing that everything had now been finished, and so that Scripture would be fulfilled, Jesus said, "I am thirsty."* 29 *A jar of wine vinegar was there, so they soaked a sponge in it, put the sponge on a stalk of the hyssop plant, and lifted it to Jesus' lips.* 30 *When he had received the drink, Jesus said, "It is finished." With that, he bowed his head and gave up his spirit.*

31 *Now it was the day of Preparation, and the next day was to be a special Sabbath. Because the Jewish leaders did not want the bodies left on the crosses during the Sabbath, they asked Pilate to have the legs broken and the bodies taken down.* 32 *The soldiers therefore came and broke the legs of the first man who had been crucified with Jesus, and then those of the other.* 33 *But when they came to Jesus and found that he was already dead, they did not break his legs.* 34 *Instead, one of the soldiers pierced Jesus' side with a spear, bringing a sudden flow of blood and water.* 35 *The man who saw it has given testimony, and his testimony is true. He knows that he tells the truth, and he testifies so that you also may believe.* 36 *These things happened so that the scripture would be fulfilled: "Not one of his bones will be broken,"* 37 *and, as another scripture says, "They will look on the one they have pierced."*

38 *Later, Joseph of Arimathea asked Pilate for the body of Jesus. Now Joseph was a disciple of Jesus, but secretly because he feared the Jewish leaders. With Pilate's permission, he came and took the body away.* 39 *He was accompanied by Nicodemus, the man who earlier*

*had visited Jesus at night. Nicodemus brought a mixture of myrrh and aloes, about seventy-five pounds. [40] Taking Jesus' body, the two of them wrapped it, with the spices, in strips of linen. This was in accordance with Jewish burial customs. [41] At the place where Jesus was crucified, there was a garden, and in the garden a new tomb, in which no one had ever been laid. [42] Because it was the Jewish day of Preparation and since the tomb was nearby, they laid Jesus there.*

Once again, the best approach is to provide suggestions for reading it more intensively. This passage recounts (1) the crucifixion, (2) the titulus at the top of the vertical beam, (3) cutting his garment into four pieces, (4) four women at the cross, (5) Jesus expressing his thirst just before expiring, and (6) the burial. John shapes all of his narratives so readers and hearers will imagine all of this happening to Jesus.

## CRUCIFIXION

The most likely location of the "Place of the Skull," or "Golgotha," is today inside the Church of the Holy Sepulchre, with the tomb too inside the church. The identification of that location was made in the 3rd and 4th Centuries. Crucifixion was a brutal, terrorizing, sadistic (not only) Roman punishment for the worst criminals, especially for conquered enemies and political opponents. Its purpose, other than sick revenge, was to deter similar rebellion or crime. A body was suspended from cross-shaped beams, or at times impaled on a single beam. The body was attached to the beams by nails or by ropes, and in most cases the crucified died by asphyxiation. A Hasmonean king, Alexander Jannaeus, had crucified 800 Pharisees in Judea. The Romans flanked Jesus with two other criminals (19:16b-18), which indicates he was crucified as a criminal.

## TITULUS

We are to look up and above the head of Jesus to the sign at the top of the vertical beam. His "crime" was claiming to be "king of the Jews." In fact, Pilate's wording in three languages ironically gives Jesus the title "king" while the "chief priests" want the accusation to read "this man claimed to be king of the Jews" (19:19–21). Pilate stands by his own wording. The accusation on the *titulus* had large enough letters for "many" of the Judeans to read it.

Jesus had labeled himself at times with terms that evoke kingship, like Son of God, even Son of Man, and Messiah. That was the final argument of the Judean leaders in 19:7, but his act of turning over tables in the temple no doubt provoked his arrest as well. His self-claims and the confessions of those who followed him best explain why Jesus was crucified as a criminal, in particular for fomenting a potential rebellion against Rome's current man in power, Pilate.

## HIS GARMENT

Crucified victims were either stripped naked or nearly naked, which is why dividing his clothes among four soldiers turned into something worthy of comment. The tunic was seamless, and they chose, evidently because of its value, not to cut it but to roll the dice. Their act, again ironically, fulfills a Bible verse from Psalm 22:18, a favorite psalm in the early church for interpreting Jesus' death. That psalm, which one should read along with our passage, is the heart felt cry of an afflicted, suffering person longing for divine deliverance, and it moves from suffering to victory. The early church, including the author of this Gospel, ransacked the Bible in order to explain the death of Jesus.

## WOMEN AT THE CROSS

All but one of the male disciples fled from the presence of the crucifixion scene. They no doubt considered themselves vulnerable to the same punishment, but four women stood by Jesus. Three of them are named Mary, by far the most popular Jewish name for a daughter. (Which was also the case in the USA until the latter half of the 20th Century.) Along with the four women, "standing nearby," was "the disciple whom [Jesus] loved" (19:26). For all the excitement Jesus had stirred up in his entry into Jerusalem, the meager number of followers near him at his crucifixion surely indicates the terror of Rome.

Jesus hands over his mother, not to his brothers who also are absent, but to this disciple who took Mary into his own home (19:26–27). One must ponder how the mother of Jesus, the one who heard from angels and who had watched him become a star attraction in Galilee and who was more than convinced he was the Messiah . . . one must ponder what she thought as she saw her Messiah-son crucified.

She's not alone: what did his mother's sister (Salome) think? Mary the wife of Clopas? And Mary of Magdala, what did she think? Their Lord and Savior, their hope was crushed. What will they do next?

## THIRST AND DEATH

A theme in John's Gospel, especially prominent at times in the events of the last week, is that Jesus was in control. While those around Jesus were convinced life had spun out of control, Jesus knew he was in the Father's hands. Which is why John informs us that Jesus knew "everything had now been finished" (19:28) or, to use another term of John's, the final minute in that final hour was about up. In order "that Scripture would be fulfilled," he writes, Jesus announces to those around him that he is thirsty. We don't know who did this, but "they" dipped a sponge in "wine vinegar" and pressed it to Jesus' mouth "on a stalk of the hyssop plant" (19:29), Jesus drank from it, then said "It is finished," and he died (19:30). A hyssop plant evokes Passover (Exodus 22:12), which gives us a glimpse of the significance of the death of Jesus.

The only text from the Old Testament that seems to fit, even if the fit is uneasy, is Psalm 69:21. That psalm, speaking of the psalmist's enemies, says they put "gall in my food and gave me vinegar for my thirst." If that is the context, the meaning has either shifted from cruelty to compassion or the soldiers are mocking Jesus again. Or, perhaps Psalm 69 isn't in view and we should consider this an act of compassion by (probably) the soldiers. John doesn't make that clear but other Gospels tell us he refused the drink because of its bitter taste (Mark 15:23; Matthew 27:34). I favor the view that the soldiers acted with cruelty here.

Jesus is the actor: he both "bowed his head and gave up his spirit" (19:30). His life was not taken from him. He gave his life (cf. 10:18).

Another Passover evocation is found here when the "Day of Preparation" is mentioned (19:31). To hurry the deaths of the crucified they decide to break their legs but, when they get to Jesus, he has already died so they don't break his legs (19:31–33). Which itself could be another Passover evocation (Exodus 12:46) or perhaps it points us to Psalm 34:20's theme of divine protection. Instead, a soldier pierced him with his "spear" and out came "blood and water" (19:34).

"The man who saw it" connects that man with the author of the Gospel (cf. 19:35 with 20:30–31; 21:24). His testimony secures the reality of the death of Jesus and the flow of water and blood, but we can't be sure what that flow of water and blood means. Lord's supper and baptism? Or the cleansing Spirit (cf. 7:38)?

All of this happened to fulfill yet another Scripture, namely, Zechariah 12:10 ("they will look on the one they have pierced"). This quotation points to the act of the soldier fulfilling a Scripture, perhaps of a gentile putting a Judean to death (cf. Zechariah 12:7–9), and perhaps too it leads us to Thomas seeing the wound (John 20:24–29).

## BURIAL

John moves quickly from Jesus' carrying the cross to his burial, all done in about two dozen verses. Tourists to Jerusalem today often visit the Garden Tomb, which has a tomb that undoubtedly stimulates visceral experiences of a real tomb and devotion to Jesus' resurrection. The tomb at the tourist site was not a "new tomb" (19:41) but was from some eight centuries before Christ. It is more likely that Jesus' tomb is, as stated above, in the Church of the Holy Sepulchre.

Two not-too-close followers of Jesus, Joseph of Arimathea and Nicodemus, acquire rights to the body of Jesus, prepare his body for burial, and place him in a "new tomb" not far from the site of his crucifixion (19:38–42). Their acts are an extravagant expenditure from their own funds.

One more time we emphasize the lack of interpretation of the significance of the death and burial of Jesus. John does not say "for our sins" or speak of forgiveness, justification, or reconciliation. He records the bare facts, but he closes with yet another glimpse of interpretation when he writes "it was the Jewish day of Preparation," which is Passover, which is about divine protection and liberation.

What we know is that this crucifixion scene is Jesus' glorification, his act of drawing people to himself, his being lifted up, his kingship and his kingdom revealed, his suffering on behalf of others, his going to the Father—he is Logos, Life, Lamb of God, Light of the world, Messiah, king and Son of God. The cross scene reveals each of those labels for Jesus being turned inside-out and upside-down.

Jesus' death liberates his followers, but at the moment of his crucifixion they were swirling in grief. Three days later the story will change, and all these labels for Jesus will suddenly rise from memory into living realities. The swirl of grief will spin into glorious hope.

## QUESTIONS FOR REFLECTION AND APPLICATION

1. Why was Jesus' death classified as a criminal death?

2. Read Psalm 22:18 and compare it with this passage on Jesus' garment. What do you notice?

3. What stands out to you about the presence of the female disciples at the cross (and the absence of the male disciples)?

4. What do you think about the reappearance of Nicodemus here?

5. What do you make of the fact that John does not use any of the words for Jesus' death that we often use in the church, like forgiveness, justification, or reconciliation?

# JESUS IS NOT
# IN THE TOMB

## *John 20:1–10*

*¹ Early on the first day of the week, while it was still dark, Mary Magdalene went to the tomb and saw that the stone had been removed from the entrance. ² So she came running to Simon Peter and the other disciple, the one Jesus loved, and said, "They have taken the Lord out of the tomb, and we don't know where they have put him!"*

*³ So Peter and the other disciple started for the tomb. ⁴ Both were running, but the other disciple outran Peter and reached the tomb first. ⁵ He bent over and looked in at the strips of linen lying there but did not go in. ⁶ Then Simon Peter came along behind him and went straight into the tomb. He saw the strips of linen lying there, ⁷ as well as the cloth that had been wrapped around Jesus' head. The cloth was still lying in its place, separate from the linen. ⁸ Finally the other disciple, who had reached the tomb first, also went inside. He saw and believed. ⁹ (They still did not understand from Scripture that Jesus had to rise from the dead.) ¹⁰ Then the disciples went back to where they were staying.*

On Easter Sunday, our pastor, Amanda, opened her sermon with these words:

**Resurrection begins in the dark**. In the pitch black of a tomb—carved into the rock, his dear, broken body as cold as the stone on which he lay. There was no one there to witness the moment. Was it sudden? A flash of light, and a new creation? Was it gradual—his side mending. The nail holes closing. His heart giving one thump—then another, and another, and faster. He takes a new first breath and fills his lungs with the breath of resurrected life. Did he open his eyes in the dark? Did he remember right away, or did it take a moment, like waking in an unfamiliar room? Were the angels there, keeping watch? Or did he wake alone, in the dark, the Light of the world? Did he stand and stretch? Did he sing a Psalm? Did he shout Alleluia into the darkness and silence of that tomb? Did the stone that had shut him in cry out, Glory?!*

A sealed tomb was dark, and that body snapped the chains of death with no one watching. I like to imagine with Amanda those details. Perhaps you do, too. We may not know many details other than some remaining burial clothing, and we may have to imagine the details, but details happened.

John says not a word about Jesus' rising from among the dead. Instead, he tells us about an empty tomb. For which there are only two explanations: either someone removed the body, first rolling away the stone, or he was raised from the dead. Take your pick because there are no other options.

## AN EMPTY TOMB

Right there, at the opening of that new tomb, we stand alongside Mary Magdalene and Peter and the faster-than-Peter

---

* Text from the written text of her sermon; used with her permission; her emphasis.

runner look into it, and there is no body. The evidence for the resurrection of Jesus is two-fold: the tomb was empty, and people witnessed Jesus after the discovery of the empty tomb. An empty tomb signifies a resurrection of the body, not a post-death apparition or appearance of the so-called "spirit of Jesus." All four Gospels, holding hands across the Mediterranean basin with the first decade of Christians, witness to an empty tomb.

Empty tomb not only signifies an absent body, but it also requires answering a question: How do you think the tomb became empty? Again, two answers: someone took the body or God raised him from the dead. The apostles explained it one way—God's work—and the opponents of Jesus explained it the other way—someone stole the body. David Ford calls it a "God-sized event" (Ford, *John*, 396).

## CONFUSION

Mary Magdalene's discovery, in the darkness, of the removed stone did not prompt her to enter the tomb. (The other Gospels tell us that other women were with her—notice Luke 24:10—and John leaks that information in John 20:2 when it says, "*we* don't know where they have put him!") Instead, she ran to "Simon Peter" and the disciple Jesus loved, informing them the body was gone. (So maybe she did look into the tomb.)

The two men took off running to the tomb. The beloved disciple peered but did not enter, Peter barged right in. Tomb confusion reigns.

Inside the tomb Peter discovers the burial cloths for Jesus, each where they were when Jesus was still in them. Remember that Lazarus emerged from the tomb with his grave clothes still on the body. Something else has happened here. How to explain when all that remains in a tomb is a person's clothing? Did he just evaporate? Go invisible? Did someone remove the clothing to steal just a body? How do you explain an empty tomb with burial cloths in place? It was confusing, but one can at least question anyone suggesting grave robbers would both steal a body and leave the clothing there in pristine shape.

John is about to tell us that the disciples "still did not understand from Scripture that Jesus had to rise from the dead" (20:9). So they return "to where they were staying" (20:10).

## BELIEF

Confusion, which needs to be communicated in our readings of these texts, seems to swamp Mary and Peter but there's something said about the beloved disciple not said of the other two. Before we speak to that, however, if we follow the text and don't assume what we know will happen, this passage never gets beyond thinking someone has removed the body from the new tomb. But something is written (20:8) that removes that explanation from a possibility.

The other Gospels do not report what is said in John; they leave the first-time reader hanging for an explanation. When he entered into the tomb and saw the burial cloths it says, "He saw and believed" (20:8). What did he believe? He believed that Jesus had been raised from the dead even if he did not comprehend the script about it in his Bible. Unlike Mary, who thinks "they" had taken the body of Jesus, John perceives in those burial cloths a body raised from the dead. He must have remembered the words of Jesus that he was going to the Father, that his crucifixion was a glorification, which included a glorified body, and that Jesus would come again and take them to their homes with him and the Father. "Lazarus was raised to life again; Jesus was raised to life anew" (Thompson, *John*, 411).

Ponder anew with me that the empty tomb means new creation has been launched in this world, that the burial cloths cannot contain the powers of the resurrection, and that what looks like defeat to begin the day morning became victory by noon. Even before he saw the resurrected Jesus and before he had pondered Scripture after Scripture, the beloved disciple trusted that Jesus was alive. Peter and Mary are not yet where the beloved disciple is, but they will get there soon.

## QUESTIONS FOR REFLECTION AND APPLICATION

1. What do you feel and sense as you picture Jesus' moments of resurrection along with Amanda's sermon?

2. What strikes you about the faster disciple noting his foot race victory?

3. How is John's response to the empty tomb different from Mary's?

4. What are some differences between Lazarus's resurrection and Jesus'?

5. Do you ever struggle to believe in a literal, physical resurrection of Jesus? Do you know anyone who does?

# JESUS APPEARS TO MARY MAGDALENE, THE DISCIPLES, AND THOMAS

## John 20:11–29

### Mary Magdalene

*¹¹ Now Mary stood outside the tomb crying. As she wept, she bent over to look into the tomb ¹² and saw two angels in white, seated where Jesus' body had been, one at the head and the other at the foot.*

*¹³ They asked her, "Woman, why are you crying?"*

*"They have taken my Lord away," she said, "and I don't know where they have put him."*

*¹⁴ At this, she turned around and saw Jesus standing there, but she did not realize that it was Jesus.*

*¹⁵ He asked her, "Woman, why are you crying? Who is it you are looking for?"*

*Thinking he was the gardener, she said, "Sir, if you have carried him away, tell me where you have put him, and I will get him."*

*¹⁶ Jesus said to her, "Mary."*

*She turned toward him and cried out in Aramaic, "Rabboni!" (which means "Teacher").*

¹⁷ Jesus said, "Do not hold on to me, for I have not yet ascended to the Father. Go instead to my brothers and tell them, 'I am ascending to my Father and your Father, to my God and your God.'"

¹⁸ Mary Magdalene went to the disciples with the news: "I have seen the Lord!" And she told them that he had said these things to her.

### The Disciples

¹⁹ On the evening of that first day of the week, when the disciples were together, with the doors locked for fear of the Jewish leaders, Jesus came and stood among them and said, "Peace be with you!" ²⁰ After he said this, he showed them his hands and side. The disciples were overjoyed when they saw the Lord.

²¹ Again Jesus said, "Peace be with you! As the Father has sent me, I am sending you." ²² And with that he breathed on them and said, "Receive the Holy Spirit. ²³ If you forgive anyone's sins, their sins are forgiven; if you do not forgive them, they are not forgiven."

### Thomas with the Disciples

²⁴ Now Thomas (also known as Didymus), one of the Twelve, was not with the disciples when Jesus came. ²⁵ So the other disciples told him, "We have seen the Lord!"

But he said to them, "Unless I see the nail marks in his hands and put my finger where the nails were, and put my hand into his side, I will not believe."

²⁶ A week later his disciples were in the house again, and Thomas was with them. Though the doors were locked, Jesus came and stood among them and said, "Peace be with you!" ²⁷ Then he said to Thomas, "Put your finger here; see my hands. Reach out your hand and put it into my side. Stop doubting and believe."

²⁸ Thomas said to him, "My Lord and my God!"

²⁹ Then Jesus told him, "Because you have seen me, you have believed; blessed are those who have not seen and yet have believed."

The tomb was empty, not because someone had removed Jesus' body, but because Jesus had been raised from the dead into the Father's glory. We can't "prove" the resurrection of Jesus, but we can explain the combination of an empty tomb and people being with Jesus as a miracle, an act of God. The resurrection stories of the Gospel affirm two major claims: the tomb was empty, and he appeared to and was touched by his followers. First, Mary Magdalene outside the tomb; second, the disciples who were behind closed doors; and third, Thomas with the disciples when Thomas touched the body of Jesus.

## MARY MAGDALENE COMMISSIONED

Mary grieves in trauma over the death and disappearance of her Lord. In grief she saw "two angels in white" inside the tomb where Jesus' body lay (20:11–12). She is asked the same question ("Why are you crying?"), once by the angels (20:13) and once by Jesus (20:15). She explains to the angels what she then believed: someone had taken the body of Jesus (20:13). She seems unimpressed to see angels. How do you explain that one? Were angels that common?

She then, unknowingly, encounters Jesus outside the tomb when he asks the same question, plus a follow-up, and she gives to Jesus the same answer (20:15). She thinks he's the gardener, so she wonders if he is the one who removed the body from the new tomb.

Time stops. Long pause.

She hears "Mary" and recognizes the voice of Jesus, as sheep know the voice of the shepherd (10:3). He speaks her name. She explodes with "Rabboni!" John loosely interprets that Aramaic word as "Teacher" but it's a bit more than that, too. It can be translated "*My* Greatness" or even "*My*

Great One" (20:16). The exclamation explodes from anxiety, depression, and confusion. All at once, all is resolved. Jesus is alive. Her exclamation declares that she, along with the Beloved Disciple (20:8), believes.

She must have embraced him for he says, "Do not hold on to me" or, better yet, "do not touch me" (20:17), as if she could hang on to this moment in time forever. Their embodied relationship must change, and the old days will not return, because he must return the Father, as he has said. With new creation launched, she is commissioned as an apostle to the apostles to inform them that Jesus is returning "to my God and your God" (20:17). So she does just that (20:18).

The resurrection of Jesus commissions people to tell others about Jesus.

## THE DISCIPLES COMMISSIONED

In the darkness of the tomb, glory inhabits the body of Jesus to transform it into a new creation body. It is the same body but also not the same. We know this because he suddenly appears in a house with locked doors (20:19). The Beloved Disciple believes Jesus is raised; Mary embraces the raised body; and now the disciples see "his hands and side" (20:20). Same body, but not the same. His wounds were visible and will be visible eternally. They "were overjoyed" expresses that they join the Beloved Disciple and Mary as believers in the resurrection of Jesus.

As Jesus instructed Mary not to touch him but to go tell the disciples, Jesus now commissions the disciples. His greeting of "Peace," repeated twice, leads to the commission. The words jump off the page: "As the Father has sent me, I am sending you" (20:21; cf. 17:18). From Father to Son to followers: there is but one mission, it is the mission of the Father, and the Son and followers are the ones sent. The story is not over. Yes, Jesus has been raised, and that's an amazing conclusion to his life, but the story must go on. The disciples are not permitted to go off on some holiday to celebrate. No, they are commissioned to spread the gospel.

That mission involves being empowered by the Holy Spirit, which makes this verse John's Pentecost (20:22). In this version of a Pentecost before Pentecost, the disciples are renewed, infused, and empowered by the Spirit, through the Son, and from the Father, to "forgive sins" (20:23). Recall that sin in this Gospel is about failing to trust in Jesus (15:24; 16:9). You may be snagged by that expression, but we need to let its words sink in. As sent by the crucified, raised, glorified Lord who accomplished redemption, disciples do nothing less than (or more than) extend the redemptive mission of Jesus. Only God forgives sins, but we need to say it like this: God alone forgives, but God chooses to use us as agents of redemption in this world. When our pastor, after we have all confessed our sins, absolves us of sin it is not because the pastor forgives but because the pastor announces, as God's agent of redemption, our forgiveness. You may remember that what was assigned to Peter (forgiveness; Matthew 16:19) was later assigned to all the disciples (18:18) and that expansion is at work in our passage too (John 20:23).

## Thomas Convinced

You can just hear Thomas's response to the disciples claiming they saw Jesus alive. *Yah, right!* Thomas contends that he would not believe Jesus was raised until he could confirm it by touching the body (20:25). Thomas has gone down in history as a doubter, and many contend doubt is the opposite of faith. That's wrong. The opposite of faith, which is coupled in the Bible to obedience, is disbelief and disobedience. Daniel

Taylor thus prefers to speak of our need to "belive" instead of "believe" (Taylor, *The Skeptical Believer*, 15). Faith for Thomas was risky because of the life he would have to live in public: to believe the crucified Jesus was raised put him in immediate danger with the powers at work in Jerusalem. To believe, then, for him required the ultimate commitment. *Am I willing to be attached to the one who could lead me to my death?*, that was his question.

Jesus obliges Thomas. Touching Jesus he blurts out from his innermost being "*My* Lord and *my* God" (20:28, italics added), a remarkable confession that he believes Jesus has been raised, and that Jesus is in fact God (1:1). Faith, Jesus instructs him, based on what is seen is acceptable but "blessed" are the millions who will believe even though they "have not seen" (20:29). The next passage (20:30–31), which we discussed to open this Study Guide, reveals that Thomas's belief perfectly expresses the aim of the entire Gospel of John. Jesus is revealed; believing is the response.

Doubt is a dimension of growing faith. Instead of denouncing doubt we should listen, pray for, encourage, and watch faith grow. Frederick Buechner, with a wink in his eye, said "Doubts are the ants in the pants of faith. They keep it awake and moving" (Buechner, *Beyond Words*, 85). Not so whimsically, a guru on doubt, Daniel Taylor, sorts out his observations about doubt discovered in a life of faith mixed with skepticism. His wisdom contains these, and these are all quotations from Taylor:

1. I have been invited not into an argument but a story.
2. This story gives me not just something to believe but something to do.
3. The real test of any story is what it asks me to love and what kind of life it requires to live.

4. The closer one gets to things that really matter in life, the further one gets from any easy notion of proof.
5. All evidence is resistible. All arguments are assailable. All arguments . . . leak. Anyone who tells you differently is Blowing Smoke.
6. Doubt is an inescapable consequence of being a finite creature in a broken world (Taylor, *The Skeptical Believer*, 7–8, 13).

A life of faith, what Taylor calls "be-living," will encounter doubts of various dimensions of the faith. Some major, some not. But all doubts disturb. Thomas reveals doubt in the innermost circle of the followers of Jesus, a circle that believed but struggled at times to continue in the be-lieving and be-living.

Notice this, too: the grandest confession of the Gospel was said by the one who had doubts: "My Lord and my God" (20:28).

## QUESTIONS FOR REFLECTION AND APPLICATION

1. What is Mary's path toward belief in the resurrection?

2. What is the significance of Jesus' commissioning of Mary?

3. How do the other disciples finally come to believe in the resurrection?

4. How are you serving as an agent of redemption in the world?

5. What is your relationship with doubt in your life of faith? How does this section encourage or challenge you?

## FOR FURTHER READING

Frederick Buechner, *Beyond Words: Daily Readings in the ABC's of Faith* (San Francisco: HarperSanFrancisco, 2004).

Daniel Taylor, *The Skeptical Believer* (St. Paul, Minnesota: Bog Walk Press, 2013). See also his book *The Myth of Certainty* (Downers Grove: IVP, 1999).

# JESUS APPEARS
# TO THE DISCIPLES

## *John 21:1–14*

**Special Note to the Reader:** On John 20:30–31, see p. 7–9.

*¹ Afterward Jesus appeared again to his disciples, by the Sea of Galilee. It happened this way: ² Simon Peter, Thomas (also known as Didymus), Nathanael from Cana in Galilee, the sons of Zebedee, and two other disciples were together. ³ "I'm going out to fish," Simon Peter told them, and they said, "We'll go with you." So they went out and got into the boat, but that night they caught nothing.*

*⁴ Early in the morning, Jesus stood on the shore, but the disciples did not realize that it was Jesus.*

*⁵ He called out to them, "Friends, haven't you any fish?"*

*"No," they answered.*

*⁶ He said, "Throw your net on the right side of the boat and you will find some." When they did, they were unable to haul the net in because of the large number of fish.*

*⁷ Then the disciple whom Jesus loved said to Peter, "It is the Lord!" As soon as Simon Peter heard him say, "It is the Lord," he wrapped his outer garment around him (for he had taken it off) and jumped into the water. ⁸ The other disciples followed in the boat, towing the net full of fish, for they were not far from shore, about a hundred yards. ⁹ When they landed, they saw a fire of burning coals there with fish on it, and some bread.*

*¹⁰ Jesus said to them, "Bring some of the fish you have just caught." ¹¹ So Simon Peter climbed back into the boat and dragged the net ashore. It was full of large fish, 153, but even with so many the net was not torn. ¹² Jesus said to them, "Come and have break-fast." None of the disciples dared ask him, "Who are you?" They knew it was the Lord. ¹³ Jesus came, took the bread and gave it to them, and did the same with the fish. ¹⁴ This was now the third time Jesus appeared to his disciples after he was raised from the dead.*

## QUESTIONS

Beside that sense that 20:30–31 was a fitting ending to the whole Gospel, I don't know what stands out about this passage to you. Is it that the Gospel continues in spite of that sense of completion at 20:30–31? Is it that Jesus now appears to them in Galilee? Is it that the disciples seem to have returned to their pre-Jesus occupations of fishing the northern parts of the Sea of Tiberias, or Galilee, and that explains why they are not all together? Is it that someone—they don't realize it is Jesus—yells from the shore to toss their nets to the other side of the boat, and how can that change the fishing situation since fish move and boats move? Is it that once again it is the Beloved Disciple who is the first to recognize Jesus and the first to get to him? Is it that Jesus is making breakfast for them? Is it that odd number "153" and what does that mean? (No one knows if that number is symbolic, or if it is, what it indicates.) Is it that the net is unbroken, and does that symbolize a unity of the followers of Jesus? Is it that the disciples are afraid to ask "Who are you?" Or, is it that Jesus turns breakfast into a eucharist-sounding event with "took the bread and gave it to them, and did the same with the fish" (cf. 21:13 with 6:11)?

Everything in this passage seems to bristle with wonder for the reader, but the question they are afraid to answer perplexes. I mean, c'mon, they had already seen him twice since his resurrection, and now they both don't recognize his voice or who is on the shore, and then, eating breakfast with him, they're afraid to ask "Who are you?" Yet, they know who he is (21:12). Are they so overwhelmed by him they are unable to speak?

## Sign-like Act

The question should perhaps be flipped: Do *we* know who he is?

That's the question.

John answers the question. Jesus takes the bread and gives it to them; then he takes the fish and does the same. The Who-is-he? question is answered when Jesus reveals who is in providing bread and fish for his "friends" (21:5). This event is another sign or the event is sign-like. His word to those in the boat leads to a haul of fish (no doubt, tilapia) that leads to breakfast that leads to dining with Jesus that leads to the question of the entire Gospel: Who is Jesus? The answer is "The One who can fill your net with an abundance of fish." Too much wine in Cana (2:1–11), and too much bread (6:1–15), both stories about Jesus' prolific supply.

Three appearances (20:19, 26; 21:12) to his followers were preceded by three questions to Peter and three denials by Peter (18:15–27), and the three appearances will be followed by three more questions, three answers by Peter, along with a three-fold restoration of Peter to ministry (21:15–25).

## QUESTIONS FOR REFLECTION
## AND APPLICATION

1. How does this event function as a sign in John's narrative?

2. What do you wonder about most when you read this passage?

3. Why do you think the disciples did not ask Jesus who he was?

4. How do you think they knew who he was?

5. In what ways does this section of the study move you closer to an answer to the question, "Do we know who Jesus is?"

# JESUS AND PETER

## *John 21:15–19*

¹⁵ When they had finished eating, Jesus said to Simon Peter, "Simon son of John, do you love me more than these?"

"Yes, Lord," he said, "you know that I love you."

Jesus said, "Feed my lambs."

¹⁶ Again Jesus said, "Simon son of John, do you love me?"

He answered, "Yes, Lord, you know that I love you."

Jesus said, "Take care of my sheep."

¹⁷ The third time he said to him, "Simon son of John, do you love me?"

Peter was hurt because Jesus asked him the third time, "Do you love me?" He said, "Lord, you know all things; you know that I love you."

Jesus said, "Feed my sheep.

¹⁸ Very truly I tell you, when you were younger you dressed yourself and went where you wanted; but when you are old you will stretch out your hands, and someone else will dress you and lead you where you do not want to go." ¹⁹ Jesus said this to indicate the kind of death by which Peter would glorify God. Then he said to him, "Follow me!"

Peter did not betray Jesus as Judas did. But he denied Jesus when it meant he could save his (Peter's) own skin and perhaps jeopardize Jesus' own safety. Jesus was arrested because of the betrayal; he was wounded by Peter's denial. What happens when you meet up with one of your closest followers or friends after that person has denied absolutely any relationship to you? Who has turned his back on you at your most vulnerable moment?

## QUESTIONS

Breakfast over, Jesus begins to ask Peter questions. The questions are direct and intimate:

> "Do you love [*agapaō*] me more than these [other disciples]?" (21:15)
> "Do you love [*agapaō*] me?" (21:16)
> "Do you love [*phileō*] me?" (21:17)

Some, mostly because they've read C.S. Lewis's *The Four Loves*, think of these two Greek terms for love as expressing two kinds of love—the first two more sacrificial and the second more friendship-based—but the terms overlap in meaning and John seems to be playing with words more than hinting at precise definitions. One need only look at the interchangeability of these terms in John 3:16 and 16:27, or 11:5 and 11:36, or 8:42 and 16:27.

## RE-COMMITMENTS

Those two terms then get played with in Peter's recommitments to Jesus:

"Yes, Lord, you know that I love [*phileō*] you" (21:15).
"Yes, Lord, you know that I love [*phileō*] you" (21:16).
"Lord, you know all things; you know that I love
[*phileō*] you" (21:17).

Both terms are intimate expressions of commitment and believing in Jesus. What grieves Peter is (1) that he had denied Jesus, (2) that Jesus is calling him to return to his first love, and (3) that he asked him three times in order to undo his three denials.

These recommitments are then summed up with "Follow me!" in 21:19 and 21:22 (and 1:43). To love Jesus is to follow him, to follow him is how one loves Jesus. (This is everywhere in 1 John.) To follow Jesus means to follow Jesus all the way to death. Have you heard that Peter, according to church tradition, was crucified upside down at the hands of Nero, emperor of Rome, in about 64 AD?

## RE-COMMISSIONINGS

Three denials, three questions, three re-commitments, and three re-commissionings. The first calling of Peter was to follow Jesus and the commissioning was to expand the ministry of Jesus to others. Now Jesus recommissions the man:

"Feed my lambs" (21:15).
"Take care of my sheep" (21:16).
"Feed my sheep" (21:17).

Another play on terms. Jesus uses two terms for Peter's task—feed (*boskō*) and "take care of" (*poimanō*—and two terms for the people in Peter's pastoral care—lambs (*arnia*) and sheep (*probata*)—with the term "feed" shifted from lambs to sheep at 21:15, 17.

## PREDICTION

Jesus then, and this is not like anything in the Gospels, predicts Peter's aging into a need for physical help and also how he will die as a victim of the powers of this world (21:18–19).

Jesus knows what would happen to Peter and what will happen to us.

## QUESTIONS FOR REFLECTION AND APPLICATION

1. What, if anything, have you been taught before about the words for love in this scene? How does this explanation compare or contrast?

2. How do you think Peter felt during this encounter with Jesus?

3. How does Jesus' recommissioning of Peter clarify Peter's job in the world?

4. Have you ever had to navigate a complicated reconciliation? Or is there a reconciliation you long for? How does this passage help you think about those situations?

5. Are you willing to follow Jesus regardless of the cost?

# JESUS AND THE BELOVED DISCIPLE

## *John 21:20–25*

²⁰ Peter turned and saw that the disciple whom Jesus loved was following them. (This was the one who had leaned back against Jesus at the supper and had said, "Lord, who is going to betray you?") ²¹ When Peter saw him, he asked, "Lord, what about him?"

²² Jesus answered, "If I want him to remain alive until I return, what is that to you? You must follow me." ²³ Because of this, the rumor spread among the believers that this disciple would not die. But Jesus did not say that he would not die; he only said, "If I want him to remain alive until I return, what is that to you?"

²⁴ This is the disciple who testifies to these things and who wrote them down. We know that his testimony is true. ²⁵ Jesus did many other things as well. If every one of them were written down, I suppose that even the whole world would not have room for the books that would be written.

In this passage, Peter seems curious if not nosy. Following both Jesus and Peter at some distance Peter spots the Beloved Disciple and asks Jesus, "What about him?" He seems to be asking what will happen to that man. Will he also be put to death by others as Peter will be?

Jesus, reminding us of how he responded to his mother in Cana, said basically *it's none of your business*. He tells Peter that his calling is to follow him and to leave what God does with others to God. The Gospel includes a note to reader kind of statement, and the reader would have been someone who knew the rumor that these words of Jesus about the Beloved Disciple were misunderstood.

There is then what scholars call an autograph-like ending to the Gospel. The Beloved Disciple is the author of the Gospel, the one "who testifies to these things" and "wrote them down" (21:24). But the author slips from third person (he wrote these things) to first person plural: "We know that his testimony is true" (21:24) which now looks like there's more than one author to this Gospel. He signs off with what scholars often say: *There's so much to say about my subject [for John, the subject is Jesus] but there aren't enough pages or books or minutes for me to put it all into print.*

Which means he's given us glimpses of the glory of Jesus. Glimpses in abundance, I'd say. Enough for you and me to answer the question "Who is Jesus?"

## QUESTIONS FOR REFLECTION AND APPLICATION

1. Why do you think Peter asks the question about John?

2. What do you think of John's comments here about himself as he writes his Gospel?

3. As you conclude your study of John's Gospel, what are your key takeaways?

4. Now that you're at the end of this consideration of the question "Who is Jesus?"—what is your answer?

5. What actions do you want to take as a result of what you have learned in this study?

# NOTES

## More Witnesses to Jesus

1. "Very truly I tell you" (1:51) occurs some 25 times in this Gospel, and serves to emphasize the seriousness and truthfulness of what is about to be said.

## Jesus Brings New Birth

1. The English word "Jew" in our translations today translates the Greek term *Youdaioi*, which could be translated "Judean," in which case it refers to persons who live in or who are from Judea. That is, a geographical location more than an ethnic group. Think of referring to Minnesotans as Scandinavians.

## A Father Witnesses about Jesus

1. Almost certainly this event is the same as Matthew 8:5–13 and Luke 7:1–10.

## A Healed Man and Jesus

1. Some less reliable manuscripts described the stirring more completely, and they are translated in the King James Version at 5:4 but omitted in modern translations. Thus "For an angel went down at a certain season into the pool, and troubled the water: whosoever then first after the troubling of the water stepped in was made whole of whatsoever disease he had."

## Jesus Disputes

1. The NIV's "challenged" has no warrant in the Greek text, which only has "said" (*eipon*). The NIV's rendering ramps up the heat of the argument unnecessarily.

2. A reminder: the Greek term behind "Jews" is *Youdaioi* and refers to people who are from Judea. As such, "Judean/Jew" is a subset of "Israel," the more expansive term. Every use of "Jew" in the Gospel of John could be translated "Judean."

3. John 8:25's ending has a nearly untranslatable sentence. It could be a statement (as in NIV: "Just as I have been telling you from the beginning") or a question ("What can I even begin to say?" or "Where can I even begin?").

## JESUS PROMISES

1. The words "to help you" are inserted by the NIV. The NIV chose to use the masculine personal pronoun ("him") instead of "it," but I use "Spirit" in my paraphrases in this passage.

## JESUS SENTENCED TO CRUCIFIXION

1. Archaeologists propose different locations for this palace ("praetorium"). The most likely locations are the Citadel, or the Tower of David today, at the Jaffa Gate, or the Antonia Fortress that was on the northern end of the temple mount.

# New Testament
# Everyday Bible Study Series

In the **New Testament Everyday Bible Study Series**, widely respected biblical scholar Scot McKnight combines interpretive insights with pastoral wisdom for all the books of the New Testament.

Each volume provides:

- Original Meaning. Brief, precise expositions of the biblical text and offers a clear focus for the central message of each passage.

- Fresh Interpretation. Brings the passage alive with fresh images and what it means to follow King Jesus.

- Practical Application. Biblical connections and questions for reflection and application for each passage.

— AVAILABLE IN THE SERIES —

James and Galatians

Acts

Philippians and 1 & 2 Thessalonians

HarperChristian Resources

# The Blue Parakeet

## Rethinking How You Read the Bible

*Scot McKnight, author of*
The Jesus Creed

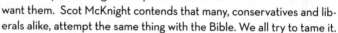

Why Can't I Just Be a Christian?

Parakeets make delightful pets. We cage them or clip their wings to keep them where we want them. Scot McKnight contends that many, conservatives and liberals alike, attempt the same thing with the Bible. We all try to tame it.

McKnight's *The Blue Parakeet* has emerged at the perfect time to cool the flames of a world on fire with contention and controversy. It calls Christians to a way to read the Bible that leads beyond old debates and denominational battles. It calls Christians to stop taming the Bible and to let it speak anew for a new generation.

In his books *The Jesus Creed* and *Embracing Grace*, Scot McKnight established himself as one of America's finest Christian thinkers, an author to be reckoned with.

In *The Blue Parakeet*, McKnight again touches the hearts and minds of today's Christians, this time challenging them to rethink how to read the Bible, not just to puzzle it together into some systematic theology but to see it as a Story that we're summoned to enter and to carry forward in our day.

In his own inimitable style, McKnight sets traditional and liberal Christianity on its ear, leaving readers equipped, encouraged, and emboldened to be the people of faith they long to be.

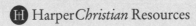
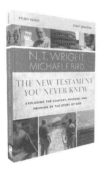
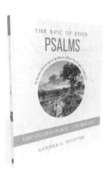
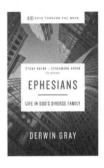

# ALSO AVAILABLE FROM
# SCOT MCKNIGHT

## *How to Know, Read, Live, and Show the Gospel*

We want to follow King Jesus, but do we know how?

Author and professor Scot McKnight will help you discover what it means to follow King Jesus through 24 lessons based on four of his writings (*The King Jesus Gospel, The Blue Parakeet - 2nd edition, One.Life,* and *A Fellowship of Differents*). McKnight's unique framework for discipleship is designed to be used for personal study and within disciple-making groups of two or more. In this workbook, McKnight will help you:

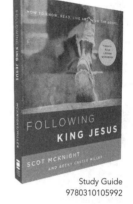

Study Guide
9780310105992

- Know the biblical meaning of the gospel
- Read the Bible and understand how to apply it today
- Live as disciples of Jesus in all areas of life
- Show the world God's character through life together in the church

Each lesson, created by Becky Castle Miller, has both Personal Study and Group Discussion sections. The Personal Study section contains a dis-cipleship reading from Scot McKnight, an insightful Bible study, and a time for individual prayer, action, and reflection. The Group Discussion section includes discussion questions and activities to do together with a discipleship group. You'll share insights from your per-sonal study time with each other and explore different ways of living out what you're learning.

Whether you have been a Christian for many years or you are desiring a fresh look at what it means to be a disciple, this workbook is an in-depth guide to what it means to follow King Jesus and to discover how to put that kind of life into practice.

Harper*Christian*
Resources